Japanese
Foreign Policy
and Domestic
Politics

The Center for Japanese and Korean Studies of the University of California is a unit of the Institute of International Studies. It is the unifying organization for faculty members and students interested in Japan and Korea, bringing together scholars from many disciplines.
The Center's major aims are the development and support of research and language study. As part of this program the Center sponsors a publication series of books concerned with Japan and Korea. Manuscripts are considered from all campuses of the University of California as well as from any other individuals and institutions doing research in these areas.

PUBLICATIONS OF THE CENTER FOR JAPANESE AND KOREAN STUDIES

CHONG-SIK LEE
The Politics of Korean Nationalism. 1963

SADAKO N. OGATA
Defiance in Manchuria: The Making of Japanese Foreign Policy, 1931–1932. 1964

R. P. DORE
Education in Tokugawa Japan. 1964

JAMES T. ARAKI
The Ballad-Drama of Medieval Japan. 1964

MASAKAZU IWATA
Okubo Toshimichi: The Bismarck of Japan. 1964

FRANK O. MILLER
Minobe Tatsukichi: Interpreter of Constitutionalism in Japan. 1965

MICHAEL COOPER, S.J.
They Came to Japan: An Anthology of European Reports on Japan, 1543–1640. 1965

GEORGE DE VOS AND HIROSHI WAGATSUMA
Japan's Invisible Race. 1966

RYUTARO KOMIYA, Ed.
Translated from the Japanese by Robert S. Ozaki
Postwar Economic Growth in Japan. 1966

ROBERT A. SCALAPINO
The Japanese Communist Movement, 1920–1966. 1967

SOON SUNG CHO
Korea in World Politics, 1940–1950: An Evaluation of American Responsibility. 1967

KOZO YAMAMURA
Economic Policy in Postwar Japan: Growth versus Economic Democracy. 1967

C. I. EUGENE KIM AND HAN-KYO KIM
Korea and the Politics of Imperialism, 1876–1910. 1967

EARL MINER, Trans.
Japanese Poetic Diaries. 1969

DONALD C. HELLMANN

Japanese
Foreign Policy
and Domestic Politics

The Peace Agreement with
the Soviet Union

UNIVERSITY OF CALIFORNIA PRESS

Berkeley and Los Angeles · 1969

University of California Press
Berkeley and Los Angeles, California
University of California Press, Ltd.
London, England
Copyright © 1969, by
The Regents of the University of California
Library of Congress Catalog Card Number: 69-16507
ISBN 9780520303829

To my parents

Acknowledgments

It is not possible to acknowledge fully the many individuals who extended valuable assistance and advice in the preparation of this study. From the time when it was first undertaken as a doctoral thesis, this book has grown and changed in a variety of ways and my personal and intellectual debts have correspondingly expanded. Almost all of the research was done during an eighteen-month stay in Tokyo, which was made possible by a grant from the Ford Foundation. To the many Japanese friends and colleagues who offered invaluable aid in coping with the truly formidable obstacles to research on contemporary Japanese politics I am particularly indebted. Professor Junnosuke Masumi offered counsel and stimulating criticism throughout my visit in Tokyo and provided me with a basic education in the politics of contemporary Japan. Matsumoto Shunichi, the plenipotentiary during most of the Soviet-Japanese negotiations, found time in his busy schedule for two long and candid interviews, which filled in critical gaps left by the published documents, and Murata Shirō, brought to my attention rare pamphlets and out-of-print books concerning the talks.

Because of the extensive revisions which were undertaken, I am particularly grateful to the following persons who read all or part of earlier drafts or discussed at length with me the substance of the book: Ernst Haas, Robert Keohane, Henry Rosovsky, Robert Scalapino, Kenneth Waltz, and Arthur Stockwin. Many of their suggestions led to basic modifications in the argument and the conclusions. I want to thank Professor Robert A. Scalapino especially, who first recognized the importance of Japanese foreign policy-making and is personally responsible for my interest and training in Japanese politics. The Far Eastern and Russian Institute of the University of Washington provided essential support for the completion of the book, both through a grant and through the helpful comments of the members of the Modern Japan Seminar. I wish to acknowledge the aid I have received from Masaaki Seki, who worked diligently and creatively as my research assistant during 1967, and Nancy Disbrow, who typed and ordered the final manuscript. Martha Weir's thorough and skillful editing managed to purge the manuscript of abundant literary infelicities. Finally, I wish to express special thanks to my wife, Margery, for her many valuable suggestions for improvement of the manuscript and for her tireless editorial assistance. I, of course, am fully responsible for all views expressed.

Contents

I

Introduction to
the Problem

This study of post-independence Japanese foreign policy-making should be viewed as a reconnaissance exercise, a preliminary effort to explore poorly known political terrain. The tangled and variable nature of postwar Japanese politics and the limited number of scholarly works in this field (in any language) make even a case study hazardous. Necessarily, the aims of this book are modest: first, to delineate the crucial features of the new Japanese political system as displayed in the first major post-independence foreign policy decision, and second, to analyze the politics of this decision in such a way as to permit comparison with similar processes in Western nations.

Postwar Japanese politics deserves far more attention than it has been accorded. The few, for the most part excellent, books in English in this field have been general surveys primarily. The kind of concrete monographic treatment accorded even to some of the most obscure developing nations has been lacking. Japanese scholars, though increasingly exposed to the latest Western social methods and theories, have, with some notable exceptions, rarely given scholarly attention to contemporary politics. The vast number of articles in Japanese intellectual magazines and journals dealing with current political problems are almost invariably journalistic, ideologically colored, or policy manifestoes. In striking contrast to the prominent place American politics holds in the curricula of universities in the United States, there are virtually no courses in Japan dealing with postwar Japanese politics. This neglect both in Japan and abroad is particularly surprising in view of the wealth of data available and the intrinsic interest of a political system in the throes of

sweeping economic and social change under radically new political institutions. The examination of a single foreign policy decision can hardly claim to close this gap, but it will raise, in a
new perspective, issues and problems that may subsequently
receive more thorough study.

Recent international developments lend increasing relevance
to Japan's foreign policy. The Vietnam war, the United States'
long-term commitment to maintaining itself as a "Pacific
power," and Japan's growing efforts to play a larger role in
Asian affairs have broadened and vitalized interest in the dynamics of Japanese foreign policy. Consequently, in addition to
its more narrow scholarly importance, an understanding of how
such policies are made is now vital to United States policy in
Asia. Three considerations make this case study particularly
instructive in this regard. First, the ultimate role of a resurgent
Japan in Asia will be shaped as much by the vicissitudes of its
domestic politics as by the more visible changes in the country's
place in the international order. Secondly, in spite of the revolutionary socioeconomic changes in Japan during the last decade
and the appearance of two new parties, there have been remarkably few changes in the broader political sphere. The left-right
split, the structure of the main parties, the dominance of the
conservatives in the Diet, even the main foreign policy issues
remain much the same today as they were in the mid-fifties.
Thirdly, any move by Japan toward a more independent foreign
policy—short of massive conventional or nuclear armament—is
likely to bring into play the same broad constellation of political
forces seen in the Soviet negotiations, rather than the mass-
centered, leftist-led crisis surrounding the renewal of the American Security Treaty in 1960.

Although the focus is on decision-making, the method I have
employed does not draw heavily on the main body of theory in
this field, which gives primary emphasis to analysis of the web
of complex bureaucracies and political organizations with
highly institutionalized procedures that characterizes modern
democratic systems. Most approaches are based on organization
theory (e.g., James G. March and Herbert Simon, *Organizations* [157]) and are especially useful in a concrete study of

decisions within a given institution. This extensive literature is of limited value for analysis of the foreign policy-making process as a part of the political system, broadly defined. Political scientists have supplemented organization theory with general systems analysis (e.g., Talcott Parson's action system and Marion Levy's structure-functional requisite analysis) thereby broadening the model of decision-making to include both the social and the political systems. Several studies have been made in this vein of foreign policy formulation (e.g., Richard C. Snyder, *et al., Foreign Policy Decision-Making* [166]; James N. Rosenau, *Public Opinion and Foreign Policy* [163]; and to a lesser extent) Karl W. Deutsch and Lewis J. Edinger, *Germany Rejoins the Powers* [144]). Apart from the theoretical difficulties involved in structuring a comprehensive scientific decision-making model (so that it is not just a setting forth of categories), the extensive detailed data required for this type of analysis presently poses virtually insurmountable research barriers to its use regarding Japan. A third method used for comparing policy-making processes, the straightforward institutional approach, is of limited value in studying Japan, where the functions of the new political institutions are not yet firmly established.

The method employed here is an adaptation of that used in *The Political Process and Foreign Policy* by Bernard Cohen; it encompasses all elements of the political system which are in one way or another involved in the making of all policy decisions. Unlike the institutional approach, it takes into consideration expressions of opinion and organizations outside formal political institutions, and unlike the more rigorously scientific analytical techniques, the variables considered are rather loosely cast (e.g., political parties, public opinion). Cross-national comparison is allowed for by the systematic explanation of categories commonly employed in the discussion of foreign policy-making in Western nations. This more flexible and interpretive approach is well suited to the Japanese situation about which so little is known, and it fully satisfies the limited aims of this book.

THE JAPANESE FOREIGN POLICY
MAKING PROCESS

Japan's role in postwar world politics has been singularly modest, despite its global strategic importance and economic preeminence in Asia. This is the result of a variety of factors: a "no war" constitution, supported by widespread feelings of pacifism despite a backdrop of continuous war or confrontation in East Asia; close military and economic ties with the United States; an overriding concern with domestic reconstruction; and the inherent limits on a middle-range power in an essentially bipolar order. Within this framework, the international actions of Japan have been further constrained by the nature of her policy-making process. It is with this last factor, the pattern of Japanese post-independence foreign policy formulation, that the following analysis of the negotiation of the Soviet–Japanese peace agreement of 1956 is most directly concerned.

The comprehensive examination of these negotiations also sheds light on the nature of the new, Occupation-spawned political order during Japan's early years of autonomy. Virtually all political forces directly participated in this first major policy decision after independence, and the conflicts over this issue broadened to involve the basic structure and processes of the entire political system. Moreover, because at this time Japanese politics were undergoing rapid and fundamental change, aspects of the decision-making process which commonly take place in muted fashion, behind the scenes, occurred openly and in exaggerated forms. In consequence, the negotiations provide a unique opportunity for exploring the dynamics of post-independence politics.

There are several advantages in using a case study to delineate Japanese foreign policy-making.[1] First, concentration on a single incident permits specific and systematic examination of each component of this process (e.g., public opinion, political parties). In this way, the still largely uncharted contours of Japanese politics may be identified and described in some detail.

Secondly, by dealing comprehensively with a single decision in accordance with an explicit conceptual framework, the inter-relations between these components can be analyzed and their effective influence on the decision more readily gauged.[2] Since various elements of the political system—the ruling party, pressure groups—are dealt with discretely in each chapter, the general picture appears in a somewhat fragmented form. Some of the cohesion possible in a more straightforward narrative account may be lost by so structuring the discussion. In addition, such separate treatment tends to give exaggerated emphasis to the uniqueness of each component and to some extent plays down the interrelationships among them. Nevertheless, bearing in mind these skewed emphases and that political influence inevitably involves intricate psychological and personal factors, not easily susceptible to analysis in the present framework, there is special value in this particular approach. Above all, it facilitates comparison with other nations by using categories commonly used in similar studies of Western countries, and it avoids treating Japanese politics as sui generis, as is so often done.[3]

However, there is an inherent limitation to this approach, since on both logical and empirical grounds no unqualified general conclusions are possible on the basis of a single example. None are attempted, but in the interpretive approach which is used, some tentative generalizations do emerge. By juxtaposing the patterns of politics seen in the Soviet negotiations with findings from other studies of the Japanese political system, the basic dimensions of foreign policy-making can be identified and seemingly permanent aspects of this process distinguished.

To provide the setting for detailed examination of the Soviet peace negotiations, characteristics of the Japanese foreign policy formulation process are broadly sketched in terms of the categories used in the analysis. As considered here, there are three main components of this process—public opinion, the political party system, and the governmental institutions responsible for the conduct of foreign affairs.

PUBLIC OPINION

One of the striking features of postwar Japanese politics is the great increase in mass participation, a development initiated and abetted by the democratic Occupation reforms. Prima facie, this suggests that public opinion has come to be an important consideration in the formulation of all major government policies, including foreign policy. In gross terms this certainly seems to be true, but a more precise appraisal of the extent and nature of its influence is necessary before the full significance can be known, especially since the general nature of the public opinion foreign policy relation in democratic politics is a matter of dispute.

Public opinion is a prominent term in most discussions of foreign policy, in part because it is closely connected with democratic ideals and slogans. Because public opinion provides a direct link between the people and specific political decisions, it seems to exemplify a basic kind of democratic procedure and at the same time dignify the individual by projecting him immediately into the governmental process. It is seen, therefore, as a good and necessary part of the political system by those supporting democratic values, and it is from this viewpoint that public opinion is most commonly discussed. Scholars and journalists try to educate it; politicians claim to speak in its name or attempt to unify it; polls try to measure it.

Perhaps a more basic reason for the conspicuous place public opinion holds in political analysis is that widespread public participation in politics is largely a phenomenon of the twentieth century. Not all commentators view the increased political importance of public opinion with favor, especially regarding its impact on foreign policy. Walter Lippmann has been particularly outspoken and eloquent in deploring the effect of the opinions of the masses on the ability of governments to confront the great issues of foreign affairs in the modern world.

> The unhappy truth is that the prevailing public opinion has been destructively wrong at critical junctures. The people have imposed a veto upon the judgments of informed and responsible officials. They have compelled the governments, which

usually knew what would have been wiser, or was necessary, or was more expedient, to be too late with too little, or too long with too much, too pacifist in peace and too bellicose in war, too neutralist or appeasing in negotiation or too intransigent. Mass opinion has acquired mounting power in this century.[4]

Lippmann's disillusionment is shared, albeit in more reserved terms, by many students of international affairs, including George Kennan and Hans Morgenthau.[5] These men offer two basic arguments in support of their view. The problems which emerge from the complex and rapidly changing international order can not easily be reduced to general slogans, such as anticommunism, on which public opinion tends to be focused; by forcing issues to be so distilled, the public serves as millstone on statesmen, inhibiting the effective solution of these problems.[6] Secondly, they describe public opinion as a *continuous* check on democratic statesmen, "who are always on trial for their political lives, always required to court their restless constituents." [7] Foreign policy decision-making is in this way stood on its head; democratic leaders become followers, and the public holds the effective reins of control.[8] In attributing such an enormous and constant influence to mass opinion, these critics are in full agreement with the central policy role evisaged for the public in the democratic ideal.

Although the importance of mass opinion is universally acknowledged, most social scientists concerned with foreign policy-making reject the notion that the public predominates. Indeed, a major focus of such studies is usually the delineation of the peculiar role of public opinion in various political systems, and its effect upon different types of policy issues.[9] In view of the variety of approaches possible, the general premises concerning the role of public opinion in foreign policy formulation, which are basic to this study of the Japanese scene, must be elaborated.

First, a distinction must be made between effective public opinion and the opinions held by the public. The public opinion polls deal with the latter. That is, they simply set forth a description of the opinions held by the people on specific issues.

Whether these opinions have influence on the decisions made by the government depends on other factors. There are two kinds of effective public opinion; that is, there are two forms in which the people can influence the decision-makers and have an impact on public policy. One is the mass mood or the climate of opinion in which the policy-maker operates, while the second is made up of the articulate expressions on policy of specific individuals and organized groups, including the media of communication.[10]

The mass mood establishes the general nature of the objectives a policy-maker may pursue. It includes broad and loosely structured opinions such as nationalism and isolationism, as well as strong attitudes directed toward specific nations or peoples, such as the Japanese attitude toward Koreans or the French feelings regarding Germans. The policy-makers may be affected by the climate of opinion in two ways. All tend to respond instinctively to attitudes which are an integral part of the political and social milieu of which they are members. In addition, as politicians, they are influenced by the overt expression of these general opinions as manifest in opinion polls and election trends. It is important to recognize that the climate of opinion exerts influence on the most general goals of foreign policy and is of importance primarily to those few decisions which are of both dramatic and far-reaching significance, such as those involved in an immediate threat of war.

When the mass mood is not clearly manifest, which is the case in most foreign affairs issues, it has only uncertain and indirect impact on the governmental decision-making process—a fact which sheds light on the democratic potential of foreign policy formulation in mass societies. Underlying this ineffectual role is the fact that the overwhelming majority of the public is uninformed about and indifferent to all but a few foreign policy issues. What Sir Ivone Kirkpatrick has termed the "invincible ignorance of the (British) public," is abundantly manifest in numerous opinion polls in the United States as well.[11] The evidence is rather startling. In a poll taken by the American Institute of Public Opinion, published in June 1950, 74 percent of the sample were totally unaware of the meaning of the term "bipartisan foreign policy"; 42 percent were similarly ignorant regarding the "Cold War"; and 95 percent could not offer even a rudimentary identification of "Point Four." [12] Again in 1955, following a heavily publicized crisis in the Formosa Straits which presented a real threat of war, only one of every ten Americans could correctly state which China occupied the islands of Quemoy and Matsu.[13] These examples can be multiplied. This extreme lack of awareness normally gives the government wide latitude for policy leadership and makes a mass veto on policy likely only in extreme crisis. Lacking structured opinions, the masses tend to react to specific issues in terms of generalized and undisciplined feelings (moods) and assume a passive role in the policy-making process.[14]

For mass opinion to have an impact on government decisions, an intermediate step, which Rosenau terms the "opinion submitting process," is necessary.[15] Through statements by organizations and private citizens, the opinion of the mass public can be selectively conveyed to the decision-makers. These expressions constitute what is here called articulate opinion. Articulate opinion, however, does not necessarily accurately reflect the nature of mass opinion—nor does it always effectively impress opinions on the policy-makers. Foreign policy decisions can be made quite independently of the mass mood. Consequently, in order to appraise its effective influence, the relationship of this opinion to the governmental policy-making process must be examined anew for each decision.

Two other aspects of the opinion-policy relationship require special comment. Because the number of people actively participating in the public discussion of foreign policy is limited, the opinions of some individuals are more influential than others. Thus, effective public opinion is stratified. Unfortunately, this fact is often overlooked in specific discussions of this subject because the evidence cited is, for the most part, taken from public opinion polls, which are implicitly based on the premise that each individual opinion has equal importance.[16] Usually, the opinions of most individuals on specific foreign policy issues are not intensely held or overtly articulated. If these opinions have political influence, it is attributable to the impact of the polls on the policy-makers rather than to the actions of the respondents.

It is true that mass opinion does have political effect through the electoral process. There, however, many other influences such as party loyalty, the personalities of the candidates, and the presence of competing issues are also operative. Even in American presidential elections in which foreign policy questions were particular points of partisan dispute, such as those in 1940, 1952, and 1960, other factors are credited with determining the results.[17]

The limited role of mass opinion in foreign policy-making in postwar Japan is vividly illustrated by events attending the renewal of the United States Security Treaty in 1960. At that time a clear and intense mass mood centering on opposition to the Treaty was manifest not only in the opinion polls, but was made dramatically articulate through the press, through huge nationwide demonstrations, and through petitions signed by more than ten million persons.[18] Nevertheless, this impressive demonstration of mass opinion had its effect not on the specific policy (for the treaty became effective), but on the policy-makers; i.e., it forced the resignation of Prime Minister Kishi and his cabinet. In the general election four months later, when the Socialists made the Security Treaty the main campaign issue, the conservatives were returned to office with roughly the same percentage of popular vote (57.6 percent) and an even higher proportion of Diet seats (63.6 percent) than they had received two years previously.[19]

Articulate opinion, the other form in which views with substantial public support influence foreign policy decisions, contrasts with mass opinion in several significant respects. Unlike the opinion seen in the polls, articulate opinion, which is made up of overt expressions of specific positions by groups, individuals, and the mass media, has an activist dimension. These views are elaborated in structured arguments and with regard to specific interests. Moreover, the aim is explicitly to influence policy, either through direct access to the decision-makers or indirectly, by structuring the public's attitude.[20] Consequently, for the policy-makers, articulate opinion is of greater meaning than the mass mood, because the views expressed are usually concrete and detailed, and the political importance of those expressing them can be readily calculated.

Among the most common agents through which articulate opinion is expressed are the opinion groups. Such formally organized associations, whose basic purpose is to bring about the enactment of a single policy or set of policies, have long played important roles in the politics of democratic nations, especially in the United States and Great Britain.[21] These groups provide liaison between the people and the government in areas where political parties fail to offer adequate representation. Because international affairs have dominated political debates since World War II, the opinion groups have increasingly focused on foreign policy issues.

In contemporary Japan such groups abound. The various friendship societies, trade promotion associations, and similar organizations are composed of people particularly interested in supporting campaigns to influence specific foreign policy issues. In the first decade after the Occupation, groups were especially active in promoting relations with communist nations, with organizations such as the *Nihon Chūgoku Yūkō Kyōkai* (Japan-China Friendship Society) and the *Ni-So Kyōkai* (Japan-Soviet Society) regularly supporting extensive public campaigns on behalf of their causes.

Another segment of articulate opinion is formed by private individuals who are able to make a special impact on issues through public expression of their views. In Japan, this is of considerable importance because of the unusual deference accorded to persons of status. This deference is reinforced by a highly personalized style of politics, in part derivative from the Confucian notion that politics and morality are properly one, and abetted by the face-to-face contact possible in the era of television. Not surprisingly, former party leaders, important businessmen, ex-senior bureaucrats, and even leading scholars seek direct influence on foreign policy through public expression of their views.*

* Specific examples regarding the Soviet peace negotiations are provided in Chapter V.

The Japanese left-wing had refined to an unusually high degree the tactic of oppositional direct action well before this technique became a conspicuous feature of contemporary American politics. Frustrated by their minority position in attempting to challenge the government effectively, Japanese leftists (with strong support from students and trade unionists) have frequently sought to exert pressure on specific policies, beyond normal governmental and party procedures, through the demonstration or *demo*. Well organized and carefully timed, *demos* not only offer the threat of physical obstruction to the operation of political institutions, but have a broader public impact by exploiting the dramatic to which the mass media are so often drawn.[22] These two tactics—the *demo*, which is often extended as a challenge to the basis of political authority, and, on the other hand, the appeals made to authority by prestigious figures—stand together as major projections of articulate opinion in postwar Japan.

As in other open political systems, the central factor determining the expression of articulate opinion is the treatment accorded to a particular issue by the media of communication. The media not only report and distill the opinions expressed by other groups; they also provide the factual background, and they are able to forcefully argue their own opinions to an audience which includes both the policy makers and the general public.[23] Postwar Japan has seen the emergence of a powerful and politically outspoken press led by the national dailies, the *Asahi*, the *Mainichi*, and the *Yomiuri*.[24] In addition, the diffusion of television in Japan is second only to that in the United States. Both the press and the networks strongly emphasize national and international politics and thereby serve as a particularly crucial link between government leaders and the articulate public.

However, the sound of the trumpet alone does not determine the outcome of a conflict. The expansion of public pronouncements on policy questions, even with the new channels of access available in the postwar political system, should not be equated with a corresponding influence of public opinion. Necessarily, the impact of the mass mood, of the opinion polls, or of any overt expression of public opinion is conditioned by the nature of the party system, the drama and timing of the issue, and above all by the attitudes of the policy-makers. In democratic polities, it is the responsiveness of the decision-makers to the public, a responsiveness dictated as much by the personalities of the leaders and the elite political culture as by the immediate political exigencies of situation, that ultimately determines the political effects of public opinion.[25]

The recent political history of Japan suggests that the government leaders react only to the most extreme expressions of public opinion. There is little in the political culture of the elite—those bureaucrats and career conservative party leaders who have served as the policy-makers—to encourage accommodation of the opposition. In fact, there is a long history of self-conscious aloofness among Japanese government officials, which is best summarized by the slogan *kanson mimpi* (officials honored, people despised) applied to prewar bureaucrats; and it is from the bureaucracy that most of Japan's conservative party leaders have been recruited. Not only is a tradition of democratic decision-making wanting, but postwar Japanese prime ministers have in fact paid little attention to public opinion on the major foreign policy issues.[26] Furthermore, the conservatives have yet to be seriously confronted with an electoral challenge, and thus have lacked a practical incentive to heed the public. Consequently, unless there is a sharp change in the strength of the parties, the emergence of attitudes within the elite that would accord more than passing attention to modest shifts in mass opinion on specific foreign policy issues would be truly extraordinary. This relative autonomy of Japanese decision-makers from public opinion, which finds parallels in the polities of the United States and Great Britain, leaves the government with wide latitude for policy maneuver.

POLITICAL PARTIES

The most important component of the Japanese foreign policy-formulation process is the political party system. Under the Constitution of 1947, the majority party in the Diet and its president, the prime minister, are allotted the central roles in decision-making. Article 73 specifically empowers the cabinet to "manage foreign affairs and . . . conclude treaties," with the approval of the Diet. Whatever the intent of the constitution writers, in practice the unwavering party discipline in Diet votes together with the responsibilities of the prime minister, both in selecting the cabinet and assuming day-to-day policy leadership, have made the politics and policies of the ruling party the main domestic influences on Japanese foreign policy. This contrasts sharply with the prewar situation, when the Emperor and his advisors, the military, the parties, and the Foreign Ministry (*Gaimushō*) all competed for policy leadership.[27] The postwar constitutional changes and the practices that have grown up around them have radically changed the locus of decision-making. Nevertheless, just how far the elitist nature of this process has been altered and in what sense the current system, in which the lines of political authority have been clarified, is more effective, remain open questions. To deal with foreign policy formulation after 1952, however, it is clear that attention must be given to the structure, the ideologies, the pressure group connections, and the inter- and intraparty patterns of interaction of the ruling and opposition parties.

Because the conservatives have continuously controlled almost two-thirds of the Diet since independence, their frequent bitter clashes with the Socialists over foreign policy in election campaigns and in the Diet have been only of peripheral meaning in terms of the effective process by which foreign policy decisions are normally made. The locus of political power has come to be the intraparty decision-making process of the conservatives. It is the most important single factor of Japanese politics exerting influence on foreign policy, and its nature has been basically shaped by the federated structure of the party.

Structurally, the Liberal-Democratic Party and its various postwar, conservative precursors have been segmented organizations—little more than alliances of factions bound together for political expediency. This is attributable to the fact that the primary unit in Japanese conservative politics is not the party but the *ha* (*habatsu*), or faction, a political group having a distinctly different character from party cliques in other nations despite the superficial resemblance. The origins of the *ha* are found in the traditional pattern of Japanese social relations. More than any other industrial nation, Japanese society is composed of tightly knit social groups finding origin and sanctification in the traditional value system.[28] Factional divisions are found in the bureaucracies, the labor unions and every sector of the society, with the party *ha* simply the most distinctive political manifestation. Leadership in a party faction usually centers on one individual, who provides funds, positions, and services extending beyond purely economic assistance for his followers. In return, they are obliged to give him their unswerving personal loyalty. Most importantly, the ties between the leader and his followers are particularistic and personal, and the behavioral norms involved are more or less explicitly understood as part of the commonly accepted social code.[29]

Though the cause and the nature of the party *habatsu* are derived from traditional social behavioral patterns, the character of the factions has also been strongly influenced by the specific conditions of post-independence politics. In 1952, the end of the Occupation brought the return of the purged prewar political leaders, resulting in the rapid development of *habatsu* within the ruling Liberal Party. Until this time, such divisions had remained dormant under the strong, one-man rule of Prime Minister Yoshida Shigeru. Fundamentally, these factions merely sought shares in the political power monopolized by the Yoshida group, the challenge being in personal terms rather than in terms of policy differences. Inevitably, however, questions of policy came to be involved in the struggle. Attempting to ward off this threat, the Prime Minister continued to hold the reins of leadership in his own hands and relied heavily on the bureaucracy to effect control of both domestic and foreign policy. Thus freed from the full responsibilities of policy considerations, the party factions in the Diet were further encouraged to compete for political power per se, without serious concern for ideological or even policy objectives.[30] When Yoshida fell from power in late 1954, effective responsibility for policy-making devolved more fully to the ruling party as a whole, but the basic nature of the factions has persisted. Although major policy issues almost invariably become the focus for conflict among the *ha,* policy differences have not been a fundamental cause of the formation of conservative party factions.[31]

Another legacy from the Yoshida era basic to the nature of the *ha* was a split between the conservative Diet members who had previously been government bureaucrats and those who had risen to prominence from the ranks of political parties. This division, affecting the vast majority of the conservatives, grew out of Prime Minister Yoshida's successful efforts to build an intraparty machine by co-opting friends from the upper-echelon bureaucracy (e.g., subsequent Prime Ministers Ikeda Hayato and Sato Eisaku), while the old party leaders remained purged from politics by the Occupation authority. The return of Hatoyama Ichirō and other party men fostered factions of largely party membership, so-called "pure politicians factions," and the formation of similar bureaucratic *ha* followed. This broad split between the party men and the bureaucrats was important in the intraparty *habatsu* conflicts during the early years after independence, although this distinction has been blurred with the passage of time.

The most important factor abetting the establishment and maintenance of *habatsu* in the party is the manner in which political funds are raised. Individual candidates cannot raise sufficient capital to meet election campaign costs without substantial aid from other sources. Since the party lacks a mass base which may be tapped for funds, the money is supplied by the various elements within the business community. A substantial proportion of these contributions are not channeled through a general party fund, but are given directly to Diet members, usually the faction leaders. Dividends are expected from these gifts in the form of political favors, which, in turn, are mainly dependent upon the faction's current standing in the party hierarchy and the prospects that its leader will become prime minister. From this perspective, these contributions may be properly viewed as wagers on the *habatsu* sweepstakes.[32] The effects of this system of fund raising on party structure are extensive. First, no person can long remain a successful faction leader without wide contacts in the business world or enormous personal wealth. Faction cohesion is in one sense rooted in traditional social values, but in another, unity is clearly dependent on what Carlyle pejoratively called the "cash nexus." Secondly, this system has made the factions financially independent political groups. Many of the larger factions maintain their own individual offices, issue separate publications, and as formally registered political organizations, are required to report regularly on their financial status to the Autonomy Ministry. Efforts by the party headquarters to break this pattern and centralize the collection of funds have failed, but until this is done, the fragmented structure of the party will undoubtedly continue.[33]

Intraparty factionalism is also abetted by the Japanese electoral system for the House of Representatives. Each electoral district is a multi-member constituency in which each voter can support only a single candidate. Proportional representation is not used and the top three, four, or five vote-getters are elected. This system places Liberal-Democratic candidates in competition with each other and in this way has encouraged factional rivalries and existing factional divisions. *Habatsu* leaders campaign particularly hard for their followers rather than all conservative candidates, and faction funds and local factional organizations (*kōenkai*) take precedence over their party counterparts.[34] How the *habatsu* leaders take advantage of the electoral system by concentrating their efforts on one or two candidates in each constituency is reflected in the wide geographical dispersion in the membership of the larger factions.[35] From this view, the factions are more than simply coalitions of Diet members horizontally allied for parliamentary maneuver. They are small parties, vertically organized, and often with national electoral roots. This, of course, vitiates efforts of the Liberal-Democratic Party to develop grass-roots support.

Finally, the *habatsu* configuration is shaped by the pressures and conflicts of the factional struggle itself. After the merger of the Liberal and Democratic Parties in 1955 and the decision a year later to select the prime minister by a secret ballot among a group composed overwhelmingly of Diet members, the structure of the factions and their pattern of interaction underwent some modification. *Habatsu* seem to have taken on a more institutionalized form and the *hanashiai* (private talks) among the faction leaders were no longer alone sufficient to settle disputes over party leadership.[36] Nevertheless, there remains some fluidity in faction membership and normally some realignment occurs in the intense competition connected with party presidential elections, especially involving *habatsu* whose leaders have recently died or retired.[37] It is difficult to go much beyond noting this phenomenon, however, because of the very approximate numerical estimates of the factions' strength and the secrecy which surrounds individual shifts.

In broadest terms, the structure of the Liberal-Democratic Party corresponds to what Duverger has called a cadre party— that is, a party centering around well known and influential individuals and skillful campaign organizers, who are buttressed by financial aid from wealthy businessmen.[38] Lacking a broad base of participating membership, the pattern of relationships among the Liberal-Democratic Diet members constitutes the controlling organization of the party; the vital question is, what influence does this structure exert on the party's decision-making process.

In light of the fragmented composition of the party, it is clear that the intraparty decision-making process is integrally involved with the factional struggle. Contention among the *habatsu* often centers on specific policy questions, with the further acquisition of political power in view. Not all factional ventures into policy formulation are for purely Machiavellian reasons, but the uncertainties and complexities attendant with all major decisions provide particularly advantageous opportunities for altering the existing *habatsu* balance by challenging the Prime Minister. Consequently, issues, particularly international issues, come to be considered not only as to their merits as policy but as to their worth in advancing the party position of faction leaders as well. Fractious individual rivalries and petty personal ambitions are thus projected into the heart of the policy-formulation process, thereby complicating the situation and virtually proscribing decisive actions.

Strong policy leadership is inherently limited by the coalition nature of the government. Somewhat more than a primus inter pares, a prime minister still is not able to give bold personal direction on specific issues unless he is willing to risk disturbing the factional balance that keeps him in power—in effect to stake his political future on the outcome. The inhibiting effect of coalition decision-making is aggravated by the traditional Japanese style of authority, that is the manner in which conflicts are solved in the society. In Japan it is widely acknowledged that this style is consensual. Although the exact meaning of this term is left rather vague, two features do seem particularly important: a formal show of unanimity among all those responsible for decision-making, and a profound dislike of face-to-face public confrontation regarding the issue.[39] The extreme and often violent form which Diet debates and votes have taken since the inception of the Meiji Constitution in part reflects the restricted place left for open opposition in traditional Japanese decision-making. Each major postwar foreign policy decision has been accompanied by protracted consultation among various faction leaders, reflecting an effort to reach consensual agreement. In part this negotiation is aimed simply at a pragmatic balancing of the coalition *ha,* but there is the accompanying need for consensual unity. The Prime Minister acts reluctantly unless he has at least the tacit agreement of all the faction leaders. When Hatoyama in 1956 and Kishi in 1960 made major decisions without such agreement, the tensions generated directly contributed to the downfall of each man.

Because foreign policy formulation is so tightly interwoven with the factional struggle, the opinions and behavior of the policy-makers are shaped by the nature of this process. Indeed, both the international dimensions of a specific issue as well as the positions of the other components of the policy-formulation process tend to be redefined in terms of the pattern of conflict within the party. Although the precise extent to which any issue may be so affected will vary, factional conflict is destined to be an important determinant in all major foreign policies as long as the Liberal-Democrats maintain their strong majorities in the

Diet. The inward pull of this process finds illustration in the Soviet peace negotiations, which display the extremely closed form that intraparty decision-making may assume.

While the conservatives dominate, they do not function completely alone in the realm of foreign policy. The opposition has been led by the Socialists * (Social-Democratic Party), who have lavished extraordinary amounts of political energy on questions of international relations. Not only have their clashes with the Liberal-Democrats been most bitter in this area, but differences over foreign policy split their own ranks from 1951 to 1955 and have remained a continuing cause of intraparty conflict. Three aspects of the Socialist Party's situation have shaped its policy and political tactics in regard to foreign affairs. First, they have been a permanent minority, never gathering much more than a third of the electorate's support. This has led to strident and often irresponsible opposition to virtually all government policy. Secondly, the Socialist Party also is a federation of factions and its fragmented structure has further inhibited effective policy opposition. Finally, the strong influence of Marxism, which colors the party's policy dialogue, has exacerbated internal party differences and led to abstract ideological pronouncements on foreign affairs that often are abstruse and remote from the concerns of the electorate. To thus broadly characterize the Socialists' position as the major opposition in foreign policy matters is a useful preface to a detailed examination of their policy formulation process and public political maneuvers in the Soviet peace negotiations.

Although the Socialists are in no way connected with the factional struggles within the Liberal-Democrats, as the major opposition party supporting distinctly different international policy aims, they are still in a position to exert indirect influence on foreign affairs decisions. The nature of this influence differs according to the policy considered. When a government position is at odds with the Socialists' basic goals and slogans, which

---

* Since 1958, the comparatively small non-Marxist right-wing has operated as a separate group, the Democratic-Socialist Party, and has regularly captured roughly seven percent of the popular vote and a somewhat smaller proportion of Diet seats.

center around independence from the United States and support for a neutral Japan, an all-out campaign is conducted challenging the policy. At the same time, the Socialist Party is able to serve as a rallying point for all opposing interests, whoever they may be. The party seeks to obstruct passage of government measures by means of parliamentary maneuvers, mass rallies, and other commonly accepted democratic tactics. However, on repeated occasions, these actions have extended to fisticuffs within the Diet and violent demonstrations without. The immediate aim of these tactics is prevention of the realization of the government's policy, usually by denying further extension of the Diet session. Influence is sought by obstructing the institutional procedures for decision-making, and, implicitly, by totally discrediting the government. The large campaigns against major foreign policy decisions are waged in terms of this fundamental challenge.* When a foreign policy issue concerns adjustment of relations with Communist nations or with most "neutralist" states, unqualified opposition is proscribed, and the Socialists' tactics are necessarily substantially modified. Then, their role is more readily comparable with the activities of "responsible" opposition parties in other open societies in regard to foreign policy matters.

An important dimension has been added to policy-making in postwar Japan by the rise of interest groups and their active participation in politics. These organizations, based upon economic or occupational groups having continuing and permanent roles in the political process,† have impact on the major foreign policy issues primarily through the political parties. Broadly viewed, labor is closely tied to the Socialists (and the other parties of the left), while the conservatives draw support from

---

* An instance such as the Security Treaty incident, in which the foreign policy making process coincides with the political process, can be considered as a logical, if extreme, consequence of the trend toward integrating international issues into domestic politics. Nevertheless, it is doubtful that a viable political system with democratic pretensions can accommodate frequently recurring incidents in which parliamentary procedures, freedom of assembly, and other basic principles are so abused.

† For elaboration of the distinction between interest and opinion groups, see Chapter IV.

the business and agricultural organizations. However, the links between these groups and the respective major parties sharply differ. This, in turn, conditions the tactics which the interest groups employ in seeking to influence foreign policy decisions.

Sōhyō (General Council of Trade Unions of Japan), the largest labor organization in Japan with nearly four million members, is the Socialists' closest political ally. It is the party's main financial prop, and the large, highly efficient organization of the union provides crucial aid during elections. The close personal ties between party and union leaders are reinforced by common ideological and policy preferences. Correspondingly, Sōhyō's participation in the process of foreign policy formulation goes hand in hand with that of the Socialist Party. The unions, together with various student groups, provide much of the mass support for the frequent Socialist-sponsored public rallies and *demos* opposing specific foreign policies of the government. By articulating opinions beyond its self-interest as labor's representative and expressing them outside established or constitutionally sanctioned channels of access to the government, Sōhyō exceeds the political role normally ascribed to an interest group. Rather, the union functions more as an opinion group.[40] As a leader of articulate opinion, it exerts indirect influence on foreign policy by expressing opposing views and, more importantly, by offering a political challenge to the life of the government through mass protests. The effective influence of labor on foreign policy has been correspondingly limited.

In contrast, the extensive formal and informal ties between the business community and the conservative party offer special channels for access to government decision-making. Paralleling the Socialist-Sōhyō relationship, businessmen have personal bonds with party leaders, share common general attitudes toward politics, and to an overwhelming degree provide the funds of the Liberal-Democratic Party. Furthermore, the continuing electoral dominance of the conservatives has increased the importance of intraparty maneuvers in policy formulation and thereby strengthened the businessmen's ability to gain influence. Yet it is a mistake to believe that businessmen are fully integrated into the process of foreign policy-making or to assume that their opinions ultimately prevail on all the major issues. Business influence is limited, and the limitations underscore the complexities of postwar Japanese politics.

Above all, it is necessary to recognize that the Japanese business world is not cut from a single piece of cloth. There is not only a diversity of economic interests, but also political opinions concerning foreign policy vary widely. On specific major foreign affairs questions, the four large employers' associations formally and publicly present the position of the biggest, most respectable business interests. Ostensibly, these pronouncements express a united position, but sharp public criticisms by leading businessmen often accompany such statements. For example, differences concerning Sino-Japanese relations have long been evident, and there were splits over Japan's policy toward the Soviet Union at the time of the peace negotiations.*

Not only is there a diversity of views in regard to foreign policy within the business world, but the means of making these opinions politically articulate are varied and of uneven influence on the conservative party. In addition to the public statements by the employers associations, prominent businessmen usually press their views privately on the political leaders who are their close personal friends. Moreover, specific companies having direct financial ties with *habatsu* are able to secure representation in the party's decision-making process through these factions. Thus, although business liaison with the Liberal-Democrats on foreign policy matters is extensive, it is also diffuse. Consequently, the party is left with considerable latitude for action on most major decisions, particularly since these decisions tend to be defined more in political than in economic terms.

FORMAL INSTITUTIONS

Finally, the ways in which those governmental institutions formally charged with handling foreign affairs affect policy decisions requires consideration. This institutional framework in-

* For further discussion of these differences in the business community, see Chapter IV.

cludes the prime minister and his cabinet, the Foreign Office (Gaimushō), and the Diet and its committees. In contrast with the complex prewar situation in which policy responsibility was ambiguously allocated, now the authority for making foreign policy clearly rests with the Diet majority party and its leaders. The Gaimushō has been made fully subordinate to the government and is designed simply to implement the policies set down by the party. A Diet law accompanying the 1947 Constitution established a system of standing committees, including one in each house of the legislature, which deals specifically with international matters. These Foreign Affairs Committees are now integral to foreign policy-formulation and thereby strengthen the place of the Diet in this process. Although the individual roles of these institutions inevitably vary from issue to issue, several significant general patterns can be noted.

The place of the prime minister and his government in foreign policy-making under the new constitutional disposition of authority is most appropriately examined in terms of the general influence of the majority party; but one effect of this institutional change warrants special mention. From their formal position of responsibility, Japanese prime ministers have taken more and more actual control of foreign policy. International issues have been a central concern of every administration, and each premier has personally assumed the preeminent role in these matters. Increasingly, effective leadership is centering in this office. Whether this trend will continue depends upon a number of uncertain variables: the personalities of the individual prime ministers, the parties' electoral strength, the structure of the Liberal-Democrats, and the drift of international politics. Equally important will be the effective procedures for operation within the formal institutional setting in which foreign policy is made.

Although specifically invested with the management of international affairs, the Foreign Office has had a limited impact on major policies. In part this weak performance is a legacy of several decades of operation on the periphery of the decision-making process. For more than twenty years preceding postwar independence, other political forces directed Japan's foreign policy. From the Manchurian incident in 1931 until the end of the war, leadership in foreign affairs was appropriated by the military. Then, in the succeeding years, the Occupation authorities were in control, with the skeletal staff of the Gaimushō performing only minor advisory and administrative duties.[41] Consequently, as Japan began to re-establish her normal place in the world community, the Foreign Office had to be completely rebuilt. Reconstruction has moved ahead, but this weak foundation retarded the ministry's development, especially during the early years of independence.

Basic to its modest postwar role is the Gaimushō's new position of subordination to the ruling party and its government. This arrangement, although common in constitutional democracies, constitutes a sharp break with practices of prewar Japan. There was in this earlier era no single established pattern of decision-making in which the place of the Gaimushō was clearly defined. As noted above, the diffuse allocation of authority under the Meiji Constitution left responsibility for policy ambiguous. Through World War I, the extra-legal *Genrō* institution overcame this constitutional ambiguity; but during the so-called party period, the Foreign Office, the military, and the party leaders all vied for policy leadership with inconclusive results, until the military took ascendance in 1931. Normally, the foreign minister was a career diplomat and, buttressed by the support of the ministry's bureaucracy, was well situated to compete with the premier or the military for policy influence. Katō Takaaki and Shidehara Kijūro stand as perhaps the most famous examples of prewar foreign ministers who championed the cause of the Gaimushō.[42] In addition, foreign affairs tended to be considered supra-partisan national matters, over which party leaders should not (and did not) exercise full control.[43] In the tangled moves and countermoves which constituted decision-making in those years, the Gaimushō was fully involved in establishing policy aims. This direct role in substantive policy-formulation led to factionalism within the Foreign Office, with each faction adopting a particular policy posture (e.g., the Anglo-American faction). Under the 1947 Constitution, such capacity for direct, semi-autonomous participation in policy-making has been drastically curtailed. The position of subordination to the ruling party is conspicuously exemplified in the selection of foreign ministers on the basis of party position and not on career in the Foreign Office.

With the center of the stage for policy-making occupied by the prime minister and the majority party, the Gaimushō has been left with simply an important supporting role. The office of the foreign minister has been freed from the intimate ties with the foreign ministry which characterized much of the prewar era. Now the foreign minister is a party man, appointed by virtue of his place within the ruling party, and fully responsible to the prime minister. With policy leadership in this way linked directly to party leadership, the Foreign Office has of necessity been concerned with the technical functions of working out policy details and of administering the country's international activities. Professional competence in these auxiliary tasks has shown steady improvement, but because Japanese international relations have been heavily concentrated on expanding economic ties with the world, the Foreign Office has had to share many responsibilities with other government offices specializing in this field, especially the ministries of Finance and International Trade and Industry. Given the essentially routine nature of the Gaimushō's main duties and the sotto voce character of Japanese diplomacy, few opportunities are available for the ministry acting in its official capacity to play a major role in policy formulation. In the near future, its most likely means of access to decision-making lies in informal contacts with the Liberal-Democratic Party, either by personal ties with party leaders (particularly ex-diplomats) or through direct alliance between cliques within the ministry and party factions. Nevertheless, both the radically different constitutional framework and the consolidation of policy control in the hands of the ruling party make it unlikely that the Gaimushō will significantly alter the style of foreign policy leadership offered Japan.

Both the Diet and the various standing committees connected with foreign affairs formally participate in decision-making and can play a crucial part in the realization of governmental policy. Active support of the chairmen of the concerned Diet committees and of the presiding officers of both houses is a particularly important element in assuring the Diet approval normally required on foreign policy decisions. If these officers oppose the policy for either substantive or factional reasons, they have the power to delay and obstruct its implementation. In 1960, for example, the Kishi cabinet would not have been able to push through Diet approval of the Security Treaty in a midnight session, without the full cooperation of House Speaker Kiyose Ichirō and the chairman of the House Steering Committee, Arafune Seijirō.[44]

For the most part, the Diet and its committees serve as arenas for bitter verbal and occasionally physical partisan struggles. The strict party discipline displayed in the Diet, which almost invariably cloaks the factional differences, and the rarely-bridged ideological policy gap separating the Japanese right from the left contribute to the sharpness of debate and inhibit a positive policy-making role. The main function of the committee hearings on international issues, which normally involve the Budget and Finance as well as the Foreign Affairs Committees, is to provide an opportunity for the government once again to state publicly its previously established policies and for the Socialists to attack them. Policy deliberation occurs among Liberal-Democratic Party leaders before submission to the consideration of the committees. Party discipline inhibits open criticism of the official stand by conservative committee members. It also assures committee approval, as membership is allocated in proportion to the total number of Diet seats held by each party. In this context, the aim of Socialist actions is to embarrass and obstruct the government and not to provide responsible criticism.* Similar obstructionist tactics recur during the plenary session of the Diet scheduled to pass on a particular policy—resulting in frequent outbursts of violence on the floor of the legislature over controversial major issues. In the long

---

* For example, during the hearings in early 1960 of a special committee to consider the Security Treaty with the United States, the Socialists kept discussion focused on two or three clauses for *over one hundred days*, while they sought to mobilize mass support behind their position.

run, the airing of political differences in public debate may well become a constructive influence on policy formulation. Currently, however, the impact of Diet proceedings on foreign policy-making is destabilizing, for the conservatives are provoked to display a "tyrannous" majority in forcing through legislation or treaty ratifications, and the Socialists' frustrations in the Diet encourage resort to mass direct action.

It is in terms of these general concepts and broad trends of postwar Japanese politics that the Soviet-Japanese peace negotiations will be analyzed. The resulting detailed delineation of Japanese foreign policy-making facilitates speculation concerning the effectiveness, the stability, and the democratic features of this process.

II

History of the
Peace Negotiations

Before analyzing the Japan-Soviet peace negotiations in terms of the domestic political process, it will be useful to fill in the broader historical setting. By establishing the historical context of the negotiations—the main currents of Japanese politics during this period, and the postwar relations which had prevailed between the two nations—we can introduce a comprehensive perspective of the talks, to be followed by more detailed analysis. Similar considerations recommend setting forth a specific chronology of the talks and a summary of the major issues involved in order to provide a factual screen on which the complex policy-making process may be more clearly viewed. It is inevitable that in choosing various single components of the political process to be the foci of discussion, violence is done to the chronological order; certain events tend to assume an exaggerated importance. These imbalances should be in part corrected by a straightforward description of the talks.

For most of the twenty-three months over which the negotiations extended, other problems occupied the center of the political stage. Japanese politics was then in an extreme state of flux. A fractious power struggle, touched off by the political demise of Prime Minister Yoshida Shigeru in late 1954, raged openly within the conservative camp throughout the entire period. The fall of Yoshida and his Liberals brought on the establishment of the Democratic Party, dividing the conservatives into two antagonistic coalitions of factions. Even with the merger of these two groups in November 1955, the new party was riven with factional strife as the leaders struggled to adjust to the still uncertain conditions left by the Occupation and its democratic reforms. Thus the decision to normalize relations with the Soviet Union occurred at a time when conservative politicians were preoccupied with intraparty power struggles.

Part of the turbulence within the conservative camp in 1955–56 was caused by the seemingly real and vital threat of a leftist government, despite the appearance of the first tangible effects of the postwar economic boom following reconstruction. This period saw the reunification of the Left- and Right-Wing Socialist Parties (split since 1951), a steady gain in Socialist electoral strength, and in 1956, the party's successful (and violent) obstruction of a politically inspired bill for election redistricting. These successes and the promise of more had effect not only on the conservatives but on the Socialists' attitudes and tactics regarding their participation in policy-making.

Internationally, this was a time of thaw in the global Cold War with the impact of peaceful coexistence especially evident in East Asia. It was most prominently manifested at the Geneva Conference, which temporarily halted the war in Indo-China, and at the Afro-Asian Bandung Conference, which condemned bipolar confrontation and apparently launched a new third force in world politics. This was also the period when Japan, in the wake of Occupation policies and the gradual attrition of the legacies of illwill left by the war, made cautious moves toward a wider and more independent international role. In addition to the effort toward reconciliation with the Soviet Union, increased contact with Communist China and the settlement of war reparations with the Philippines figured prominently in Japanese foreign policy during 1955 and 1956.

From the end of World War II until mid-1954, the Soviet Union's policy toward Japan was quite hostile. Its last-minute entrance into the war yielded possession of substantial northern territories previously occupied by the Japanese, but the Russians were blocked from effective participation in the Occupation by the United States. In consequence, Moscow's attitude toward Japan quickly came to be cast in terms of Stalin's rigid concept of the Cold War. No contact was made with the Japanese government, which was always the object of bitter criticism, and political influence was sought only among the "people," through the support of various left-wing groups in Japan.[1] When, in 1950, the Soviet Union signed the Treaty of Friendship and Alliance with the newly-established Peoples' Republic of China, Japan was pointedly singled out as a potential aggressor.[2] At the San Francisco Peace Conference, the Soviets demanded a package settlement requiring the neutralization of Japan and the recognition of Communist China.[3] When these conditions were rejected by the United States, they refused to sign the treaty. Japan and the Soviet Union thus continued to be legally in a state of war and few gestures were made to improve relations during the subsequent three years.

The shift in Soviet policy which occurred in 1954 seems to have been primarily based on two factors: the results of the Geneva Conference on Indo-China, and the more flexible attitude of the Soviet leaders who succeeded Stalin. International tension in the Far East was temporarily eased in the period following the agreement at Geneva in July of 1954. For almost the first time since the end of World War II, the immediate threat of an all-out East-West military confrontation in Asia was removed, and the prevailing international temper throughout much of the area was "neutralism" and cooperation—the spirit that was to dominate the Bandung Conference in early 1955. To deal with this new situation, Moscow (and Peking) shifted to a policy of peaceful coexistence. The Soviet approach to Japan was guided by this general policy shift, and on the same day that the note was handed to the Japanese government requesting the opening of peace negotiations, the Soviets unilaterally ended the state of war existing between themselves and both East and West Germany.[4] By this time, it was also evident to Moscow that little profit would accrue from continuing the policy of almost complete isolation from the Japanese, and this further encouraged moves toward reconciliation.[5] Rapprochement essentially involved political, not economic, questions, particularly acceptance of Japan's alliance with the United States and consideration of Soviet-Japanese relations independent of Sino-Japanese relations. Concession on these two points constituted the substance of the change in the Soviet approach.[6]

The first concrete evidence of this new attitude appeared on

September 12, 1954, when Foreign Minister Molotov announced that the Soviet Union was ready to normalize relations, provided that Japan showed a similar willingness.[7] One month later, a joint Sino-Soviet declaration explicitly stated the desire to coexist with the Japanese government in terms of the principles of "equality and reciprocity." [8] Following still another positive statement by Molotov,[9] the Soviets formally took the initiative on January 25, 1955, and dispatched a note requesting that negotiations for the normalization of diplomatic relations be opened.[10] In this way, the issue of normalization was introduced to the Japanese political scene—initiated by Russia primarily as part of a broader policy shift made in the context of global Cold War strategy.

At the time that the Soviet Union made these gestures, the Japanese political world was undergoing far-reaching changes. Yoshida, the prime minister for six years and the man most closely identified with United States policy, was clearly in the twilight of his political career. A series of domestic incidents, including a scandal which reached into the cabinet, had brought his popularity to an all-time low [11] and brought his many critics within conservative ranks into unified and open opposition. The Democratic Party, which had been formed in October 1954, was truly a potpourri of political opportunists, who were united by little more than their desire to topple his cabinet. As president they selected Hatoyama Ichirō, an old and ailing prewar party veteran, who, after his depurge in 1951, had already made several abortive attempts to unseat Yoshida. With the aid of the two Socialist parties, the Democrats brought down the government on December 7, 1954, transferring the mantle of political leadership to a motley coalition headed by Hatoyama.

The issue of Soviet relations was projected directly into the center of this unsettled situation. Immediately after entering office, Hatoyama proclaimed normalization of relations with both the Soviet Union and Communist China as a central policy goal, and it quickly became one of the major political slogans of the Democratic Party.[12] Not only did it precipitate a bitter public controversy with the rival Liberal Party, since the position sharply diverged from that of Yoshida, but the fulfillment of this vague pledge came to be a trying policy responsibility for Hatoyama. Thus, from the very beginning, the issue was drawn deeply into the maelstrom of Japanese domestic politics.

Establishment of the Democratic cabinet offered the first opportunity for substantial revision of Japan's foreign policy after independence, since the Yoshida governments had done little more than extend the America-centered policies of the Occupation. Hatoyama's aim to normalize Soviet relations was only one part of a general program to settle issues in Asia outstanding from World War II and to play a broader and more independent role in the postwar world.[13] Independence in fact meant greater freedom from the United States, and Hatoyama did advocate revision of Article IX of the Constitution to allow Japanese rearmament. It is mistaken, however, to construe the efforts toward rapprochement with Moscow as a fundamental change in Japan's international position. It was sought only on the condition that the San Francisco Treaty and the military alliance with the United States remain unaffected. The aim was a modest one, but it was not fully accepted even within the Democratic Party; Foreign Minister Shigemitsu openly differed with the Prime Minister. Although it was formally denied, Shigemitsu had from the beginning supported a much firmer approach to the Soviets. For example, he insisted that Moscow take the initiative in normalizing relations and demanded that the thorny issues of territory and detained Japanese be solved before the establishment of diplomatic contact.[14] On these points, Hatoyama was in clear disagreement, despite the fact that his overall position had not yet been fully formulated.[15] Consequently, in the period immediately preceding contacts between the two governments, Japan's Soviet policy was far from definitive; even the basic position remained a subject of controversy within both the government and the conservative camp. The general political crisis and the minority position of the Democratic Party in the Diet virtually proscribed strong policy leadership, further complicating the issue.

THE FORMAL NEGOTIATIONS

After the first Soviet note, several months of bickering over procedural matters followed, but the formal talks were finally scheduled for London in early June. During these months, no changes were evident in the attitude of either nation, despite the overthrow of Soviet Premier Georgi Malenkov in February and a Japanese general election in the same month, from which the Democrats emerged as the leading, but not the majority party in the House of Representatives.[16]

On June 1, the London talks opened. Jacob Malik, then an ambassador to England, represented the Soviet Union, and Matsumoto Shunichi, a career diplomat having close ties with Hatoyama, was the Japanese plenipotentiary. Both the draft treaty submitted by the Soviets and the memorandum presented by Japan were intended as merely starting points for negotiation. The Soviet proposal included a demand for the military neutralization of Japan, a stipulation which Molotov had earlier implicitly renounced and which Tokyo could never accept.[17] At the same time, Japanese insistence on the return of all northern territories occupied by the Soviets as a result of World War II was a condition not only unacceptable to the Russians, but not legally susceptible to bilateral settlement according to the terms of the San Francisco Treaty.[18] Within two months, both sides had greatly modified their initial demands.

In early August the Soviet Union abruptly made a major policy shift and pressed for an immediate treaty settlement. Malik dropped the demands for neutralization, offered to return the Habomai and Shikotan Islands, and tentatively agreed to acceptable solutions for all other issues. Since Matsumoto had negotiated in London with the understanding that Japan's minimum territorial demands could be satisfactorily met with the return of these islands, the prospects for agreement seemed bright.[19] However, at that time the Japanese Foreign Ministry without warning issued a pamphlet which unqualifiedly asserted that, for both historical and legal reasons, the South Kurile islands of Etorofu and Kunashiri belonged to Japan.[20] In a draft treaty prepared by the Gaimushō which followed, Japan demanded the return of these islands and proposed that title to South Sakhalin and the North Kuriles be settled at a subsequent international conference.[21] The Soviets flatly rejected this claim, and shortly thereafter (in late August) the formal talks were broken off, stalemated over this issue.

During the four months in which the talks were recessed, the Japanese position did not discernibly change. The platform of the newly merged Liberal-Democratic Party, issued in November, simply reiterated the official government policy, calling for return of the South Kurile islands as part of a general treaty settlement.[22] Yet the merger had been one of forced expediency, prompted by the earlier unification of the Socialists in October; and, formal pronouncements to the contrary, the long-standing dissension among the conservatives over Soviet policy continued beneath the surface.

Two actions by the Soviet Union prior to the next series of talks were to have a significant impact on the negotiations. On September 14, a provisional agreement was signed with West Germany restoring diplomatic relations and repatriating German detainees, but postponing settlement of their territorial problem. For the Japanese, the lesson to be learned from this closely parallel situation was obvious. Foreign Minister Shigemitsu declared that the government would not consider a similar solution, but in the face of continued Soviet intransigence, the so-called Adenauer formula, which sidestepped the territorial issue, offered an obvious method by which Japan could salvage something from the protracted talks, without being forced to the humiliation of modifying its position.[23] In early December, the Soviet Union again vetoed Japan's admission to the United Nations. Because the Soviets had already agreed to reverse this stand after a peace treaty, the veto reactivated pressures in Japan for an early settlement.

With these changes in the background, but neither side formally altering its position, the London talks reopened on January 17, 1956. Shortly thereafter, the Soviets did informally propose an Adenauer solution, but it was promptly rejected.[24] The succeeding weeks brought about agreement on the specific details of a treaty—except for the territorial question. Finally, it became evident that this impasse could not be broken by a decision in London, and on March 20, it was mutually agreed to suspend the talks indefinitely.[25]

The Soviets then embarked on a skillful diplomatic maneuver that ultimately forced the reopening of the talks under conditions more favorable to themselves. The following day, March 21, Moscow announced that fishing restrictions would be enforced on Japanese vessels in the northern Pacific and Bering Sea for the season beginning May 15.[26] The reaction in Tokyo was immediate because of the economic and political importance of the fishing industry and its special ties with the Hatoyama faction in the Liberal-Democratic Party. Consequently, on Japan's initiative, an emergency fishery conference was scheduled for late April. Agricultural and Forestry Minister Kōno Ichirō, the most powerful political figure in the cabinet and outspokenly committed to the early normalization of relations, was dispatched to Moscow to negotiate a temporary fishery agreement. Once the talks were under way, the Soviets pressed to expand their scope, tying concessions on the fishery issue to the question of diplomatic relations. Kōno was highly amenable and the fishery pact signed on May 15 was contingent on the resumption of general negotiations on July 31. Furthermore, although fishing was allowed for that season, the conditions of the agreement would apply in the future only after the effectuation of a peace treaty or the restoration of diplomatic relations by a provisional formula.[27] The Russians had thus enormously increased the incentive for some settlement at little cost to themselves.

With the prospects for a definite decision on the government's Soviet policy thereby greatly increased, the cleavages over this question which had lain beneath the surface of the conservative alliance broke out into the open, bound up with a power challenge to the Hatoyama-Kōno leadership. A substantial proportion of the party, led by ex-Prime Minister Yoshida and Foreign Minister Shigemitsu, criticized Kōno's diplomatic maneuver and gave full support to the treaty conditions previously proposed by Japan.[28] On the other hand, the Hatoyama mainstream alliance, anxious to bring about the early normalization of relations, was clearly receptive to an Adenauer-type agreement.[29] Direct consideration of the policy issue by the conservatives was put off until after the mid-July House of Councillors election, in which the Liberal-Democrats made a poor showing; thus Hatoyama's party leadership was further weakened. When the issue was finally confronted, the conflict was not over policy alternatives, but over the membership of the Moscow delegation—a controversy primarily involving factional and personal consideration and only indirectly the substantive questions. Thus, on the eve of the talks, the government's position had not been defined and Shigemitsu, the compromise choice as plenipotentiary, was invested with "discretion" to negotiate with the Soviets.[30]

On July 31, in Moscow, formal negotiations for restoring diplomatic relations opened for the third time. The territorial question was the only unsettled issue. Shigemitsu first offered to drop the demand that the sovereignty over South Sakhalin and the North Kuriles be decided in an international conference, but he persisted in claiming the return of the South Kuriles.[31] This proposal was bluntly rejected. On August 10, Khrushchev and Bulganin told him directly that the return of the Habomais and Shikotan was positively their final offer. Confronted with this ultimatum, Shigemitsu, who was on record as opposed to territorial concessions and an early settlement, made a complete personal volte-face and wired Tokyo that he had no alternative but to accept the Soviet terms.[32] Capitulation to this degree exceeded what the conservative leaders considered "discretion," and undoubtly it would have had a disruptive impact on the intraparty situation, especially in view of Hatoyama's commitment to an "honorable" settlement. In consequence, Shigemitsu was ordered to break off talks until after the international conference on Suez in London; in a special meeting on August 13, the Prime Minister and his cabinet decided to reject the Soviet offer.[33] Four days later the Foreign Minister was instructed to return to Japan after the Suez meeting, and Hatoyama expressed his intention to go personally to Moscow to break the stalemate.[34]

Shigemitsu bitterly condemned these decisions as prompted by domestic politics rather than international considerations.[35] The details of this situation will be explored later, but here two points are important. On August 10, Hatoyama announced that he would retire when Japan-Soviet relations were settled and his successor chosen. This statement intensified the already-raging struggle for conservative party control, and it further involved Soviet policy as an issue in the fray. Secondly, the conspicuous influence of intraparty bickering on an important foreign policy decision dropped public support of the government to an all-time low and completely alienated the business community.[36] Hence, the climax of the Soviet-Japanese negotiations coincided with a domestic political crisis.

In late August, United States Secretary of State John Foster Dulles further complicated the situation by threatening permanent American occupation of Okinawa if Japan ceded Etorofu and Kunashiri Islands to the Soviet Union.[37] Up to this point, the United States had not taken a strong stand on the territorial issue, although it had frequently consulted with the Japanese government at crucial junctures in the negotiations. Dulles' gesture was ostensibly designed to strengthen Japan's position, but since Tokyo was still in the process of formulating its position, it became merely another unsettling element in already confused circumstances.

With Shigemitsu's return to Japan, the Liberal-Democrats finally began to consider directly the merits of alternative policies toward the Soviet Union. It was painfully evident that policy toward the Soviet Union and party problems had become so interdependent that an acceptable decision on the former required resolution of the latter as well. Consequently, when the party accepted the mainstream faction's Adenauer-formula policy on September 6, it was necessarily linked with issues such as Hatoyama's early retirement and the retention of the existing cabinet.[38] Opposition from both the Yoshida and Shigemitsu factions continued to be strong; but when the tentative Soviet acceptance of the new proposal had been facilitated by another trip to Moscow by Matsumoto, Hatoyama and Kōno were able to depart for direct negotiations in Russia.[39]

The talks in Moscow, conducted in a cordial atmosphere, were somewhat anticlimactic. On October 19, just four days after the negotiations began, the Joint Declaration was formally signed.[40] Diet ratification followed on November 15, and the ratified documents were formally exchanged on December 11, thus completing Japan's first major post-independence foreign policy decision. Nearly two years had passed since the issue had first been raised, and a solution had come only after an agonizing and comprehensive test of the Japanese political system.

THE JOINT DECLARATION

To assure that the final product of the negotiations is understood from the outset, the substantive aspects of the Joint Declaration must be outlined.[41] The specific issues of the agreement which excited political activity in Japan will be met later in their appropriate places.

First of all, provisions were made to normalize diplomatic and economic ties. Articles 1 and 2 terminated the state of war between the two nations and provided for the establishment of diplomatic and consular representatives to facilitate the conduct of "peaceful and friendly relations." To this end, a separate protocol for the "promotion of trade and the mutual extension of the most-favored-nation treatment" was simultaneously signed,[42] and a pledge to work for a more comprehensive commercial treaty was included. The fishery agreement signed in May was also made effective with the Declaration's ratification.

With the exception of the territorial question, all issues outstanding from World War II were settled. Japanese nationals detained in the Soviet Union were to be immediately repatriated and all reparations claims were mutually renounced. The territorial settlement, which had proven to be the biggest stumbling block to rapprochement, was postponed. Negotiations for the conclusion of a peace treaty encompassing this issue were to continue after normal diplomatic ties had been resumed. With the conclusion of such a treaty, the Soviet Union agreed to return the Habomai and Shikotan Islands. Subsequent efforts toward such an accord have proved fruitless.

Japan's position in the international community was fully accepted. The Soviets had earlier balked at Article 5 in the San Francisco Treaty, which reaffirmed the right to individual and collective self-defense stipulated in Article 51 of the United Nations Charter, and on which the accompanying Japan-U.S. Security Treaty legally rested. However, this article, together with pledges to settle peacefully all international disputes and to refrain from interference in each other's internal affairs, was affirmed. The Soviet Union's pledge to support Japanese entrance into the United Nations resulted in the unanimous approval of Japan's membership application by the Security Council on December 12 and formal admission one week later.

Through this Joint Declaration, Japan appeared once again on the stage of international politics. Yet the stumbling manner in which the entrance was made brought Japan's future role into question. To this story we now turn.

III

The Conservatives

Any effort to understand the dynamics of Japanese policy-making in the Soviet negotiations must begin with the role of the conservative party. We have seen that policy control rested overwhelmingly in the hands of the ruling party and influence came almost entirely through access to the process of decision-making within the party. The role of the conservatives will be considered from two perspectives: the focus in this chapter mainly on intraparty policy formulation, and the remainder of the study touching on the relationships between the party and the other components of the political system.

The striking feature of conservative party policy-making was the influence of the factional struggle upon it. To examine this complicated process, I will investigate first the structure of the party and the pattern of factional interaction. Then the history of conservative policy on this issue will be traced, particularly demonstrating how the question became ensnared in the factional battle over party control. This battle proved to be the most important single factor in determining the shifts of Japan's position during the talks.

PARTY STRUCTURE AND THE DYNAMICS OF POWER

EARLY HISTORY

It is possible to appraise the situation among the Japanese conservatives during the 1955–56 period only against the backdrop of their extremely complicated postwar history. Within a few months following the surrender, the prewar party leaders prepared to re-enter politics, presumably to function under much the same conditions that had prevailed prior to the sweeping wartime changes of the militarists. Indeed, the two largest conservative parties established in late 1945, the Liberals (*Jiyutō*) and the Progressives (*Shimpotō*) were essentially regroupings of the prewar *Seiyūkai* and *Minseitō*, respectively.[1] Hatoyama Ichirō, a *Seiyūkai* veteran who had served as minister of education and had been narrowly defeated for the party presidency in the late thirties, assumed leadership of the Liberals. After his party won a plurality of seats in the first postwar House of Representatives election in April 1946, Hatoyama seemed assured the premiership. But then the extent of the Occupation political reforms was made dramatically clear to the conservative politicians. On the eve of his appointment, Hatoyama was declared an undesirable candidate under the January 4, 1946 Occupation purge directive, and was barred from holding any public office.[2] The Liberals were thus left in a peculiarly difficult situation. A leader acceptable to the remaining faction leaders in the party and to the Americans as well had to be found. In the context of these unique circumstances, Yoshida Shigeru was projected to the forefront of Japanese politics. Hatoyama personally persuaded Yoshida, a distinguished career diplomat with no previous party commitments or experience, to be his successor as party president and prime minister—with the understanding that the reins of the party would be returned to Hatoyama as soon as the purge had ended.[3] In this fashion the "Yoshida era" dawned on Japanese politics.

Yoshida entered the world of party politics with extreme reluctance,[4] but he proved to be a singularly effective leader. For the next eight years he personally dominated the Liberal Party and, with the exception of one sixteen-month interval, the Japanese government as well. Two factors were responsible for his success in maintaining power. First, no important rivals were able to challenge him as long as the purge kept virtually all veteran Liberal leaders out of politics. Secondly, operating in the shadow of the tutelary authority of the Occupation, Liberal Party unity was not subject to the divisive pressures later concomitant with full responsibilities for policy formulation. Under

these circumstances, Yoshida was able to concentrate on systematically developing his own *habatsu* of party Diet members;
almost all of these were ex-bureaucrats, new to politics in the
postwar period, and indebted to him for their political careers.[5]
This organization, built up in the political vacuum of the Occupation, retained control of the Liberal Party and the government for more than two years after independence and was a
potent force in conservative politics for much longer.

The main conservative opposition, initially called the Progressives, met with uneven success in challenging the Liberals.
This group opposed Yoshida's party mainly for tactical and
personal reasons, although in 1947 it made an effort to appear
as a middle-of-the-road party in support of a platform of "re-
formed capitalism." Despite depletion of the party's ranks by
the purge, and the strong appeal of the Socialists in the traditionally Minseitō urban districts (from which its electoral support was largely drawn), a strong showing was made in the
April 1947 general election. The following month, this group
(now called the Democratic Party) joined with the Socialists in
a coalition government for sixteen months.[6] This government
collapsed in the wake of a corruption scandal which implicated
several cabinet ministers, and public support of the Democrats
fell off sharply in the next election. Nevertheless, the party continued to poll nearly sixteen percent of the vote in subsequent
elections and held a similar proportion of Diet seats. Although
it was never again a threat to the hegemony of the Liberals, the
party continued to be a considerable political force.

With the end of the Occupation in 1952 and the return of the
purged party leaders, the situation within the conservative camp
altered. As the returning politicians sought to re-establish their
positions, clear and intense factional divisions emerged within
both parties. Liberal Party unity was further undermined by
Yoshida's refusal to relinquish the party presidency to Hatoyama, which precipitated a bitter personal power struggle leading ultimately to a sweeping conservative realignment.

Before achieving its goal, the movement to unseat Yoshida
met with two years of frustration and failure. Hatoyama, left a
semi-invalid by a stroke in 1951, made his first overt challenge

in the Liberal Party presidential election of the fall of 1952. Because his effort was frustrated by the circumstances within the party, he broke away a few months later and founded the Japan Liberal Party (*Nihon Jiyūtō*), in the hope of mounting a successful electoral challenge. However, after an overwhelming defeat in the April 1953 Upper House election, Hatoyama and most of his followers gradually returned to the old Jiyūtō and the struggle once again assumed intraparty dimensions.[7] Yoshida emerged from these public encounters triumphant, but not unscathed. The open challenges plus the persistent and increasing factional agitation clearly had a corrosive effect on his leadership. Consequently, in April 1954, at his instigation, a council was established to promote a new, unified conservative party—including the opposition conservative group, now called the *Kaishintō* (Reform Party). The result of this move was completely contrary to the intent. Rather than fostering party harmony in a manner favorable to the mainstream Liberal faction, it had precisely the opposite effect, i.e., consolidation of all conservative opposition to the Prime Minister. The organization collapsed in early July following the withdrawal of government support, but it was immediately succeeded by a similar group with an explicitly anti-Yoshida orientation under the leadership of Kishi Nobusuke, Ashida Hitoshi, and Ishibashi Tanzan. It was through this latter association that the foundation was laid for the establishment of the Japan Democratic Party (*Nihon Minshutō*), which was to unseat the Liberals before the end of the year.[8]

The development of organized opposition among the conservatives coincided with a sharp drop in Yoshida's public popularity. A scandal involving shipping interests had brought into question the integrity of many top Liberal leaders, and the Prime Minister aggravated matters by blatantly employing the powers of his office to prevent the arrest of Satō Eisaku, then a party leader and later the prime minister.[9] Business circles, long among Yoshida's staunchest supporters, also began to question openly his ability to control the political situation. Moreover, an opinion poll in September showed that public support for his government had fallen to an all-time low. Ignoring these por-

tents, Yoshida departed on a lengthy foreign tour, and his conservative opponents hastened to administer the coup de grâce.

Following complicated negotiations among the leaders of the
opposition factions, again centering on questions of personality
and position, the Democratic Party was formed on November
24, 1954. At its inception, the Minshutō essentially was a parliamentary coalition, composed of six *habatsu* united by their
opposition to Yoshida.[10] The nature of this alliance was almost
exclusively expediential; policy, much less ideological considerations, was of marginal significance. Moreover, the autonomous
nature of the factions, both financial and organizational, rendered the general party organs established at this time virtually
meaningless in a functional sense. Structurally, the party was a
loose agglomeration of politically independent groups—a factor
that shaped the selection of its leaders.

The choice of Hatoyama to lead the party resulted from the
interplay of a variety of influences. His earlier efforts to unseat
Yoshida and his position as the senior party figure made him a
leading candidate, despite the fact that he had shared the initiative in the movement to found the Minshutō with several others,
particularly Kishi. Secondly, if the Democrats were to retain
control of the government after the success of their parliamentary challenge, it was imperative for them to score an electoral
victory. Hatoyama was the best-qualified individual in the party
to lead such an effort. Not only was he a widely known and
extremely popular public figure, he was also a highly effective
campaigner. Finally, the precarious nature of the coalition proscribed the selection of a strong or ambitious leader, but at the
same time required the choice of a broadly accepted individual
able to prevent the early disintegration of the party. In terms of
these criteria, Hatoyama was uniquely suited. He possessed an
affable personality and, more importantly, his poor health and
advanced age made an early retirement likely. His selection
permitted at least temporary quiescence of *habatsu* rivalries
while the immediate problems of securing and consolidating
control of the government were achieved. Clearly, a fundamental reason that Hatoyama was acceptable as president was the
assumption that he would not lead either strongly or for long.

Consequently, even though he was formally the Democratic leader and proved to be the most popular political figure in the country, from the outset Hatoyama did not have control of the intraparty situation. This fact took on increased significance as he came to be personally identified with policies favoring the normalization of Soviet relations.

The vice-presidency of the new party and consequently the deputy prime ministership went to Shigemitsu Mamoru as leader of the Kaishintō. Shigemitsu's personal background as well as the immediate considerations underlying his appointment to these high posts shed light on his subsequent role in the Soviet talks. He was an outstanding example of a prewar bureaucrat. Prior to his entry into party politics, he had had a brilliant and colorful career in the Foreign Ministry. Thrice he had served as foreign minister, and it was he who represented the Japanese government in the formal surrender ceremonies on the deck of the *Missouri* in 1945. His record accorded him a status as an elder statesman which could be rivaled only by Yoshida, even though he had been convicted and purged as a Class A war criminal. While in Sugamo Prison, Shigemitsu declared his intention to enter party politics after his release. With the bravado befitting an aspirant *genro,* he declared his ambition to become prime minister so that he might "tutor the Japanese people in democracy." [11] He briefly considered joining the Liberal Party but was persuaded by Oasa Tadao and Ashida Hitoshi to enter the Kaishintō in June 1952, and shortly thereafter he was elected its president. Despite this auspicious beginning, Shigemitsu was neither comfortable nor adept in the rough world of party politics. As president, he did not build up his own *habatsu,* but sought to preserve party unity while remaining aloof from factional politics. [12]

Under his leadership, the Kaishintō did not gain appreciably in Diet strength, and by mid-1954 it was clear that the party could expect to participate in a government only as part of a coalition. At the same time, it also became evident that any successful effort by dissident Liberals to bring down Yoshida required the cooperation of the Kaishintō and its seventy-one Diet members. When such cooperation was sought in the fall of

1954 by the Hatoyama group, the Kaishintō included in its minimum price for cooperation the appointment of Shigemitsu as vice-president of the Democratic party—a demand which was justified both in terms of his party's strength as well as Shigemitsu's personal stature.[13] For Shigemitsu, the merger offered hope that his political ambitions would finally be realized. Indeed, he accepted the vice-presidency of the Democratic Party with the full expectation, if not the promise, that he would succeed Hatoyama as prime minister.[14] Shigemitsu also served as deputy prime minister and, largely through his own insistence, was named foreign minister as well. He held these positions for the duration of Hatoyama's term in office. It is important to recognize that in his eyes these posts were stepping stones; continued frustration of his ambition to head the government and differences with the Prime Minister over Russian policy combined to shape directly and dramatically the course of Soviet-Japanese negotiations.

Within two weeks after its birth, the new party, a motley factional coalition without strong leadership, formally took over the reins of government. To bring down the Liberals, which remained the largest party in the Diet, the Democrats had to secure the cooperation of the Socialists. This was achieved through a promise to hold a general election two months after the establishment of a Democratic government. Following passage of a no-confidence motion, Yoshida decided against dissolution, and the first Hatoyama cabinet was formed on December 7, 1954.

THE HATOYAMA ERA

The two years in which Hatoyama served as prime minister constituted a period of sweeping and fundamental change for the Japanese conservatives. They emerged formally united into a single party, but only after it had been demonstrated that the *habatsu* was their primary political grouping. What is significant is not that factions were present, but the extent to which the *ha* dominated conservative politics. Side by side with this divisive force was the pressure for unity induced by the growing electoral challenge from the united Socialist Party. In 1955 and

1956, a Socialist victory seemed possible if not imminent, as their popular support was then sharply rising. These cross pressures forced the conservatives to confront internal party problems. Particularly crucial was the question of leadership in a party which was now clearly invested with the responsibility for policy formulation, structurally fragmented, and operating under a concept of authority calling for consensual (i.e., overtly unanimous) agreement from its members. This situation begot a kind of *immobilisme,* which in the Soviet talks projected the factional struggle deeply into the policy-making process. It was broken (i.e., a decision made) only by the action of the Prime Minister when he freed himself from further political responsibilities by announcing his imminent retirement.

When the Democrats first came into power, their two overriding concerns were maintenance of party solidarity and strengthening of the party's Diet representation in the forthcoming general election. Since Hatoyama's caretaker government was in power at the sufferance of the Socialists, there was little latitude for intraparty dissension. Nevertheless, to assure that cohesion was maintained, cabinet positions and top party posts were allocated to give suitable representation to the six party factions.[15]

The effort to build momentum for the approaching election focused on a concerted campaign to distinguish the Democratic Party from the Liberals in terms of policies as well as personalities. Even though the Democrats themselves remained divided on the details of policy toward the Soviet Union, normalization of relations with Russia became the main slogan with which the party was identified. That this policy was set forth largely as a slogan finds corroboration from several sources. It was introduced by Shigemitsu, who was known to be cool to early Soviet ties, when he was inaugurated as foreign minister. Emphasis was given to the re-establishment of "friendly and peaceful relations with China and Russia" as part of a general revision of Yoshida's diplomacy.[16] Hatoyama extended still further the theme of a "more independent national policy . . . to normalize relations with Asian Communist nations" as a posture fundamentally different from that of the preceding Liberal government. The Prime Minister made such a policy a major theme in his campaign speeches, even declaring that Japan should take the initiative in normalizing ties with Russia.[17] In response, the Liberals were bitterly critical of any premature "appeasement" of the Soviets, and the resulting public debate perceptibly widened the already deep rift in the conservative camp. Since the Democrats themselves were divided over the details of policy toward Moscow, what was important was not the actual divisions fomented by this campaign, but the fact that Soviet policy was projected into the midst of the intra-conservative power struggle—where it remained for the next two years.

While the general election in February 1955 proved highly successful for the Democrats and an overwhelming personal victory for Hatoyama, the situation within the conservative body was left largely unaltered. Hatoyama himself polled more votes than any previous postwar candidate, and the strength of his faction went up sharply. However, his mainstream alliance still remained outnumbered by the old Kaishintō group, and a rumored move by his followers to replace Shigemitsu as Foreign Minister proved abortive.[18] Although the Democrats became the largest party in the Diet with 184 seats, they were left short of a majority and obliged to secure Liberal cooperation in order to act. The seeds of bitterness sown during the election campaign fully sprouted during the subsequent Diet session. The Liberals harassed and obstructed virtually every aspect of the government's legislative program. Criticism of the efforts to normalize Soviet relations was unrelenting, and the party flatly refused to give suprapartisan cooperation when the formal talks with the Soviets opened in June.[19]

In view of this background, it is clear that the preliminary merger talks begun in July by the two conservative parties were prompted not by widening areas of agreement and understanding but by the threat posed by the Socialists. It had become apparent that the Socialists' own merger talks, initiated several months earlier, would end successfully. This meant that a new unified opposition party would be formally inaugurated in mid-October. The countermove for conservative unity was initiated largely by three men: Democrats Kishi Nobusuke and Miki

Bukichi, and Liberal Ōhno Bamboku. The latter two individuals, who played the leading roles, were the doyens of Japanese party politicians; their careers extended far into the prewar period. Both were traditional politicians par excellence, masters at *machiai seiji* (behind-the-scenes politics—literally, geisha house politics), and it was on this level that the effective negotiations occurred. Not all factions were receptive to the move for unification, and there was some conflict as to whether Hatoyama or Liberal President Ogata Taketora would serve as leader of the new party. The underlying requisite for successful unification was the creation of an atmosphere in which recent foes would consent to be bedfellows, if not for affection, for reasons of mutual advantage. Through the skillful mediation of Miki and Ōhno this was achieved.[20] Relations with the Soviet Union was the one policy issue that played a role in the merger, in large part because it had already become deeply and publicly ensnared in the factional rivalries. The official policy of the newly merged party, calling for a treaty settlement returning the Southern Kurile Islands, seemed a triumph for the "go-slow" factions. But it proved a short-lived victory indeed. Except for policy toward the Soviets, the date for the formal merger (November 15) was set *before* discussion of the party platform and organization was undertaken—further indicating that this was a hastily arranged marriage of convenience.[21] Under these circumstances, the nature of conservative politics could not be, and was not, greatly changed by the formal party organs and procedures.[22]

The Liberal-Democratic Party was essentially a broadened coalition of *ha* with the party institutions merely providing new stages on which the old factional battles could be waged. The cast was larger, the drama basically the same. Although the cabinet (formed on November 23 by Hatoyama) did not reflect the scrupulous balancing of faction representatives found in the two previous Democratic Governments, the allocation of party posts inevitably involved consideration of *ha* interests.[23] Selection of the party president was not susceptible to *habatsu* compromise and the issue was left unresolved. A special proxy committee composed of Ogata, Hatoyama, Miki, and Ōhno served as the transitional executive while further negotiations continued. The platform was designed to promote party unity, and the goals and principles were enumerated in broad terms. As will be indicated specifically in regard to the policy toward Russia, it was not an accepted guide to policy formulation.

Information concerning conservative factions, although necessarily incomplete and of limited accuracy, is sufficient to permit sketching in broad strokes the structure of the Liberal-Democratic Party. At the time of the merger, the nature of the *ha* leadership was in the midst of transformation. In the prewar period the *habatsu* members had been bound to the leader (*ryōshū*) by ties of personal loyalty similar to those traditionally operative in the Japanese family.[24] Furthermore, the influential men usually did not hold prominent posts in the party or government hierarchy, but wielded their power in behind-the-scenes maneuvers.[25] After 1945, vestiges of this kind of leadership still remained prominent in conservative politics, particularly following the depurge of prewar politicians. Miki Bukichi, Ōhno Bambuko, and Hatoyama himself were among the most notable examples of what are commonly called *chōrō* (elderly, superior persons). However, in the altered postwar setting, the role of the *chōrō* gradually came to be challenged by a new kind of political leader, the *jitsuryokusha* (literally, real power man). Miki Takeo, Ikeda Hayato, and particularly Kōno Ichirō were among the first to emerge as *jitsuryokusha*—comparatively young, having access to political funds, and openly maneuvering for positions of influence as *ryōshū* of powerful *habatsu*. The same factors which lay behind the development of the postwar *ha*—the policy-making role of the Diet, fund-raising practices, and the like—also explain in broad terms the appearance of the new kind of political leaders. This change seems best understood in strictly situational terms, i.e., under the altered political conditions, a new species of Japanese conservative leader survived more readily. There is no way to determine precisely when the old gave way to the new, but the rise of the *jitsuryokusha* was manifest in the more public and more intensified factional battle following the merger, especially the open and acrimonious *habatsu* clashes in the summer and fall of 1956. Behind-the-scenes negotiations were still important in resolving conflict, but the style of politics was changing—postwar *ha* were replacing pre-war *ha*.[26]

At its inception the Liberal-Democratic Party was not only divided into approximately ten *habatsu,* but these in turn were allied into mainstream and anti-mainstream groupings—a division which has become a permanent feature of the conservative political terrain. Essentially, the two major groups are coalitions of factions in competition for the party presidency. The factions in a coalition may share similar policy orientation, but more basic bonds are alliances between various *habatsu* leaders in their attempts to gain control of the party. At one extreme are the allies of the prime minister, and at the other are those in full opposition, while in the center are factions whose commitments shift from one bloc to the other. The negotiation and compromise required to maintain a majority coalition is the essence of the factional system. Policy leadership necessarily depends on maintaining a delicate balance among the *habatsu* and inevitably encompasses personal factors beyond substantive considerations of policy. On most issues the mainstream *versus* anti-mainstream split is of little import, and only if a policy matter is sufficiently significant and controversial to bring into question the position of the prime minister do the lines of these groups become openly drawn. Even in such circumstances there is considerable fluidity because of the subjective basis on which these coalitions rest.

During the period from the merger until the Soviet-Japanese Joint Declaration, the question of Hatoyama's successor was almost constantly open, leaving the components of the mainstream and anti-mainstream groupings more visible. The nucleus of the mainstream consisted of the Hatoyama, the Miki Bukichi–Kōno, and the Kishi factions, and the opposition always included the old Yoshida (headed by Ikeda Hayato) and the Ogata (later Ishii Mitsujirō) *habatsu.* The other *ha* tended to be correspondingly allied along the lines of the old Democratic and Liberal parties (the former constituting the mainstream, the latter the opposition), but there were some notable exceptions. Three former Democratic Party factions, the Ishibashi, Ashida, and Miki Takeo *ha,* normally worked with the anti-mainstream group. Both Ishibashi and Ashida had broken primarily because of personal dislike for and disputes with Kōno, while Miki, because of a strong stand against the merger, was denied representation in the third Hatoyama Cabinet and in this way was forced into opposition.[27] On the other hand, former Liberal Ōhno Bamboku's large *habatsu,* for tactical and personal rather than policy reasons, came to be closely identified with the mainstream.[28]

Although the power configuration remained essentially unaltered during the first months after the merger, the sudden death of Ogata in late January resolved the problem of electing the party president in favor of the mainstream group. Ogata's supporters were unable to unify around a single candidate in the two months preceding the presidential election and challenge Hatoyama effectively. He ran unopposed and was elected by an overwhelming, though not unanimous vote.[29] Although this left the cabinet and the formal party organization intact, the underlying cleavages were also unaffected.

Internal antagonisms placed severe limitations on Hatoyama's capacity to provide positive leadership as was clearly demonstrated when he and Kōno sought to force an early normalization of Soviet-Japanese ties. The Russians had provided the opportunity for this maneuver by imposing fishing restrictions, thereby transforming the entire question of Soviet relations into an urgent domestic political issue. Despite Gaimushō and intraparty opposition, Kōno, who as Minister of Agriculture and Forestry had some jurisdictional claim, was appointed chief delegate of the special fishery mission, with the clear intention (public promises to the contrary notwithstanding) that his negotiations in Moscow would range beyond the subject of fish.[30] The resulting fishery agreement, which required the reopening of the general talks by the end of July, fulfilled their plans, but the repercussions produced among the Liberal-Democrats were damaging. Indeed, this policy triumph proved to be a Pyrrhic victory in terms of intraparty politics.

Two closely related considerations were the targets of the conservative attacks on Hatoyama: his authority as party leader, and the substance of the policy he advocated. He had on several occasions announced his "responsibility" for settling Soviet-Japanese relations. Consequently, there were implications of a definite decision on this matter contained in the fishery pact, and these inevitably provided a critical test of his authority as prime minister. Because a major policy decision seemed imminent, incentive was provided for all the anti-mainstream factions to attack the government privately and publicly on its handling of the problem. In addition, much more vocal opposition came from those groups which had consistently favored a full-fledged treaty settlement. Although official party policy held for a final settlement also, the mainstream *ha* had set the stage for a frontal clash by indicating on several occasions that an Adenauer-type settlement would be acceptable in order to break the stalemate.[31] Initially, opposition was mainly in the form of critical public statements by individuals such as Yoshida and Foreign Minister Shigemitsu, and the party's Foreign Policy Research Committee.[32] In retaliation, Kōno let it be known that he favored a cabinet reshuffle to consolidate the mainstream's control. By early June, the factional battle had reached such serious proportions that the Executive Board barred discussion of Soviet relations during the House of Councillors campaign which began later in the month, and in comic-opera fashion, threatened to keep the Prime Minister from electioneering because of "repeated slips of the tongue" concerning the subject.[33] Thus Kōno and Hatoyama's effort to press for an early settlement weakened rather than strengthened their party position and set forces into motion that threatened the very existence of the conservative coalition.

Pressures of the election campaign imposed a brief respite, but then the intraparty situation deteriorated even more rapidly. A major stabilizing influence on the party was removed on July 4 with the death of Miki Bukichi, the mainstream's leading strategist in the world of *habatsu* politics.[34] Shortly thereafter the Liberal-Democrats made a poor showing in the upper house election; their popular vote dropped sharply, and the Socialists achieved control of one-third of the Councillors' seats for the first time since independence.[35] This was a particularly serious setback for Hatoyama since it undercut his prestige as a successful vote getter, one of the major reasons for his position as party president. With the mainstream weakened in these ways, the Yoshida group boldly demanded the immediate resignation of the Prime Minister.

In the midst of the crisis, still another incident brought severe censure to the party leadership: the stumbling manner in which the members of the delegation to Moscow were selected. Two factors in particular lay behind the confusion. First, the ambiguity surrounding the party's policy toward the Soviet Union meant that the attitudes of the plenipotentiaries dispatched could heavily influence the direction of the talks. Hence the "go slow" and "early settlement" groups vied for representation. Secondly, personality conflicts, so fundamental to the behind-the-scenes *habatsu* politics, intruded, transforming the episode into an unseemly, almost farcical public display. Both Sunada Shigemasa, an ally of Kōno, and Satō Naotake, an ex-diplomat and non-party member of the Upper House, were designated plenipotentiary and then withdrawn for political reasons. Ultimately, Foreign Minister Shigemitsu, who under standard practices of international diplomacy would have served ex officio as plenipotentiary, was the compromise choice to head the delegation. He had been consistently cool to the idea of any negotiation at this time, and his presence on the mission was balanced by Matsumoto Shunichi, London plenipotentiary and close adviser to Hatoyama. Nevertheless, Shigemitsu was piously accorded "the full and unified support of the party" and left following a gala, highly publicized bon-voyage party given by the Liberal-Democrats.[36]

When, on August 10, Hatoyama announced his intention to retire, it did not come as a surprise. The value in his continuing as party leader was clearly open to question, and a settlement with the Soviet Union, a primary aim of his administration, seemed within reach. However, almost immediately complications appeared, postponing his departure from the political scene. The intensified *ha* battle touched off by his retirement statement coincided with an unexpected turn in the Moscow talks, which were again suspended without an agreement. The fluid events of the succeeding weeks constituted a major crisis for the conservatives. The *habatsu* struggle became synonymous with the foreign policy-making process as political conflict revolved around the question of Soviet relations. Therefore, it is now appropriate to turn back to the entire question of the development of conservative policy toward Russia.

FOREIGN POLICY FORMULATION PROCESS

POLICY SHIFTS AND PARTY INFLUENCE

There are many points at which conservative politics and the formulation of Japan's policy toward the Soviet Union touched and commingled, but to explore each of them through a comprehensive chronology would confuse as much as it would clarify. Consequently, in describing conservative decision-making, focus is narrowed to analysis of the five policy shifts between 1954 and 1956. Even this more concentrated approach does not rigorously demonstrate causal relationships, but it does shed light on the interaction between policy changes and intra-party politics.

A recapitulation of the initial moves toward normalizing Soviet ties in late 1954 and early 1955 clarifies the relationship between conservative politics and the first important policy shift. After forming the first Democratic Government, Hatoyama explicitly made normalization of relations with the Soviet Union and Communist China a major policy goal.[37] This was Japan's first official move away from the stance of unqualified confrontation.[38] Motivating their desire for greater flexibility were both the genuine conviction of the Prime Minister and his advisers as to the merit of a more pragmatic, independent foreign policy, and the previously noted necessity of becoming more clearly distinguished from the Liberals in the forthcoming general election.[39] Initially, this diplomatic shift was only one of several policy aims set forth by the government; equal priority was assigned to both Chinese and Soviet relations. Only after the Russians specifically announced their willingness to normalize ties and Hatoyama indicated his receptiveness in several speeches did it become an issue of importance. Following a number of critical public exchanges with the Liberals, the subject assumed still greater proportions when, on the eve of the campaign, Soviet emissary Andrei Domnitsky bypassed official diplomatic channels to deliver a note to the Prime Minister requesting that formal talks be opened. Both the timing of this move and the covert manner in which the note was delivered to Hatoyama himself led to still greater public discussion.* Thus, the Prime Minister and his faction became closely identified with the issue, making it imperative that the government press for a positive solution to the problem. Therefore, in succeeding months, Hatoyama took the lead in the preparations for the formal talks in London in June.

The crucial events involved in this change to a more conciliatory policy toward the Soviet Union—the broad statement of the government's goals, public political speeches, pronouncements from Moscow, and *à couvert* maneuvers by an "unofficial" Russian delegate—indicate the loose nature of conservative decision-making during this period. Contributing to the unusual disorder of these maneuvers was the failure of the Democratic Party to take a clear stand on the question. A forthright position was, however, virtually proscribed by the strong opposition of leading Democrats, such as Foreign Minister Shigemitsu and faction leader Ashida Hitoshi, as well as by the extremely tenuous structure of the newly formed party. Any move by Hatoyama to force acceptance of his more conciliatory views would have jeopardized the very existence of the Democratic coalition. Despite the absence of intraparty communications, the Prime Minister and his associates gave emphasis to policy leadership on this issue, necessarily operating in an ad hoc and independent manner. Two actions especially illustrate the autonomous fashion in which they operated: Hatoyama's statements urging early rapprochement, which were in contrast with Shigemitsu's publicly expressed views,[40] and the Prime Minister's eager acceptance of the Soviet note after the same message had been rejected by the Foreign Ministry.[41] Hatoyama did successfully achieve his short-term aims: he introduced the

* For elaboration, see the section on policy groups in Chapter V.

issue into the election campaign, with dramatic effect, and scheduled the normalization talks. But because these were accomplished without consultation with, or much less with the broad agreement of the Democrats, party divisions deepened. In addition, of course, the campaign to promote relations with the Soviets severely aggravated the rift with the Liberals over this issue.

It is clear from these tangled events in Tokyo that Japan's policy change toward Moscow was not a carefully calculated diplomatic action. The shift toward normalization was first introduced in the form of a slogan, primarily for domestic political effect, and the government's moves in the weeks immediately following were guided largely by considerations of internal politics. As a result, the Soviets held the diplomatic initiative from the outset, and from an international viewpoint, it was in response to their maneuvers that the changes in Japanese policy took place. Japan's role was an extremely passive one.

When the London talks opened in June, Hatoyama's faction was still in control of Soviet policy, but little had been done to repair the fragmentation of the conservative alliance. Not only was there a split within the Democrats, but Liberal opposition on this matter had intensified, becoming increasingly overt and uncompromising as time passed. In late May, the Prime Minister made a carefully timed bid for suprapartisan cooperation, but was flatly refused.[42] This setback came on the eve of the talks during a highly publicized meeting between Hatoyama and Liberal Party President Ogata. It publicly demonstrated that the Liberals were as much committed to obstructing a settlement as the leading Democratic faction was to promoting one. The hope for successful negotiations lay, therefore, in rapid movement toward mutual agreement in London, and even more, in the protection of the issue from any domestic political compromise at home.

That the government was pressing for an early agreement is evident from its position on the crucial territorial question. The first Japanese proposal (in the form of a memorandum to the Soviets) called for the return of all formerly Japanese lands occupied by the Soviets at the end of World War II, but Pleni-

potentiary Matsumoto Shunichi had been given additional in-
structions specifying that three distinctions in regard to the
disputed territory were also factors in the negotiations.[43] First,
the Habomais and Shikotan were to be claimed unconditionally
as inherently Japanese, and most importantly, *the return of
these islands was to be considered satisfactory grounds for a
treaty.* Second, priority was attached to the Southern Kuriles,
which were demanded for "historical reasons" but were not
deemed essential for an overall settlement. Finally, the Northern Kuriles and Southern Sakhalin were claimed simply for bargaining purposes.[44] Consequently, when on August 5, the
Soviets suddenly modified their proposal and offered the return
of the Habomais and Shikotan as well as acceptable conditions
for all other outstanding issues, an agreement seemed imminent.
However, at this point, the Japanese government abruptly revised its position, and extended the minimum territorial claim to
include the Southern Kuriles. The revision surprised and
angered the Russians, who indignantly branded the new terms
totally unacceptable. Within two weeks the talks were suspended.

The reason for the sudden Japanese reversal can be found
lodged in the interstices of the conservative coalition. When the
Liberals and the Democrats initiated merger talks in July, a
common policy toward the Soviet Union was a major point of
contention. Although detailed supporting evidence is not available, the expanded territorial claim in the London negotiations
seems to have been the direct result of a government compromise with the Liberals intended to foster unification of the two
conservative parties. In November, this revised territorial position was embodied in the platform of the newly merged conservative party at the public insistence of the Liberals, although
agreement on this issue had been achieved in the unification
talks held four months earlier. Kōno admitted as much when, in
a conversation with Matsumoto in London in late August, he
told the plenipotentiary that the sudden alteration of the government's policy had been caused by "pressures of domestic politics." [45] Furthermore, there seems to have been little attention
given to the international consequences of this action. Matsu-

moto, invested with plenary authority, was as surprised as the Soviets at the sudden policy change.[46] He had never been consulted on the matter, an oversight which would hardly have occurred had the shift been a considered move by the government. In this instance, the slighting of international considerations thanks to intraparty conservative politics was to prove costly to Japan.

At this time, Soviet internal politics were in a transitional state. Khrushchev was still striving to consolidate his own power position. Foreign policy was directly involved as he sought acceptance by other party leaders of a softer international approach, including normalized relations with Western Germany and Japan.[47] The modified proposal made to Japan in early August, involving return of the Habomais and Shikotan, should be seen in this light. Japan's expanded territorial claims greatly embarrassed the Soviet leader since his position in the Kremlin was also involved. This led to early suspension of the London meetings and assuredly contributed to the subsequent intransigence of the Russians on the territorial question.

Despite two additional months of talks in London in early 1956, the deadlock continued until the Soviets sought to break the stalemate by introducing a new consideration, restrictions on Japanese fishing in the northern seas bordering Russia. Immediately, the Japanese fishing industry used its close personal and financial ties with the Hatoyama faction to press for early redress of this action.[48] The efforts of this group, the general public outcry over a tangible national grievance, and the eagerness of the Prime Minister to stabilize relations with the Soviet Union resulted in an emergency fishery conference in Moscow in late April, convened at the insistence of the Japanese. Ostensibly, the sole purpose of this meeting was settling the fishery question for that year, a point made clear in statements by the Foreign Ministry, the Liberal-Democratic Party's Executive Committee and Foreign Policy Research Committee, Hatoyama, and Kōno, who was chosen to lead the delegation.[49] The opposition's concern that the scope of the mission be clearly and openly delineated came from the fear that Kōno and the Prime Minister would use this opportunity to break the impasse in the

general negotiations—a distrust which proved to be well
founded. The Soviets' timing in imposing fishery restrictions
(i.e., the day after the London talks were suspended) and
their insistence on making the fishing settlement contingent
upon the normalization of diplomatic ties indicates that they
shared Hatoyama's intent. The conditions of the settlement, embodied in Kōno's agreement, placed the issue of Soviet relations
in a new perspective, making an early settlement along the lines
of the Adenauer formula much more likely.

As in the events which led to the opening of the 1955 negotiations, the Hatoyama-Kōno faction was able to change the direction of policy at this time by exploiting the power of initiative available to it through control of crucial formal positions in
the government. To have followed through with a binding policy
decision, however, would have required the support of a deeply
divided party, and Miki Bukichi vetoed any effort to force the
issue in the face of intraparty opposition, since it was likely to
precipitate a conservative split.[50] Instead, despite the greatly
increased pressure for a policy commitment, nothing was done.
In the following weeks, the conservatives were occupied with
the House of Councillors election and the selection of the Moscow delegation. No serious consideration was given to the substantive questions involved in Soviet relations. Because the
party failed to make a decision, the responsibility for formulating a new policy was left in the hands of Plenipotentiary–
designate Shigemitsu. He was dispatched to Moscow with "discretion" to negotiate, but no guidelines were offered, other than
the government's formal position on which the previous formal
talks had twice foundered and which obviously remained unacceptable to the Russians.

In Moscow, the Soviets were predictably unyielding on their
territorial position, but Shigemitsu, to the surprise of everyone
and the consternation of Japanese conservative leaders, accepted the Russian proposal for a treaty returning only the
Habomais and Shikotan—the same offer the government had
rejected in London and which he personally had often condemned. But this dramatic shift in Japanese policy was never
effected, for within three days the Cabinet turned down the

proposal and suspended the negotiations; the delegation returned to Japan shortly thereafter. Before considering what,
determined these decisions in Tokyo, a brief recapitulation of
Shigemitsu's overall role in the negotiations will be instructive
in comprehending his dramatic about-face.

Shigemitsu's actions at first seem confusing, but they reflect
the ambivalence of his position. Despite his place in the government, from the first he sought to slow down and obstruct the
progress of the negotiations. On several occasions he issued
public statements directly at odds with previous pronouncements by the Prime Minister, thus embarrassing Hatoyama and
inhibiting his efforts to foster an early settlement. Contrary to
Hatoyama, he declared that Russia, not Japan, should take the
initiative in any moves toward an early settlement. Shigemitsu
openly differed with the Prime Minister on the need for a treaty
settlement rather than an agreement simply restoring diplomatic
relations.[51] Such statements were as muted as possible, but
they made evident to all that the Foreign Minister and
Hatoyama were in fundamental disagreement on the substance
of policy.

Shigemitsu also used his powers and prerogatives as foreign
minister to impede the formal dealings of the government with
the Soviets: the Domnitsky note had been rejected by the
Gaimushō for reasons of protocol; in June 1955, he purposely
gave a distorted emphasis to the Soviet offer in London by
describing it as being "similar to the contents of the peace treaty
proposed by Mr. Gromyko in San Francisco"; [52] and he made
an abortive effort to block Kōno's trip to Moscow for the fishery
negotiations. Two considerations lay behind his obstructionist
tactics—a perception of the international situation that involved
greater distrust of the Soviets and assigned high priority to close
Japanese-American relations,[53] as well as a distaste for the
manner in which the negotiations were being conducted. While
in the Foreign Ministry, Shigemitsu had acquired a reputation
as a highly meticulous negotiator and could not but be instinctively repulsed by the free-wheeling, pragmatic diplomatic
techniques employed by Kōno and Hatoyama.[54] Hatoyama, at
crucial points during the talks, purposefully by-passed the

Gaimushō and Shigemitsu to deal directly with the Russians.*
For these reasons, Shigemitsu became a detractor of the government's conciliatory Soviet policy.

Yet his opposition was scrupulously restrained; it successfully
avoided an open split, and ultimately made possible his selection as plenipotentiary of the Moscow delegation. This restraint
is best understood in terms of his responsibilities and ambitions
in party politics. A rigid and provocative stand against
Hatoyama over Soviet policy undoubtedly would have jeopardized his place in the cabinet and undermined his aspirations for
the prime ministership by narrowing his support in the party.
His ambitions remained, but his position within the conservatives steadily worsened as factional rivalries grew, for in the
world of *habatsu* Shigemitsu continued to be ineffective. By the
middle of 1956, it was clear that to contend for party leadership
he could not rely on intraparty maneuvers but would need a
foreign policy coup of some sort. It is in these terms that his
sudden policy switch in Moscow should be viewed. It seems to
have been an abortive attempt to capture the prestige that
would accrue from the settlement of what had become a tire-
some and divisive issue in Japan, thereby bolstering his strength
in the party.[55] The events following his recall to Tokyo drolly
corroborate this interpretation. Two emissaries from Japan met
with him en route home—one a government representative, to
insure that he would not issue any statements concerning the
intraparty split, and the other a party ally, to inform him of the
current maneuvers within the Liberal-Democrats. The results of
the Soviet talks were for the moment secondary.[56] With the
support of former Kaishintō members, Shigemitsu blocked
moves for a cabinet reshuffle that would have added to his
public embarrassment. Nonetheless, his political future was de-
stroyed. Even this short-lived shift in official policy, though
engineered single-handedly by career-diplomat Shigemitsu, was
yet shaped by intraparty considerations, and its rejection is similarly explained. The factional struggle within the Liberal-
Democratic party greatly intensified after the Foreign Minister's
return and now focused on the Soviet question.

* For elaboration, see Chapter VIII.

Immediately following Shigemitsu's departure from Tokyo, the conservative *habatsu* leaders had begun concentrated discussions of Hatoyama's retirement and the advantages of a cabinet reshuffle. Coming at a time when a display of national unity was universally supported, these meetings were strongly condemned by the press and leading business groups. When on August 10 the Prime Minister made public his intention to retire, the responsibility for naming his successor was left completely in the hands of other Liberal-Democratic leaders, signifying that efforts to resolve intraparty differences had failed. Four days later, the Soviet offer tentatively accepted by Shigemitsu was rejected both by the Executive Board of the party and by the cabinet, despite the fact it met the minimum demands initially specified by the government in the London talks and that as plenipotentiary, Shigemitsu had been given full discretion to negotiate. However, to have acquiesced under such conditions would have rendered absurd the preceding year of talks with the Soviets, deprived Hatoyama of a graceful way of retiring, left a major section of the conservative camp bitterly dissatisfied, and risked substantial public opposition. Hatoyama's announcement five days later that he would personally go to Moscow to reopen negotiations provoked vehement conservative opposition. Soviet policy then became fully entangled in the factional battle for party control, and the struggle to settle both questions was carried on during succeeding weeks in full public view.

For Hatoyama, a satisfactory end to his political career required that ties with the Soviet Union be normalized. This issue more than any other had come to be identified with his government, and he had taken the lead in the efforts to secure an early agreement. Indeed, failure in this regard would have a peculiarly individual flavor, since he had repeatedly proclaimed full responsibility for gaining a settlement, thereby risking personal embarrassment if not dishonor. His formal retirement announcement made all the more imperative the need for an immediate final effort. At the same time, it placed him in a unique position to provide policy leadership. In undertaking a course of action, he was freed from the pressures to develop party agreement and to protect his own position. Consequently, Hatoyama was strongly motivated to act and was also able to force the issue with little regard for the normal inhibitions to positive policy formulation. His decision to visit Russia and his behavior in the face of the controversy surrounding this move must be viewed in the context of his unique situation.

Kōno strongly supported the Prime Minister's plan, but as an ambitious and powerful *habatsu* leader he was also concerned over its impact on the party situation. He pressed for an immediate cabinet reshuffle to replace Shigemitsu and strengthen the position of the mainstream faction for the impending showdown on policy and for the coming party presidential election.[57] The main outcome of his proposal was to still further emphasize the play of factionalism upon the policy issue.

The opposition was built around the hard core of the anti-mainstream group—the followers of Yoshida, antagonistic to the Prime Minister personally and strongly against the policy of normalization. Their tactics forced total confrontation in the spheres of both politics and policy. Not only was the proposed Moscow trip vehemently condemned, but the Prime Minister's immediate resignation was demanded, ostensibly on the grounds that he bore full responsibility for the increasingly chaotic situation in the party and the recent electoral setbacks.[58] They sought to obstruct the government in both the cabinet and party meetings, while maintaining a continuous barrage of criticism in the press. Finally, in late September, by establishing the Situation Consultation Committee (*Jikyoku Kondankai*)—a loose alliance of anti-mainstream conservatives—a direct but abortive challenge to party unity was made in a manner closely paralleling that used to topple Yoshida in 1954.[59] This persistent opposition made impossible even the semblance of party consensus on Soviet policy and kept attention focused on the question of Hatoyama's retirement.

The complex relationship between Hatoyama's foreign policy and his retirement was further graphically illustrated in the vacillating alliances of two groups normally allied with the mainstream faction. Virtually all former Kaishiuntō members were at first opposed to the Prime Minister's trip because it was linked with a cabinet reshuffle affecting Shigemitsu, their former president. However, once the plan for such a change was dropped and a direct affront to their prestige within the party circumvented, the majority switched to support Hatoyama— despite Shigemitsu's continued objections to new talks at this time.[60] Kishi Nobusuke, party Secretary-General and the leader of the largest faction, also momentarily moved into opposition toward Hatoyama's trip. Personally, he heavily favored a pro-United States, anti-Communist international posture (as conclusively demonstrated in the Security Treaty incident of 1960), and undoubtedly he was impressed by Dulles' blunt threat of expanded American claims to Okinawa should Japan accede to Soviet territorial demands. Nevertheless, considerations of party politics seem to have been even more important than this broad policy inclination in guiding his actions. He was the leading candidate to succeed Hatoyama, and to maintain this position, it was particularly essential that he pick the "right" side in the dispute centering on Soviet relations. This task was far from easy. In the turbulent state of affairs during late August and early September, it was not clear whether the Prime Minister could control the situation. Furthermore, Kishi's chief financial backer, Fujiyama Aiichirō, and the business world in general, had shifted to opposition to immediate negotiations and were demanding Hatoyama's resignation.[61] In the face of these pressures, Kishi relented and issued a statement denouncing the Prime Minister's plan. That his move was prompted by sheer expediency became clear just a few days later when he returned, chameleon-like, to the side of the government, once the intra-party political tides again seemed to be running in favor of Hatoyama.[62]

What is significant is not that conservative party politics shaped Japanese policy toward the Soviet Union, but the *degree* and *manner* in which it did. As events moved toward a climax, the issue came to be almost completely defined in terms of intraparty considerations; the direction of policy was independent even of American strictures. Hatoyama set the stage for such development with his proposal to visit the Soviet Union without any indication of a change in official policy. In effect, this merely meant the substitution of one negotiator for another, again avoiding a confrontation of the substantive issues in question. In the spate of top-level party conferences following his statement, concern was not with minimum conditions for a satisfactory settlement with Russia, but over the impact of the Prime Minister's move on the *habatsu* balance in the party.[63]

Thus the final decision was not reached through channels of responsible party leadership. Rather, acceptance of the Adenauer formula came only with the resolution of differences within the mainstream group, especially with the retention of the entire cabinet and Hatoyama's promised retirement.[64] Hatoyama was able to pursue successfully his foreign policy only through personal capitulation to the exigencies of party unity. It was not an act clothed with the authority of the Prime Minister's leadership of government and party. Moreover, as will be elaborated, the nature and momentum of the intraparty decision-making process made it a self-contained decision, only peripherally affected by political forces outside the party.*

FORMAL PARTY ORGANIZATIONS AND POLICIES

Because policy formulation was so much confined within the Liberal-Democratic Party, some attention must be given to the structural effect of the official party organizations and policies. Their role, while significant, did not fulfill their original purpose. The formal party structure and procedures did not provide authoritative channels for the resolution of conflict. Instead, they became instruments in the policy-making process, manipulated by *habatsu* leaders and the close advisers of the Prime Minister. In particular, the official organizations figured prominently in the efforts to check the actions of Kōno and Hatoyama.

The most bitter opposition to the Prime Minister came ironically from the group specifically responsible for drafting the party's foreign policy, the Foreign Policy Research Committee (*Gaikō Chōsa Iinkai*). It was composed of former diplomats,

* On public disapproval of Hatoyama's journey to Moscow, see Chapters IV and V; on the obstructive efforts of business interests, see Chapter VII.

who all had strongly anti-Communist orientations, and was headed by Ashida Hitoshi, a career Foreign Office official and a former prime minister. Ashida, by virtue of his position as a faction leader in the Kaishintō, had been named chairman of the committee in the Democratic Party. He was retained in this post after the conservative merger, in part because his policy views accorded with those of the Liberals, and he directed the attack on Hatoyama's conciliatory posture.[65] The Prime Minister's position was consistently rejected by the committee; it gave its uncompromising support to the "official" policy, that which maintained the larger territorial demands. In spite of the committee's formal title and the vigorous performance of its duties, it was able to exert little direct influence on policy through authorized channels. Instead, under the aggressive leadership of Ashida, it acted through public statements, carefully timed, strongly worded, and issued in the name of the Liberal-Democratic Foreign Policy Research Committee.[66]

The committee's antagonism exposed the sharp party split over the policy issue and undoubtedly embarrassed the government, but there is no indication that its efforts were in any way decisive. Significantly, the agreement with the Soviets was achieved in the face of constant and extreme hostility from this committee, the authorized voice of the party on foreign affairs.

The official Liberal-Democratic Party policy toward Russia was a compromise to facilitate the conservative merger, and there is some doubt that it was ever taken seriously by Hatoyama and Kōno. On several occasions the Prime Minister publicly expressed his disagreement, and, more importantly, it did not greatly inhibit his efforts to foster an early agreement. In making the fishery settlement contingent on the reopening of diplomatic negotiations, Kōno acted directly contrary to official party policy.[67] Similarly, in September the shift to the Adenauer formula was not formally ratified before Hatoyama's departure for Moscow by any of the responsible party organizations: the Foreign Policy Research Committee, the party Policy Committee, or the party Executive Board.[68] In short, shifts in government policy were made in spite of, not because of official party policy.

The actions of the party Executive Board, the principal organ for directing party affairs, displayed no independent capacity to control the *habatsu* and in that way shape policy. In August, when factional rivalries intensified and were focused on Soviet policy, the Executive Board meetings became a major arena for these conflicts, but such meetings merely were an extension of previous informal conferences of *ha* leaders.[69] The inability of this organization to affect the policy-making process was demonstrated in September and early October. With the Board deadlocked over his proposed trip, Hatoyama simply circumvented it by gaining official approval from the more tractable cabinet and then departed [70]—demonstrating once again that the formal decision-making apparatus of the Liberal-Democrats was incapable of constraining the policy formulation process.

TRADITIONALISM AND DECISION-MAKING

Among the most striking features of conservative decision-making is the persistence of traditional structures for the resolution of conflict. In the most general sense, Japan stands as an example par excellence of a society which has modernized through the positive use of traditional culture and social structure,[71] and it is hardly surprising to find vestiges of these practices in the conservative party, even in the context of the constitutionally democratic and "developed" political setting of the postwar era. The kinds of practices which have survived and their adapted forms are of interest. In the Soviet negotiations, four examples of modified traditional behavior (Almond calls it the "traditional-modern dualism") [72] were prominently displayed by the Liberal-Democrats: the personality-centered *habatsu* grouping, the personal (Confucian) sense of responsibility, the concept of consensual authority rather than majoritarian, and a leadership pattern which centered around the *jitsuryokusha*. Together they gave a peculiarly Japanese style to the pattern of decision-making.

Political parties in all open societies are divided internally, but Japanese factions are unique in several respects. Whereas most factions are based upon ideological or territorial divisions or are directly tied to economic or social groups outside of the party, *habatsu* center around a single individual, are buttressed by traditional attitudes of personal loyalty, and in both origin and function are almost exclusively party organizations. The personalism so characteristic of Japanese politics was especially manifest during the Soviet negotiations in the extreme nonpolicy cast of the *ha,* which functioned essentially as power blocs loyal to their leaders. There was little evidence that the factions were a transient political grouping destined to give way to the "more limited, programmatic, and functionally defined allegiances represented by modern interest groups and political parties" that Ward speaks of.[73] Whatever the roots of party factions in traditional social attitudes and practices may be, the *habatsu* appeared in the Soviet negotiations as fully integral factors of the early postwar political order, and they seem destined to be permanent features of this system.

Hatoyama's traditional concept of a leader's responsibility elicited his dogged determination to see that the issue of Soviet relations, which he had raised, be resolved, in spite of compelling physical and personal reasons to retire. In asserting his responsibility, Hatoyama was not declaring that he held the office constitutionally vested with responsibility for this sort of decision. His statements are significant in terms of traditional (Confucian) ethics. Responsibility of this kind is not based on an election mandate, but rather is of a personal nature, requiring adherence to an abstract ideal. Leaders are responsible to the people because of moral demands, not because they derive their authority from the people. Consequently, Hatoyama assumed moral responsibility for satisfactorily solving this problem, and failure would likewise be cast in personal, moral terms and could not be dismissed as merely an unavoidable policy frustration.[74] The practice of this personal conception of moral responsibility in the position of the prime minister, where authority was constitutionally limited and functionally discrete, inevitably produced a unique kind of leadership.

Legitimate authority is consensual in many non-Western nations and open confrontation to resolve conflicts is avoided in numerous states both modern and modernizing, yet the decision-making practices of the Liberal-Democrats have a distinctiveness of their own. *Machiai seiji* finds support not only in the political culture of the Japanese political elite, including the dislike of face-to-face confrontation and the need for a display of unity,[75] but is related to the peculiar composition of this elite and the processes of politics that have emerged in the postwar era. Private consultations are the heart of the decisional process, producing policies that in a basic sense preclude further serious Diet debate and which the majority party transforms into law. In contrast, the crudely analogous cloakroom politics of the United States Congress is basically an addendum to policy debate and as a pattern of decision-making that is primarily public, it involves individuals from both parties and is constrained by institutional checks. The nature of behind-the-scene talks among Japanese party leaders also shapes the style of policy leadership provided by the faction *ryōshū* who participate. The replacement of the prewar *chorō* by the *jitsuryokusha* illustrates how a traditional behavioral pattern was adapted to the changing circumstances of Japanese political life. In keeping with traditional practices, policy may still be made in a private and collegial fashion, but the elite is now composed of those skilled as party politicians, especially in raising funds and maneuvering in the continuous *habatsu* struggle within the party.

These hybrid structures and practices have little correspondence with the form of democratic decision-making embodied in the Constitution or the kind of functionally differentiated behavior and associations by which modern politics is frequently defined. Nevertheless, they were integral features of the political system in 1956 and are appropriately viewed as distinctive features of the still-evolving style of Japanese politics in the postwar era.

SOME CONCLUSIONS

A full appraisal of the impact of the Liberal-Democratic Party on Japanese policy toward the Soviet Union must await the consideration of the remaining components of the policy-formulation process. However, some tentative conclusions

which seem implicit in the foregoing are stated here to sum-
marize and clarify this somewhat complicated discussion.

Certain aspects of conservative politics in the years of 1954
through 1956 belong only to the immediate post-independence
period. Most obvious was the enervating effect of the lingering
shadows of defeat and the Occupation upon conservative political leaders as well as the public. Deprived of effective political
responsibility for seven years (many of them purged from all
public life) and living in a society still in the midst of economic
reconstruction, the leaders' primary preoccupation was with
establishing a niche in the new order. The almost obsessive
scramble for power and position within the government and the
party, with a secondary concern for substantive policy considerations, must be seen in this light. Not only were priorities
given to questions of domestic political strategy, but Japan's
heavy dependence on the United States plus the still fresh
stigma and weaknesses left by the debacle of the East Asian
War obviated any bold foreign policy actions by conservative
leaders. With the passage of time these conditions have substantially changed.

The very newness of the political and constitutional order
also contributed to the fluidity of politics in the ruling party. It
was not just the lack of congruence between past practices and
attitudes and the prescribed pattern of democratic decision-
making that was unsettling. The *Realpolitik* of the new circumstances inevitably gave rise to new political practices and organizations. Both the powerful political machine built up by
Yoshida in the hot-house conditions of the Occupation and the
sudden return of purged party leaders serve as prime examples
of unique and complicating factors. This was the period in
which the new *habatsu* were formed and when the implications
of mass democratic politics were first realized by Japan's ruling
elite. Although these factors are essential to understanding the
Soviet negotiations, it is imperative to emphasize that they are
non-recurring.

Other characteristics of the political system manifested in this
foreign policy decision seem likely to be more permanent features on the Japanese political landscape—having survived vir-

tually intact during the succeeding decade in the face of enormous socio-economic changes. First, the *habatsu* that emerged in this period continue to be the fundamental political unit among the conservatives, perpetuating the fragmented structure of the party. Moreover, the factions have maintained an essentially non-ideological, indeed, non-programmatic cast. Although at any given point each faction will take a policy position, this should not obscure the fact that they are geared almost exclusively toward gaining party control. Secondly, as demonstrated in the Soviet negotiations, the tight intermingling of the *ha* conflicts with foreign policy-making complicates and inhibits the formulation of policy. Finally, the inevitably weak coalition leadership is weakened still more by the persistence of the notion of consensual decision-making among the conservatives. *Habatsu* politics, despite its crassness, is constrained by the vestiges of tradition. The fundamental role of these elements in the peace talks should not be considered unique. Rather they are suggestive of the future impact of domestic politics on Japanese foreign policy formulation.

The Liberal-Democrats clearly played the crucial role in shaping Japanese policy in the negotiations. To determine more precisely the extent to which their control was autonomous, however, the actions of the chief opposition party, the Social-Democrats also require consideration. But first let us turn to an altogether different component of the decision-making process.

IV

The Climate of Opinion

During the course of the peace negotiations, the voice of Japanese public opinion was faintly but continuously audible. Only rarely did that voice rise to express clear demands on specific issues; and even then, on basic questions such as the status of the northern territories, the public voice had little discernible impact on policy-formulation, On the whole, public opinion provided the background against which the policy-making drama was enacted; but in order to fully comprehend this drama, some understanding of the setting—the structure and action of public opinion—is essential. Two aspects of public opinion must be examined: the climate of opinion and articulate opinion. First, the broadly held attitudes of the general public will be analysed.

The history of nineteenth- and twentieth-century relations between Japan and Russia suggests the early origins of the image of the Soviet Union which colored Japanese sentiment toward the negotiations. From the time of Japan's emergence from the self-imposed isolation of the Tokugawa era, the country has been almost constantly confronted by international challenges from her big northern neighbor. A treaty fixed their common boundaries in 1875, but in the following years, conflict still arose from the expansionist designs of both nations toward Northeast Asia—particularly Manchuria and Korea. As a result, Tsarist Russia played a villain's role in all the major military ventures undertaken by the Japanese in their rapid progress to ascendancy in East Asia. Japan was ceded the Liaotung Peninsula in Manchuria as part of the spoils of victory in the Sino-Japanese War of 1895; but the Russians, after gaining the support of France and Germany, forced the retrocession of this territory to China. Then just three years later, in a crude power-play, the Russians forced the Chinese to grant them control of the peninsula. Soon their imperialist rivalry erupted into the Russo-Japanese War of 1904 and 1905, the immediate cause of which was the struggle for control of Korea. The terms of the Treaty of Portsmouth, although far from satisfying to the Japanese after their military triumphs, did establish the two countries' spheres of influence on the Asian continent, thereby preventing further violent clashes until after the Bolshevik Revolution in 1917.[1]

Japan's relations with the Soviet regime were little better than those with Imperial Russia. Large-scale participation in the Allied military intervention against Bolshevik troops in Siberia in 1918 totally alienated the Communist government, and only the withdrawal of Japanese troops in 1923 and lengthy negotiations brought about the restoration of diplomatic relations in 1925.[2] Other than two bloody border incidents in Manchuria in 1938 and 1939,[3] the full-scale Japanese military operations in China during the thirties did not involve the Soviets. However, Russia's fear of Nazi Germany and Japan's unwillingness to risk a Siberian invasion led to the signing of a five-year nonaggression pact in 1941. The Japanese militarists and the Soviet Communists were uneasy bedfellows from the beginning, and this pact was based on nothing but expedience.[4] It was broken by the Soviets on August 8, 1945, five days before the end of the war, enabling Moscow to pick up all the territorial concessions promised by the Allies at Yalta—and more. This action evoked an extremely bitter response from Tokyo, for the hopelessly beaten Japanese had been naively trying to use the good offices of the Soviets to sound out the United States on terms for surrender. Aggravated by the incarceration of thousands of Japanese civilians and military personnel captured in Manchuria and North Korea, Japanese antipathy toward Russia was extremely strong during the immediate postwar years throughout all levels of society.

Thus Japan's modern history has seen in Russia a menacing Asian neighbor, a challenge to the nation's security if not an enemy in war. This picture has been deeply impressed upon the Japanese populace, not only through recent personal experience

but also in history books, war shrines, films, and the mass communication media. Until the expanded contacts in the years
following the peace agreement, there was little to mitigate this
highly negative image. The limited amount of cultural `inter-
change had little impact, and Russia, unlike China, never played
a major role in Japanese trade until after 1960. Such a background explains the national opinion poll of May 1949, in
which 80 percent of those showing a preference viewed Russia
as the foreign country most disliked.[5] These widespread un-
friendly attitudes toward Russia affected the efforts to restore
normal diplomatic relations.

TABLE 1

DESIRE FOR A PEACE TREATY

Do you think the Japa- nese government should conclude a peace treaty with the Soviet Union?	*May 9–11 1952* [a]	*August 10–12 1952* [b]	*June 16–17 1953* [c]
Yes	54%	41 2%	47%
No	20	19 6	16
Don't know	26	39.2	37

[a] *Asahi shimbun,* May 17, 1952.
[b] *Shimbun yoron chosa renmei,* cited in Cole and Nakanishi, *Japanese Opinion Polls* [139] p. 681.
[c] *Asahi shimbun,* June 24, 1953.
All are national, stratified, random samples.

After the outbreak of the Korean War, public attitudes toward the Soviet Union rapidly grew to encompass more than the
historically rooted feelings toward Russia as a nation-state. The
Soviet Union loomed as one of the two major protagonists of
the Cold War, and Soviet-Japanese relations came to be considered largely in terms of the immediate question of the peace and
security of the country. In national surveys taken in May and
August 1952 and June 1953, while the Soviets were still pursuing a "hard" policy toward Japan, more than twice the number positively favored a Soviet peace treaty as were positively
opposed (see Table 1). The impetus for rapprochement was

linked to the broader problems involved in Japan's role in the
new international order. A majority of those respondents in the
Asahi surveys who did favor a treaty cited the desire to maintain peace as the basis for their position; the desire to finally
terminate the state of war, and all it symbolized, was the other
most frequently listed reason.[6] Sympathy for Soviet policies in
the Cold War clearly was not an important factor. In both the
second *Asahi* poll and in a July 1953 survey by the *Simbun
Renmei,* questions were asked specifically on this point. No more
than one percent favored Moscow's foreign policy line; in both
of these polls, roughly 37 percent of the sample favored a pro-
American policy, and a like percentage favored neutralism.[7]
Thus, when the question of Soviet-Japanese relations was cast
in terms of current international issues, the Japanese public was
willing to accommodate itself to global realities, even though
negative attitudes were held toward Soviet policy.

Public sentiment toward the Soviet Union from 1952 to 1954
can be best understood in terms of the political temper of the
times, particularly as related to foreign affairs. Achievement of
independence was accompanied by an inevitably negative reaction to the long years of complete subordination to the United
States. The political troubles and finally the collapse of Yoshida
and his Occupation-spawned political machine were intricately
involved with the appearance of what can be called a mild form
of Japanese nationalism. In international affairs, the drift of
public opinion was toward a more independent position for
Japan. Although 55 percent of the public favored a pro-
American posture in 1950, this figure had fallen to 36 percent
just three years later.[8] But before Japan could play a positive
role in world politics, unresolved issues left from World War
II—including a peace agreement with the Soviet Union—
remained to be settled. Pacificism, which was rooted in the still-
recent wartime disasters, powerfully promoted by the Occupation in its early years, and legally sanctified by the Constitution,
was another significant feature of the climate of opinion during
this period. It was most prominently manifest in the opposition
to rearmament and in the desire to ease tensions in Asia by
normalizing relations with Communist China as well as the Soviet Union.[9] The high percentages of support for these positions

suggest that the early efforts of the Hatoyama Government to normalize relations with the Soviets found wide public acceptance.

Once the negotiations had begun, the opinion polls concentrated on the specific questions being discussed at the time of the surveys. From the responses, a rough profile of prevailing attitudes can be reconstructed, but the nature of the data imposes limitations. Many surveys posed questions concerning the same issue from different angles, making comparison of the results difficult. Territorial questions were often too detailed to yield meaningful answers from the respondents. Furthermore, separate treatment of each issue produces a distorted impression of the climate of opinion; it is necessary to indicate how the public balanced individual questions against each other. Nevertheless, by delineating public attitudes toward the main issues, some insight is provided into the opinion-milieu and its influence on the policy-making process.

THE TERRITORIAL ISSUE

From the time of the London stalemate in August 1955, restoration of diplomatic relations became inextricably tied to the solution of the territorial issue. Thus the two questions were almost always treated as one by the pollsters, as well as by the public.[10] Probably the best measure of public opinion on the whole question of normalization lay in its attitudes toward an Adenauer-type agreement. Such an agreement, bypassing territorial differences, had clearly become the most feasible path to an early accord. In surveys taken in 1955 and 1956, the overwhelming number of respondents indicating a preference approved of such a settlement (Table 2). But this latitude for policy leadership was not exploited. As we have seen, settlement was achieved by the government in accordance with the Adenauer formula, but only after the prolonged political crisis centering on the conservative intraparty struggle. Concerning this basic question, public opinion and the policy-formulation process seemed to function independently, in parallel planes, with no discernible interconnections.

TABLE 2

RESTORATION OF SOVIET-JAPANESE DIPLOMATIC RELATIONS
BY THE "ADENAUER FORMULA"

Do you think that diplomatic relations should be established first and the solution of the territorial problems be postponed?	*November 1955* [a]	*April 1956* [b]	*September 1956* [b]
Yes	53%	55%	49%
No	28	20	21
Don't know	19	25	30

[a] *Asahi shimbun,* December 7, 1955.
[b] *Yomiuri shimbun,* April 20 and September 22, 1956.
All are national, stratified, random samples

Despite its readiness to postpone a territorial settlement, Japanese public opinion was firmly opposed to any concessions to the Soviet Union on the territorial question itself. Initially, the government demands encompassed all of the northern territories controlled by Japan prior to the war, and the public strongly endorsed this claim (Table 3A). When the official policy was revised, limiting the immediate demand to the South Kuriles plus the Habomai and Shikotan Islands, this too received strong support (Table 3B). At the same time, the public remained overwhelmingly opposed to the Soviet proposal to return only the Habomais and Shikotan, even though this would have speedily brought about the normalization of relations. Yet in view of the nature of the issue, this consistent support for the government's position is not particularly surprising. Survey questions specifying "the return of former Japanese territory" or requiring the determination of what is "ours" and "theirs" were unlikely to elicit responses altruistically declaring for the Soviets. In addition to these psychological inhibitions, the obvious seizure of these lands by the Soviets in 1945 and the historical validity of the Japanese claim made this hostility inevitable. Prima facie, the opinion trends evident in these surveys could not be ignored by the decision-makers with impunity.

Before casting final judgment, however, it is necessary to examine the extent of commitment behind these opinions. The public's interest in the territorial dispute seems to have fluctuated in close accord with the attention the issue received in the mass media. In the summer of 1955, before there was a deadlock on this matter and when no single problem had acquired special prominence, only 15 percent of the population named it

TABLE 3A

TERRITORIAL QUESTION, JULY AND OCTOBER 1955

How much of the Soviet-occupied territory should be returned to Japan?	July 30–31 1955 [a]	October 14–16 1955 [b]
All former Japanese territories (Kurile Islands, southern Sakhalin, and the Habomais and Shikotan)	53%	64.6%
Kurile Islands and the Habomais and Shikotan	23	9.9
Southern Kuriles and the Habomais and Shikotan	—	2.8
The Habomai and Shikotan Islands	5	2 0
Don't know	19	20.7

[a] *Yomirui shimbun,* August 9, 1955.
[b] *Mainichi shimbun,* October 24, 1955.
Both are national, stratified, random samples.

as the most important issue in the negotiations. This figure rapidly rose to 41 percent in October of that year when the question received extensive news coverage as the stumbling block to negotiations. In June 1956, after Kōno's fishery agreement, only 33 percent considered it the most important issue, despite the fact it was still the sole obstacle to a general settlement At that time, with some sort of agreement likely in the near future, the return of detainees was considered most important; and the fishery question, which had been the focus of national attention for the preceding two months, was mentioned as often as the territorial issue (Table 4). Although the polls show that public support for the government's territorial position was consistently high, the fluctuations in concern for this question imply that the opinions expressed were not held with

TABLE 3B

TERRITORIAL QUESTION, NOVEMBER 1955 TO AUGUST 1956

Should Japan accept the Soviet offer to return the Habomais and Shikotan only?	Yes	No	Don't know
November 20–21, 1955 [a]	13%	58%	29%
April 12–14, 1956 [b]	14	61	25
June 15–17. 1956 [c]	10.9	61.4	27.7
August 27–28, 1956 [d]	15	50	35

[a] *Yomiuri shimbun*, December 1, 1955. "Do you think it is good or bad to accept the Russian offer to return Habomais and Shikotan?"
[b] *Yomiuri shimbun*, April 20, 1956. "Should Japan compromise with Russia concerning the South Kuriles question?"
[c] *Mainichi shimbun*, July 12, 1956. "Should Japan accept only Habomais and Shikotan or insist on the return of the South Kuriles?"
[d] *Asahi shimbun*, September 2, 1956. "Should Japan claim only Habomais and Shikotan or insist on the return of the South Kuriles?"
All are national, stratified, random samples.

great intensity. Opinions born of shallow commitment, expressed largely because of an interviewer's prodding rather than from sustained and serious concern, are rarely of direct political effect. In any event, since the timing of the changes in the government's territorial policy clearly was not correlated with the shifts seen in the polls, popular opinion was of no discernible import in the making of policy on this issue.

JAPANESE DETAINEES

Repatriation of the Japanese detained in the Soviet Union after the end of the war was an issue on which almost all Japanese were agreed. The only question was as to the best

TABLE 4

MAJOR ISSUE IN THE SOVIET-JAPANESE PEACE NEGOTIATIONS, JULY 1955–JUNE 1956

What is the most important issue between Japan and the Soviet Union?	July 30–31 1955 [a]	October 14–16 1955 [b]	November 26–27 1955 [c]	June 15–17 1956 [d]
Return of detainees	43%	40.9%	27%	53.3%
Return of former Japanese territory	15	41.2	23	33.6
Conclusion of peace treaty	9	—	2	—
End of state of war	8	—	2	—
Restoration of Soviet-Japanese trade	7	9.7	1	15.4
Solution of fisheries problem	3	6.0	2	32.2
Entrance into United Nations	1	2.9	—	—
Establishment of cultural relations	—	3.8	—	—
Don't know	14	8.1	54	20.6

[a] *Yomuri shimbun*, August 9, 1955 "What is the most important issue outstanding between Japan and the Soviet Union?"

[b] *Mainchi shimbun*, October 24, 1955. "With which question involved in the negotiations are you most concerned?" Two answers to this question were accepted.

[c] *Asahi shimbun*, December 5, 1955 "Which claim do you desire Japan to press for most strongly?" Two answers to this question were accepted

[d] *Mainchi shimbun*, July 12, 1956. "What do you think is the most important question in the Soviet-Japanese negotiations?" Two answers to this question were accepted.
All are national, stratified, random samples.

means of effecting the return as quickly as possible. This issue
was regularly listed as that about which the public was most
concerned (Table 4). In surveys taken in October and November 1955, 84 percent and 76 percent of the samples expressed a
desire that the detainees be returned immediately.[11] Hatoyama
had made repatriation one of his major slogans in his argument
for early normalization; and his public commitment, together
with the virtually unanimous positive feeling of the public, undoubtedly served as a prod for reaching some sort of settlement.
The Joint Declaration provided for the immediate return of the
detainees, thereby satisfying what was to the public, as well as
the government, the *sine qua non* of any agreement.

NORTHERN FISHERIES

During most of the negotiations, the question of fisheries in
the northern seas commanded a very small part of the public's
attention. In the surveys taken in 1955 regarding the most important issue in the talks, the fisheries problem was barely mentioned (Table 4). However, after the Soviet Union unilaterally
imposed restrictions on fishing in March 1956, the question
received heavy publicity in connection with Kōno's mission to
Moscow for an emergency fishery conference. Because of this
publicity and because the pact signed by Kōno made future
solution of the fishing problem contingent on a general settlement of relations, the issue rose in importance in the eyes of the
public. The percentage of persons naming it as the most important unresolved issue shot up to 32.4. The fisheries question was
directly instrumental in producing a final agreement, but pressures growing from a strong national sentiment cannot be considered influential in this regard. What impact the public's
attitude on this matter did have seems to have been through the
threat of electoral reprisal posed by voters directly involved in
the fishing industry, a threat of which Kōno was especially
aware.[12]

DEPTH OF OPINION

The effective influence of public opinion depends, in large part, on the kind of knowledge and political involvement which the opinions reflect. Were opinions concerning the Soviet-Japanese negotiations rooted in an intense concern for the issues or were they merely off-hand, instinctive reactions to interviewers' questions? Were they informed opinions? In appraising the public opinion, equal significance clearly cannot be accorded both to opinions based on careful analysis or reflecting a deep and direct concern and to those representing unthinking responses to pollsters. It is not possible to go behind the survey results to probe rigorously the factors underlying individual attitudes, but by examining all of the survey data a rough evaluation can be made of the general nature of the political commitments on which public opinion rested.

The outstanding characteristic of Japanese opinion in regard to the peace negotiations is represented by the high percentage of "don't know" answers occurring in the surveys. Although the data in the tables is not representative in any rigorous sense, the percentages of respondents who did not answer are typical of other polls not used here. Even though the questions usually involved selecting an answer from several alternatives, almost invariably more than 20 percent of the sample replied, "don't know." When the respondents were asked to provide information not specified by the questioner or to exercise more independent judgment in replying, the results were often appalling. For example, in a November 1955 *Asahi* survey, 62 percent of the sample could not name even one item that had become a point of contention in the talks.[13] A *Yomiuri* survey taken during the same month showed that 48 percent of those who considered themselves "familiar with the Soviet-Japanese negotiations" could not select (from six choices) or provide independently a description of the Soviet attitude toward the talks.[14] Fifty-five percent of a *Yomiuri* sample taken in April 1956 were not able to choose one of seven possible reasons that the negotiations had gone badly.[15] These illustrations can be multiplied. They

imply a poorly informed public having a very superficial understanding of the issues.[16]

At first glance it is startling, but this lack of awareness concerning the issues in the Japanese-Soviet negotiations is very
comparable with that displayed by both the American and
Japanese publics regarding other important foreign policy questions. Despite the sizable attention devoted to the Vietnam War
and the related issue of Communist China in the American mass
media in recent years, a survey by the Survey Research Center
of the University of Michigan in mid-1964 indicated that the
American public remained remarkably poorly informed on
these matters. Twenty-eight percent of Americans did not know
that China was governed by a Communist government, and only
43 percent had ever heard of Nationalist China.[17] Perhaps
more surprising was that one out of every four persons was
wholly unaware of the Vietnam War.[18] A survey on China
taken in Japan by the Kyōdo News Agency in June 1967
yielded similar results. Even in the wake of the sensational
coverage accorded the Cultural Revolution in the Japanese
mass media in the immediately preceding months, *roughly one
out of three persons in Japan was unaware that a Communist
government controlled China.*[19] Thus, however much the widespread ignorance regarding the Soviet peace talks inhibited any
policy influence by the public, it seems a characteristic feature
of public opinion on foreign policy issues in Japan and in the
United States.

That the opinions which the public did express in the polls
lacked firm commitment is evident from the substantial shifts
that occurred regarding many issues during the course of the
talks (Table 4). The fluctuations of priority given the territorial
and fishery issues have already been noted, and further evidence
is provided by the variations in the proportion of "don't know"
answers in the polls taken in October and November 1955 and
June 1956. The unusually high level of such replies to the
November 1955 *Asahi* poll is best understood in terms of the
focus of political debate in Japan at that time.*

---

* Although the question in this survey was differently worded, this
alone is not sufficient to account for the enormous variation in the
"don't know" responses.

When this survey was taken, the London talks had been suspended for more than two months; in the meantime, other political events, including the merger of the conservative party, had crowded the question of Soviet relations from the center of public attention. When the issue was again in the headlines, in June 1956, the number of people able to offer some opinion as to the important questions rose sharply.

Such instability reflects the tenuous nature of the Japanese public's attitudes toward the issues of the Soviet peace talks. The survey questions referred to events that were, for the public, transient phenomena—problems which flashed briefly before their eyes only during the immediate negotiations and then passed beyond the range of attention. In the absence of a broader, more permanent frame of reference into which these questions could be fitted, they were understood almost exclusively in the context of the talks themselves and thus were governed by oscillations in the day-to-day situation of the negotiations as reported by the mass media. The results were shallow opinions, affected by the course of events rather than influencing its direction.

The development of a clear and strong climate of opinion regarding the Soviet peace talks was inhibited by two aspects of the behavior of the conservative political leaders: the ambiguous and varied policy positions taken by the government, and the protracted, complicated intraparty struggle, which became increasingly involved with the foreign policy issue. At various times during the talks, four different policies were officially supported by the government. Initially, return of all of the northern territories by means of a peace treaty was demanded; then a treaty settlement encompassing the Southern Kuriles was forwarded; Shigemitsu, as plenipotentiary in Moscow, shifted to a treaty agreement including only the Habomais and Shikotan; finally, an Adenauer-formula settlement was agreed upon. With these frequent and often abrupt changes, no single national policy emerged about which opinion could crystalize. As the behavior of the American public during the Korean War demonstrated, when a government does not explain its policies clearly, the public tends to be confused or fragmented in its views.[20]

In addition to these shifts in official policy, the open struggle among the conservative factions over the question of diplomatic ties with Russia further blurred the situation and hindered consolidation of popular opinion. By August 1956, it was unclear even to the closest observer whether the settlement was being blocked by truly irreconcilable policy differences between the two nations or by Liberal-Democratic Party wrangling. Policy issues became identified with, and obscured by, the personal battle for control of the conservative party. For example, in an August 1956 *Asahi* survey, 15 percent of the sample favored a settlement involving the return of only the Habomais and Shikotan (50 percent opposed), but in the same poll 34 percent favored "Shigemitsu's plan" for concluding the negotiations (32 percent opposed).[21] Since Shigemitsu's plan was precisely for the surrender of Japanese claims to all territory except the Habomais and Shikotan, this blatant inconsistency indicated either ignorance or misunderstanding of the dimensions of the Foreign Minister's proposal. Whatever the explanation, it illustrates how the extremely confusing situation surrounding the government's actions further obstructed the emergence of an informed public opinion.

CONSERVATIVE PARTY ATTITUDES

Whatever small influence the polls might have had on policy was further mitigated by the attitudes of conservative party leaders toward public opinion and by the self-contained nature of the intraparty decision-making process. It is true that normalization of relations with the Soviet Union was introduced by Hatoyama as a campaign slogan and remained at the fore of political debate in Japan for nearly two years. However, when this issue moved toward a climax in mid-1956, the public was excluded from the sphere of policy-making, first deliberately by Liberal-Democratic Party leaders and later through the introversive pull of the factional battle.

In early June 1956, the conservatives made a remarkable decision to prohibit public discussion of policy toward Russia during the impending electoral campaign for the House of

Councillors. After Kōno's fishery agreement made diplomatic
normalization a problem of immediate and dramatic political
importance, it quite naturally should have become a focal point
of the upper house election to be held in mid-July. With Kōno's
return, however, the conservatives' house was placed in a state
of complete disarray over the issue. At a news conference in
early June, Hatoyama contradicted both the official party policy
and a statement made the preceding day by Foreign Minister
Shigemitsu. Party Secretary-General Kishi Nobosuke then publicly indicated that the Prime Minister might be barred from
campaigning in the forthcoming election lest further slips of his
tongue exacerbate the already acute divisions within the party
concerning this issue.[22] Five days later the party's Executive
Committee decided to allow Hatoyama to campaign, but only
after it was agreed that no conservative candidates would dis-
cuss Soviet-Japanese relations during the election.[23] Thus, for
the sake of conservative party unity and short-run electoral tactics the issue was removed from public discussion, excepting the
Socialist monologue.

Following the election, the Japanese political scene was
dominated by Shigemitsu's climatic trip to Moscow and intensification of the factional battle for control of the Liberal-
Democratic Party. As resolution of the first major post-
Occupation foreign policy problem neared, the conservative
party decision-making process became a self-contained struggle
among *habatsu* leaders. Bathed in the brightest possible light of
publicity, the Liberal-Democrats' performance could not have
appeared more shabby. In the wake of almost continuous petty
factional wrangling as well as the abortive efforts by Shigemitsu
to reach an agreement, public support for the government
slumped to only 29 percent.[24] Public disillusionment had
reached such proportions that even when Hatoyama finally assumed the initiative and declared his intention to go to Moscow
himself to bring about a settlement, he had the support of only
30 percent of the people (42 percent opposed).[25] Throughout
these weeks, public attitudes were seemingly wholly ignored by
the decision-makers as the momentum of the intraparty struggle
induced a kind of myopia. It is indeed ironic that when Hato-

yama displayed positive policy leadership and a decision was made, it was in the face of a clearly disapproving public.

SOME CONCLUSIONS

It is not surprising that a climate of opinion strong enough to influence the policy-makers did not and could not emerge. The highly negative, historically rooted feelings toward the Soviet Union and the overwhelming antipathy toward Communist policy were countered by the equally strong attitudes favoring peace, settlement of issues still outstanding from World War II, and a desire for Japan to play a more independent role in world politics. Public attitudes toward specific problems involved in the talks were not intense and were shaped by the specific turns of events during the negotiations rather than shaping them. This absence of strongly supported opinions allowed policy initiative to rest almost completely with the government. Only if the reins of public opinion are extremely taut are they able to affect the decision-making process over the short run. In the Soviet-Japanese negotiations, they definitely hung slack.

The nature of the climate of opinion together with the attitudes of the conservative leaders, abetted by the closed nature of the party's decision-making process, served to vitiate the influence of popular attitudes. Yet the public's voice is more than an amorphous climate of opinion determined by periodic opinion polls. Individuals and organized groups make specific efforts to impress their views on policy-makers, and it is the nature and effectiveness of their activities that will now be considered.

V

Articulate Opinion

Given the nature of the climate of opinion during the negotiations, the gap between the public and those involved in the policy-making process could be breached only by the articulation of specific views by interested groups and individuals. The prolonged period of the talks permitted extensive and varied expressions of opinion, and their examination completes the picture of public opinion and further illuminates the basic features of the policy-formulation process.

Articulate opinion is considered as "the active and articulate expressions on policy of specific individuals and organized groups including the media of mass communication." [1] Its components in the Soviet-Japanese negotiations, if distinguished according to the substance of the views expressed, fall into two broad groupings. By far the more important of the two factions comprised those concerned with the general question of the normalization of relations; including an ad hoc group of former diplomats, the national business associations, and formally organized groups specifically interested in improving Soviet-Japanese ties. Secondly, there were numerous groups more narrowly concerned with individual issues outstanding between the two countries. All of the elements of articulate opinion sought to influence policy through public expression of their views (i.e., press releases, petitions, and pamphlets), supplemented when possible by direct personal contacts with the decision-makers. Although the avenues of political access open to each group depended on its membership and structure, to a considerable extent their tactics were shaped by the specific features of the foreign policy-making process as it evolved over two years. The press played a central role in the activities of almost all these groups, and it is examined both as a medium and originator of articulate opinion.

THE SENIOR DIPLOMATS

A distinctively Japanese flavor was given to the public policy debate by the actions of a group of former top-ranking Foreign Ministry officials. After Kōno's May 1956 fishery agreement made a decision concerning diplomatic relations inevitable, these men, led by ex-Prime Minister Yoshida Shigeru, undertook a series of public actions in support of a "prudent policy" (*shinchō seisaku*) approach, a euphemism meaning opposition to early rapprochement with the Soviet Union. Although their efforts can be viewed as part of the movement within the conservative camp to obstruct a settlement, the basis of the group was more than a common set of policy convictions or an interest in furthering the ambitions of a particular party faction. All of its members had enjoyed distinguished diplomatic careers, and they were prompted to joint action largely in order to protect the traditional prestige and power of the Gaimushō. This was, in their eyes, threatened by the direct style of diplomacy, that ignored protocol and circumvented the Foreign Ministry, employed by Hatoyama and Kōno. Thus, although the senior diplomats were concerned with substantive policy issues, they also raised questions about the nature of the policy-formulation process itself.[2]

The first and most important action taken by the group came at a May 24th meeting of the Foreign Policy Research Committee of the Liberal-Democratic Party. This committee was not only the spearhead of the "go slow" forces among the conservatives but was dominated by ex-diplomats, notably former Prime Minister Ashida Hitoshi (chairman), Okazaki Katsuo, and Suma Yakichirō, who were happy to provide their friends with a prominent platform from which to articulate views they shared. Unofficially, the meeting was sponsored by ex-Foreign Minister Yoshizawa Ken'ichi and former Soviet Ambassador Tanaka Tokichi; it was attended by sixteen former Gaimushō officials, including Foreign Minister Shigemitsu. It was held just two days before Kōno's return from Moscow in order to seize the initiative in the anticipated policy debate. Therefore, the resolutions approved and distributed to the press were recommendations for the immediate moves to be made by the government. The Adenauer formula was rejected as a possible basis for settlement; a resumption of the London talks was called for, and return of the South Kuriles was demanded—the same conditions which the Soviets had repeatedly and categorically rejected and which had twice led to a breakdown in the talks.[3] Two further meetings were subsequently held by this group. On July 2, seven of the diplomats presented these views to a special group of business leaders, with extensive coverage in the press.[4] Another meeting on September 30 again strongly condemned an Adenauer-type settlement and the by-passing of the Gaimushō in diplomatic negotiations, and urged cancellation of Hatoyama's imminent trip to Moscow.[5]

Supplementing these joint actions, several of the men made individual statements. Yoshida contributed special articles to the press (the *Sankei Jiji* May 1956 and the *Asahi Shimbun* July 1956) in which he upheld the more cautious line described above and criticized Hatoyama's policy.[6] His onetime Foreign Minister, Okazaki Katsuo, issued a strong public denunciation of the Adenauer approach immediately after the fishery agreement was signed.[7] Ashida Hitoshi and Nomura Kichisaburō, the latter ambassador to the United States at the time of Pearl Harbor, expressed particularly vehement opposition to any territorial concessions in speeches at mass rallies and in public statements.[8]

The arguments offered by these men were, on the whole, undistinguished both in content and in presentation. All expressed their strong belief in the historical and legal validity of Japan's territorial claims, buttressed by a sense of national honor coupled with a general dislike of the Russians. They were fearful of the consequences of ties with the Soviets, both because of potential domestic Communist subversion and because of its effect on the alliance with the United States. These were standard arguments supported by many conservative Japanese, and they were little embellished by the international expertise of former diplomats. The impact of their statements, if there was any, came from the prestige of the speakers, not from the weight of their argument.

More significant than the substance of their opinions were the tactics the senior diplomats employed. All of these men were part of the "establishment" in Japan by virtue of long and distinguished careers in the government. Occupying permanent positions of respect and having wide personal contacts in the social and political worlds, their status promised success in efforts to influence policy. But in fact this potential was never realized, for their campaign was poorly organized and channels to the policy-makers did not open. The intermittent, uncoordinated manner in which the senior diplomats undertook the campaign reflects the loose structure of their group and suggests that most of these gestures were made in hurried fashion, largely on an *ad hoc* basis. Although they had private access to the important decision-makers, their recourse to public statements and to joint actions as an opinion group of foreign-policy experts would seem to indicate that the avenues of effective policy influence through personal contacts were nonetheless almost totally blocked. They tried to remove these barriers by bringing additional pressure on the government through critical public statements. It was not expected that such pressure would accrue from mass public support, but rather that it would grow from the challenge the criticisms presented to the government's promotion of a "national consensus" concerning Soviet policy. Gaining at least the tacit support of prominent officials in the legitimate political order was an important, but hardly decisive, consideration in the practices of prewar decision-making. These older diplomats had been nurtured on the ideals of the bureaucracy of that earlier era, a time when the parties played a clearly subordinate role in policy-determination, and their appeals seem to have been rooted in this older notion of decision-making.[9]

But there is no evidence that the timing or substance of government policy was affected by these actions. The preeminent position of the party was itself enough to curtail their influence. Because Yoshida and several others were directly involved in the intraparty struggles, their efforts were viewed not as dispassionate advice from diplomatic experts, but essentially as another tactic of the anti-mainstream group. The statements of the ex-diplomats were not without effect, however. They did serve to widen the split within the conservatives, and for the public, they further complicated the already bewildering number of policy choices.

THE BUSINESSMEN

Japanese business organizations were also prompted to undertake public action concerning the question of Soviet relations shortly after Kōno signed the fishery agreement. In a meeting on May 28, leaders from the four employers' associations—*Keizai Dantai Rengōkai* (Federation of Economic Organizations), *Nihon Keieisha Dantai Remmei* (Japan Federation of Employers' Associations), *Nihon Shōkō Kaigishō* (Japan Chamber of Commerce), and *Keizai Dōyūkai* (Economic Friends' Association)—decided that business circles should make a definite public stand on this issue as the negotiations entered their final stage.[10] To acquire a more complete understanding of the problem and to unify opinion within the business community, they agreed to hold a series of conferences with advocates of, or experts on, the various policy alternatives. Consequently, until Shigemitsu departed for Moscow, the businessmen did not participate in the decision-making process through their usual channels, their close financial and personal ties with the conservative party. Rather, access was sought as an opinion group, by means of conferences and public statements.*

A distinction is made here between the "opinion group" and the "interest group." An interest group is defined as a vocationally based, bureaucratized organization having permanent ties with the government (including the parties) and continuing channels of political access. An opinion group, on the other hand, is any voluntary association acting to achieve a single

---

* For a summary of the postwar history and structure of these organizations, see Chapter VII. Subsequent reference to the first three of these will be with the shortened forms of their names, *Keidanren, Nikkeiren,* and *Nissho,* respectively.

policy objective by means other than those resulting from continuing relationships with the government. An interest group is
commonly defined in terms of the "shared attitudes" of its
members,[11] but the present differentiation is according to the
type of role played in the political process, an approach more
suitable to the aims of this study. Interest groups, of course, can
act as opinion groups, and both the Japanese employers' associations and the fishing industry also functioned in this additional
role during the Soviet negotiations.*

When the national organizations began formal consideration
of the issue, business opinion split into two groups, roughly
paralleling the policy divisions within the Liberal-Democrats.
All businessmen shared a general dislike of the Russians, and
contrary to the enthusiasm of recent years, few then held out
hope for the development of substantial trade between the two
countries. In fact, the issue of trade was not seriously raised at
this time, the problem of normalization being considered almost
exclusively as a political question. On other issues, however,
there were distinct differences of opinion.

The faction supporting a "prudent" policy approach included
most of the older, more conservative business leaders, and it
was led by Ishizaka Taizō, managing director of Keidanren,
and Moroi Ken'ichi, director of Nikkeiren.[12] Two considerations of international politics seemed central to this group. First,
fear was expressed that rapprochement would damage the alliance with the United States, thereby weakening Japan's security
and possibly reducing her trade with America. Secondly, distrust of the "sincerity" of the Soviets was so strong that doubts
were raised about the meaning of any legal agreement con-
cluded with them. Equally strong was a suspicion that further
turmoil would be added to the already unstable domestic political scene when the Soviets possessed an embassy from which to
conduct Communist subversion. Finally, a highly nationalistic
posture was assumed concerning the return of the northern territories. This is graphically illustrated in Ishizaka's public ad-
monition immediately prior to Shigemitsu's departure for Moscow, "a territorial settlement preserving Japan's honor must

* See Chapter VII.

be made . . . even if the detainees and fishermen are sacrificed." [13]

Opposing them were businessmen favoring a policy virtually identical with that of Kōno and Hatoyama. The group was headed by Fujiyama Aiichirō, the president of Nisshō, and included the younger executives affiliated with Keizai Dōyūkai.[14] Their so-called realistic approach was cast in highly pragmatic terms, focusing on the immediate benefits which could be derived from a solution of the specific issues—protection of the fishery interests, return of detainees, relaxation of international tension, and entrance into the United Nations. Fujiyama argued that the "good sense" of the Japanese public would prevent any threat of subversion and saw no danger to the United States alliance from an accommodation with the Soviets, which was eventually inevitable. These men were also adamant over Japan's right to the South Kuriles, but viewed an Adenauer-type agreement as a satisfactory temporary solution.[15] Their underlying attitude was more positive, reflecting a desire for Japan to play an active and independent role in world politics, in spite of the country's weak international position.

These differences were adjusted through a series of conferences extending until mid-July, normally attended by ten to fifteen of the top leaders from the employers' associations. The first such meeting, held on June 4, involved discussion with Suzuki Kyūhei and Fujita Iwao, prominent members of the fishing industry, who had served as members of Kōno's delegation. Somewhat surprisingly, attention focused more on the diplomatic aspects of their Moscow mission than on the question of fisheries, which sheds light on the nature of business interest in the negotiations.[16] On June 25, Kōno himself conferred with this group of business leaders at great length. He not only spelled out in detail the results of his talks with the Soviets and his own policy position, but appraised the impact of the issue on the intraparty situation and the domestic political scene. No definitive statement was made by the businessmen after the meeting, but future events indicated that Kōno had successfully assuaged the fears of the more conservative leaders concerning his intentions and abilities.[17] To balance this point of view, at

the next conference on July 2, Yoshida Shigeru and six of the
senior diplomats forcefully expounded the prudent policy approach.[18] On the following day there was a morning meeting
with Sunada Shigemasa, a close advisor of Hatoyama, and in
the afternoon Dr. Hans Kroll, the West German ambassador to
Japan, explained the nature of the Adenauer formula.[19]

These meetings apparently narrowed the differences within
the business world to the point where a unified stand was possible. After the talk with Ambassador Kroll, Ishizaka called a
special press conference and declared that in the event that
Japan's territorial claims could not now be met, he thought it
would be advantageous to postpone settlement of this issue and
restore diplomatic relations.[20] In short, an Adenauer-formula
solution was acceptable to the leader of the conservative business group. In quick succession, the Consultative Committee of
Keidanren, the directors of Keizai Dōyūkai, Fujiyama Aiichirō
(the president of Nisshō), and a representative for Nikkeiren
issued statements expressing their agreement with Ishizaka.[21]
Having adjusted opinion among themselves, the businessmen
now hoped to contribute to similar public unity. The joint formal statement of July 24 was explicitly aimed at "unifying public opinion" as well as at encouraging Shigemitsu on his mission
to Moscow.[22]

The individual expressions of opinion which usually followed
the conferences of the business leaders suggest a low level of
political awareness and involvement. Statements made at the
first meeting on May 28 were, for the most part, vague
homilies based on scant information and showing little prior
attention to the problems of the negotiations.[23] Even after the
issue had been directly considered for several weeks, the quality
of these statements did not markedly alter. The comments usually fell into two groups. The conservative element speculated
on the possibility of Communist subversion and the potential
threat to the United States alliance, while the pragmatists dwelt
on calculations of the short-run benefits from the early solution
of concrete problems.[24] Use of broader, more sophisticated
frames of reference or consideration of policy questions other
than those delimited by the ambiguous notion of "national in-

terest" rarely occurred. The formless, almost apolitical attitudes apparently prevalent among the businessmen inhibited formulation of a clear policy position and thereby mitigated any influence they could exert on the government as an opinion group.

Again like the senior diplomats group, these extensive efforts by the employers' associations had no discernible decisive influence on government policy. In Moscow, Shigemitsu pointedly ignored their basic demand for return of the South Kuriles, and he did not press for an Adenauer-type settlement. The dimensions of this campaign put into clearer focus both the nature of the business-conservative party relationship and the role of articulate opinion in policy formulation during the negotiations. The very fact that the businessmen sought to influence policy through public statements suggests that in this case they, like the senior diplomats, did not have effective access to conservative decision-making. Had such contacts existed with the Liberal-Democrats, the series of conferences and public statements would have been unnecessary. Nevertheless, these meetings did ultimately produce a clear, rational policy position. To ignore the specifically articulated views of a powerful and respected group in the society is to run political risks distinctly different from taking policy actions independent of the amorphous climate of opinion. However, in the Soviet negotiations the government took these risks and suffered few immediate penalties.

POLICY GROUPS

The *Ni-So Shinzen Kyōkai* (Japan-Soviet Friendship Society) and the *Ni-Chū, Ni-So Kōkkō Kaifuku Kokumin Kaigi* (National Council for the Restoration of Diplomatic Relations with China and the Soviet Union), organizations formally established to promote closer ties between Japan and the Soviet Union, quite naturally made efforts to bring about an early settlement. These opinion groups illustrate the large number of organizations which have sprung up in postwar Japan solely to agitate for enactment of a single policy or set of policies. Almost invariably they oppose the government, and during the

1950's, those concerned with foreign policy supported causes
primarily favoring the political left-wing, with leading figures
from the Socialist and Communist parties holding prominent
positions in such groups. Membership in these organizations
involved direct political action supplementing that of the parties, thereby broadening and complicating the political process.
Their varied structures and the wide range of tactics open to
such voluntary associations are well illustrated by examining the
behavior of the Soviet-Japanese Friendship Society and the National Council during this period.

The Soviet-Japanese Friendship Association was formed on
April 22, 1949 as the merger of several small organizations
founded immediately after the war, including the *Ni-So Bunka
Renraku Kyōgikai* (Japan-Soviet Cultural Liaison Council),
Sovieto Kenkyūsha Kyōkai (Soviet Researchers' Society), and
So-Kikansha Seikatsu Yōgo Dōmei (League for the Protection
of the Livelihood of Repatriates from the Soviet Union).[25]
From the outset, it was apparent that the new organization was
under Communist and Russian control, as indicated both by the
extensive overlap between its directors and the leaders of the
Japanese Communist Party and by its undeviatingly pro-Soviet
policy line.[26] According to the founding charter (and in line
with the foreign policy tactics of the Soviet government), the
organization was to engage in a full range of activities promoting Russian contact with the Japanese "people." In fact, a limited amount of cultural exchange, a variety of publications, and
periodic public rallies were sponsored.[27] By 1955, this group
had available an organization suited to making a significant
public appeal on behalf of diplomatic normalization, but no
campaign of this sort was undertaken. Instead, the serious
efforts to influence the talks were left in the hands of the National Council, and the Friendship Association played only a
modest supporting role.[28] In view of the limited impact of
public opinion on the direction of policy, this was a well-
calculated maneuver.

In its membership, aims, and tactics, the National Council
for the Restoration of Diplomatic Relations with China and the
Soviet Union differed sharply from the Friendship Association.

It was an *ad hoc* organization established simply for the purpose of normalizing diplomatic relations between Japan and her two Communist neighbors. Lack of strong support from politicians in either the conservative or progressive camps had thwarted the attempt of Dr. Majima Ken to set up a similar group in 1953, but his persistent efforts finally met with success. On October 28, 1954, two weeks after the joint Sino-Soviet communiqué proclaiming peaceful co-existence, the Council was founded.[29] Although the Soviet government early gave its unofficial approval to the National Council, control of the group was shared by a strange mélange of individuals from the political and economic worlds of Japan. The president was multi-millionaire octogenarian, Kuhara Fusanosuke. In the prewar period he had served as president of one of the major parties, the *Seiyūkai,* and had close ties with the ultranationalists. While he did not exercise leadership in the Council's activities, his personal influence and financial support proved real assets. His motive in participating seems to have been rooted in a vague scheme to promote harmony in northeast Asia preparatory to the development of a supranational state centering around Manchuria.[30] Others participated for less utopian reasons. Hiratsuka Tsunejirō and Ōnishi Rensaka, directors of the Council, were leaders in the fishing industry and thus were directly concerned with preserving Japanese access to the northern fishing grounds. In addition to several Socialists, conservative politicians such as Ishibashi Tanzan and Kitamura Tokutarō expressed support for the Council.[31] Dr. Majima, secretary-general, skillfully directed the day-to-day operations of the Council, using the wide range of political access afforded by the varied membership.

Very few efforts were made by the National Council to arouse public sentiment concerning the issue. Irregular public statements by individual directors, a limited number of pamphlets, and an occasional public meeting constituted the sole activities of this sort. Endorsement by several groups with large membership bases suggests that the Council was a mass organization,[32] but these contacts were merely nominal and were not reflected in its tactics of influence. In consequence, although the

National Council was formally the leading opinion group whose sole *raison d'être* was a Soviet-Japanese settlement, its activities were not centered on eliciting public pressure to bring this about.

The main role of the National Council was in providing behind-the-scenes liaison between the Kōno-Hatoyama conservative mainstream faction and the unofficial Soviet mission in Tokyo. In August 1953, a delegation from Moscow took up residence in Tokyo to develop contacts with sympathetic left-wing groups and to provide intelligence on the general political conditions. It was not recognized by the Japanese government.[33] Once the Soviet Union began overtures for normalization, the activities of this mission and particularly its chief, Andrei N. Domnitsky, rapidly expanded. Majima and his associates maintained close touch with Domnitsky, and through the personal connections of the conservative politicians in the National Council, they also acquired access to Hatoyama's closest confidants, particularly Sugihara Arita. In turn, through this chain of contacts, Domnitsky was able to carry out direct negotiations with the leaders of the mainstream faction, thereby circumventing the restrictions inherent in formal diplomatic exchanges and by-passing the antagonism of the Foreign Ministry in general and Shigemitsu in particular.[34] For example, the first Soviet note concretely proposing normalization talks was personally delivered to Hatoyama by Domnitsky after Shigemitsu had refused to accept it, ostensibly for reasons of protocol.[35]

While it is impossible to document accurately the scope and nature of private negotiations facilitated by the National Council during the two years of the talks, once the formal negotiations in London were stalemated and the question of fishing rights assumed particular importance, the role of private diplomacy did seem to expand. Both Hiratsuka and Ōnishi were closely connected with Agriculture and Forestry Minister Kōno, thus assuring that Domnitsky was intimately aware of Kōno's attitude and his position in the Liberal-Democratic Party. Indeed, it appears that this was at least a partial consideration in the Soviet imposition of fishing restrictions.[36] Sergi Tichvinsky, leader of the quasi-official Soviet fishing mission established after Kōno's agreement, conferred with Kōno and other top government officials prior to Hatoyama's trip to Moscow.[37] By concentrating on personal and private diplomatic contacts, the National Council was thus able to operate very effectively in the diffuse, disorderly pattern of the negotiations. Its ability to arrange timely meetings and continuously keep the issue before sympathetic decision-makers within the Liberal Democratic Party did much to pave the way to the final agreement.

In this way, the National Council undoubtedly played an instrumental role in bringing about a final settlement, without becoming deeply involved in the accompanying public controversy. In large part its influence was made possible by both the unusually fluid circumstances of the 1955–56 political scene and the personalities of the party leadership of that time. The diffuse nature of Japanese foreign policy-making continues, but it is improbable that it will retain the looseness of this transitional period permanently. It seems likely that the private, behind-the-scenes tactics so successfully employed by the policy opinion groups in the Soviet talks will be less important in the future, but to ignore the potential importance of private liaison in diplomatic negotiations would be a serious error. When the world was closest to nuclear war during the Cuban missile crisis, the Soviets chose to communicate with the United States government through the diplomatic correspondent of an American broadcasting company.[38] Whatever the future for articulate opinion, in the personality-centered, elitist politics of Japan, a place for "private diplomacy" is assured.

ISSUE GROUPS

In addition to the organizations concerned with the general problem of normalization, there were also a variety of groups specifically pressing for the solution of individual issues involved in the talks. Both the tactics and the substance of appeals by such groups were necessarily cast in somewhat different terms. The decision-makers could not judge such appeals separately but had first to balance them against each other and then consider them in the context of the larger political question of Japan's place in the postwar international order. Moreover, there were inherent limitations to the effectiveness of the demands of such narrowly based interest groups when weighed against the needs of society as a whole. Virtually all of these organizations employed similar tactics, seeking access to the policy-formulation process through petitions to the government and public rallies.

A regionally based movement to restore the Soviet-occupied northern territories was initiated shortly after the end of World War II.[39] Centering in Hokkaido, the impetus came from residents who had been displaced from their homes in the northern islands and the fishermen whose livelihood has been seriously disrupted by the Soviet occupation. The first organization to promote return of the territories was set up in late 1945 and others followed. In December 1950, all these groups united to form the *Henkan Konsei Dōmei* (Reversion-Seeking League) with the goal of "mobilizing public opinion to bring about the return of the northern territories by establishing a peace treaty with the Soviet Union." Headed by Itō Seiya, President of the University of Hokkaido, this association held public meetings and submitted petitions to General MacArthur's headquarters, the Diet, and the Foreign Ministry.[40] Throughout the Occupation, the Hokkaido prefectural assembly also supported this movement, passing numerous resolutions demanding immediate reversion of all the Soviet-held islands. In 1952 and 1953, two other major organizations were established for this same purpose: the *Hoppō Gyōgyō Sakushin Hokkaido Kisei Kai* (Hokkaido Society for Promoting North Seas Fishing) and the *Konshitsu Chiho Heiwa Suishin Keizai Fukkō Dōmei* (League for Promoting Basic Peaceful Economic Recovery).[41]

After the formal Japanese-Soviet talks began, the tactics of these organizations did not greatly change, but the tempo was considerably intensified. In particular, petitions and resolutions were repeatedly dispatched to Plenipotentiary Matsumoto, Prime Minister Hatoyama, and to the Diet.[42] The claims of the groups were based almost wholly on pragmatic self-interest, not on the nationalistic, anti-Soviet, anti-Communist attitudes which underlay the similar territorial position of the prudent policy faction in the Liberal-Democratic Party. Demands were made for return of all the northern territories or at least the immediate reversion of the South Kuriles. However, when it became evident that the Soviets were adamant, the territorialists readily modified their stand to salvage what was possible under the circumstances. Indeed, when Hatoyama signed the Joint Declaration, containing only a promise of the future return of the Habomais and Shikotan, the *Hendan Konsei Dōmei* wired their thanks.[43]

Although the territorial question proved the biggest stumbling block to an agreement and was the center of the conservative intraparty battle, the efforts of these opinion groups played virtually no direct part in the controversy. Rather, the main import of their activities was to keep the territorial issue constantly before the eyes of the policy-makers, in the face of competing factors in the political arena.

Other efforts to influence the government's policy were undertaken by various smaller issue groups. The *Ryōdo Mondai Kokumin Remmei Jumbikai* (Preparatory Committee for a Peoples' League on the Territorial Problem), a group centering around several leaders of the Hokkaido movement and prominent political figures favoring a prudent policy approach, sponsored a mass meeting in Tokyo in August 1956, while Shigemitsu was still in Moscow. At the meeting, which was widely publicized because of its timing and the well known persons who participated, the policy of the Soviet Union was bitterly condemned in nationalist and anti-Communist terms.[44] Another special opinion group, the *Rusu Kazoku Dantai Zenkoku Kyōgikai* (National Council of Organizations of Families of Japanese Detainees) was established to hasten the repatriation of Japanese still held in the Soviet Union. By petitions and public meetings, the policy-makers were reminded of this issue for which extensive public support was also manifest in the opinion polls.[45]

The main actions of the fishery circles were, however, somewhat different. Efforts to influence policy were undertaken as an

interest group (not as an opinion group) through their direct
and continuing ties with the conservative party.* Nevertheless,
they were moved to protest publicly when the Soviets unilaterally imposed restrictions on their activities in the northern seas.
In spontaneous gestures of frustration, they made unfeasible
demands for the immediate normalization of relations or a private fishery agreement between themselves and the Moscow
government,[46] but these actions ceased once Kōno was dispatched to the emergency fishing conference.

Although it is difficult to gauge the impact of these groups,
they did keep the policy-makers aware that segments of the
public were deeply concerned over specific issues. At the same
time they kept the issues alive in the minds of the public and
offered organizations through which political action could be
taken. By thus providing a threat of potential electoral reprisal
and by keeping selected issues constantly on the political stage,
the issue groups did affect the milieu in which the decision-
makers operated.

THE PRESS

The media of mass communication, especially the press,
constitute the main channels linking the decision-makers and
the public. They influence foreign policy formulation in two
ways.[47] First, the media provide the policy-makers with a day-
to-day image of public interest in each issue by reporting overt
actions and statements concerning policy and by evaluating individual questions in editorials and special commentary.[48] Normally this constitutes almost the entire public policy dialogue,
for the decision-makers in turn use the press to disseminate
information and publicize their own views. This leads to the
second way in which the media affect policy. As the primary
source of information for the public, they are able to condition
the nature of public response to particular issues through the
kind of coverage accorded them. By establishing the focus of
attention, the press indirectly determines how the public will
participate in the policy-formulation process. In terms of these

* See Chapter VII.

two functions the role of the Japanese press in the Soviet negotiations will be appraised: as a forum in which articulate opinions found expression, and as a conveyor of the information on which both these opinions and public sentiment were based.

It is first necessary to make clear the basic features of the Japanese press in the postwar period. Two characteristics are particularly striking: the extent to which national papers dominate the field, and the emphasis given to news concerning national and international affairs. The total circulation of the dailies is extremely high (averaging nearly two per household in 1958) and almost half of this is made up by the national newspapers, led by the *Asahi,* the *Mainichi,* and the *Yomiuri.*[49] The more comprehensive morning editions normally have eight to twelve pages, the first two devoted to politics. In the national papers, these political reports are, for the most part, written by the staffs in the Tokyo offices and are thus uniform in the local editions published throughout the country. Consequently, in contrast to the situation in the United States, the public is exposed to a sizable dose of national and international news every day.

There are several distinctive characteristics of the style of news coverage. Reporting tends to be thorough and comprehensive—often undiscriminatingly so. For this reason, significant information concerning policy questions frequently is buried amidst the trivial, particularly in detailed accounts of the attitudes and machinations of the party faction leaders. All of the national papers are considered politically independent, but this is manifest not so much in the substance of their editorial opinions as in the detached, critical attitude to which all events are subject.[50] Although the major dailies editorially tend to lean to the political left, it is this self-consciously hypercritical posture rather than Communist or extreme leftist sympathies among the reporters and editors that seems to be the basic factor behind the consistently anti-government position taken.[51] Furthermore, most interpretive appraisals do not directly confront the substantive issues or attempt to organize the vast number of undifferentiated facts which are reported. The discussions are usually abstract, vaguely cast in terms of moral principles or perhaps the sweeping implications which a specific policy might have for the world international order. Few guideposts for realistically assessing the concrete issue are offered to the reader.

In the Soviet negotiations, the press reported in full detail the vicissitudes of the formal talks and the related domestic political maneuvers. Although the issue was more or less continuously reported, the intensity of coverage fluctuated widely, following closely the dramatic changes in the formal talks. The confused account which resulted paralleled the uninformed and uncommitted state of public opinion indicated in the preceding chapter—a correlation implying the strong imprint of the press on public opinion [52] and suggesting yet another reason for the gap between the public and the policy-formulation process.

Did the press serve satisfactorily as a forum for a policy discussion? The papers themselves did not editorially fully participate in such discussion. They did not take positive and definitive stands on either the controversial policy questions or the corrosive factional wrangling within the Liberal-Democrats. To be sure, the intrusion of petty, intraparty power struggles into the formulation of the nation's foreign policy was deplored by all, but no campaign for reform or to "turn the rascals out" was initiated. From the beginning, the contention among Hatoyama-Kōno, Yoshida, and Shigemitsu was in large part fought in the pages of the press, and when the negotiations reached their climax in the summer of 1956, the papers gave sensational attention to the concomitant internal party struggle. Statements by the various opinion groups and by individual politicians were publicized, but such expressions of articulate opinion were tucked in amidst a bewildering array of related data, and thus their impact on the policy-makers was substantially reduced. The resulting policy dialogue was weak and confused, making the formation of any clear opinion difficult. In no way did the press serve as a catalyst, providing order and clarity in what was a highly chaotic situation.

Articles and editorials in virtually all the leading monthly journals strongly condemned the press' performance as "irresponsible." Criticism centered on the sensational, "insidedopester" treatment of the factional bickering and especially on the absence of any effort to unify public opinion on behalf of the national interest. Most remarkable was the agreement among commentators of virtually all shades of political persuasion in blaming the press for failing to bring about a national consensus on this matter. For example, *Sekai,* the leading monthly for the left-wing intellectual position, and normally militantly anti-nationalist, editorially denounced in unequivocal terms the cynically detached attitude displayed by the papers. The press posture was contrasted with its behavior at the time of the first Russo-Japanese peace agreement in 1905 when a concerted campaign by the newspapers protesting the "national humiliation" imposed by the terms of the Treaty of Portsmouth incited the Tokyo populace to three days of violent rioting, culminating in the burning of Hibiya Hall.[53] In virtually all of the many editorials and articles dealing with the press treatment of the Soviet negotiations, conservative and socialist authors alike were similarly aroused.[54] The common critical theme claimed that the media bore an obligation to foster unity of public opinion on the issue and could be held accountable for the Babel which developed—even though the government had provided no clear policy to which the people could be rallied. Such insistence by wide sectors of the articulate public on the need for building a national consensus, with the implicit assumption that the press carried a responsibility to lead this effort, had a peculiarly Japanese flavor. Certainly it was another vestige of the traditional imperative for unanimity in decision-making, and in a very real sense it was a modern echo of prewar Japanese nationalism.

These charges of press irresponsibility raise questions not only about the actual performance of the media in the negotiations but also about the general issue of the appropriate role of the press in democratic foreign policy-making. This latter question is a matter of considerable controversy,[55] but one primary requirement that can be advanced for a responsible democratic press is the necessity of transmitting information on particular issues in such a way as to promote intelligible and constructive policy dialogue. This requirement involves both describing and evaluating, that is, reporting and editorializing. By undifferentiatingly reporting *all* the facts in the Soviet negotiations, the Japanese newspapers did not provide the basis for clear and relevant policy discussion. Inevitably the tangled tale of intra-party rivalries commanded the bulk of the coverage and most of the headlines. The newspaper editorials left undisturbed the resulting muddled picture. Whatever the shortcomings of the newspapers' performance in terms of the criteria of a democratic ideal, the chorus of criticism demanding that the press more actively propagandize for a national consensus is even more striking. Perhaps the role of the Japanese press in the peace talks is best understood as a reflection of the fluidities and uncertainties of the new political order and of the extreme complexities that developed around the normalization of Soviet-Japanese relations.

Articulate opinion in the Soviet negotiations was distinguished by great variety in the nature of the groups involved, in the kinds of opinions expressed, and in the ways in which these views were set forth. The general effect was to enrich and complicate the policy dialogue, but the perceptible influence on policy shifts was rather small. Only the elements of articulate opinion that successfully cultivated direct contact with conservative party leaders had discernible impact. Press coverage, which is particularly crucial for opinion influence, inhibited the effect not only of articulate but of general opinion on foreign policy-making. Having explored the rather peripheral role of public opinion in the policy-formulation process, it is now appropriate to turn to consideration of the actions of the opposition Socialist Party.

VI

The Socialists

The position of the Socialist Party on the Soviet-Japanese negotiations was conditioned both by fundamental changes in its
political status during this period and by the similarity of Socialist policy with that of the government. The reunification of
the Left-Wing and Right-Wing Socialist factions into a single
party, together with the sharp rise in popular support, led to a
fundamentally altered political position. At the same time, the
government's efforts to normalize relations with Russia, the first
move away from an American international orientation, found
strong support in the party, thus proscribing unqualified opposition. In consequence, the Socialists sought access to foreign
policy formulation through highly pragmatic tactics which re-
vealed their capabilities as a constructive opposition and the
dimensions of their internal policy-making process.

POSTWAR BACKGROUND

The *Nihon Shakaitō* (Japan Socialist Party) was formally
organized in November 1945 by prewar labor and left-wing
party leaders such as Suzuki Mosaburo, Kawakami Jōtarō, and
Nishio Suehiro. A conglomerate of the diverse forces of the
proletarian movement from an earlier era, it perpetuated the
personal rivalries and the strong ideological orientation of the
traditional Japanese left, centering on Marxism-Leninism.[1] Under the aegis of liberal Occupation policies, the *Shakaitō*
quickly emerged as a major political force, capturing over
twenty-six percent of the vote in the April 1947 general election
and participating for the next sixteen months in a coalition
government. Its rapid political rise was paralleled and buttressed by a spectacular growth in the Japanese labor move-

ment. Following the prewar pattern, close financial, ideological, and personal ties developed between the unions and the Socialists. Such connections grew, and labor became the main source of organizational and mass political support, supplementing the weak formal structure of the party.[2] However, close interrelationship has not had a purely salutary effect as it has inhibited the Socialists' expansion beyond a single pressure-group base and made the vicissitudes of the labor movement integral to the party.[3]

The sixteen months in which the Socialists shared the responsibilities for governing proved to be a frustrating and ultimately disastrous experience. As partners in a coalition, they lacked power to initiate their own program. They were further restricted in this regard by the sudden shift to more conservative policies by the Occupation, which in 1948 sought to resuscitate the Japanese economy in order to meet the mounting challenges of the Cold War in Asia. In October of that year, the coalition government collapsed in the wake of corruption, scandal, and intraparty strife, and in the following general election the Socialists' popular support was halved. Four years passed before their vote again exceeded twenty-five percent, suggesting that the party was destined to remain a permanent minority. Its distance from political responsibility encouraged the ideological direction of the party and had an introversive effect, fostering contention within the socialist movement.

The strong ideological cast of the Japanese left, abetted by the dominant role of intellectuals, is one of its most striking features. As in European socialist movements, there is no doctrinal consensus; the spectrum ranges from classical Marxism on the left, which has a powerful hold on most of the Socialists, to Fabianism on the right. Two effects of this situation must be noted. First, doctrinal disputes have been a major source of intraparty division, and most *habatsu* have a discernible, if not distinct, ideological hue. Secondly, policy issues are viewed through an ideological prism giving a theoretical bent to most Socialist positions and imposing a rigidity which makes compromise with other parties extremely difficult. In foreign policy the central theme has been neutralism, calling for less dependence on the United States and more ties with Communist states in the short run, and ultimately complete disarmament and non-alignment.[4] Each specific issue in foreign affairs is considered in terms of the principle of neutralism—in most instances, touching off substantive arguments over the specific meaning of this concept. That differences over a policy can be taken with great seriousness is illustrated by the 1951 dispute over acceptance of the San Francisco Peace Treaty, which produced a party split lasting four years. What may seem from afar to be a joust with ideological windmills is in the world of Socialist politics deadly serious.

Personal factionalism of the type seen in the conservative camp underlies and complicates such divisions over policy and ideological matters. Rooted in the same traditional attitudes and leader-follower relationship which gives rise to factionalism in all Japanese organizations, the Socialist *habatsu* are built around individuals able to provide funds and support from a nonparty political base. Normally, this is through special connection with a labor union. In view of this factional structure, the struggle for control of the party involves personal rivalries in much the fashion of the conservatives, although these are usually expressed in terms of policy and ideological differences.[5]

When the Soviet negotiations opened, the Socialists were divided into the Right-Wing and the Left-Wing parties as a result of the 1951 rift, and these were split into a total of five major factional groupings. Both of the *habatsu* in the Right-Wing group, the *Shamin-kei* and the *Nichiro-kei,* had deep roots in the Japanese labor movement and tended to be ideologically sympathetic with democratic socialism. However, the *Shamin-kei,* headed by Nishio Suehiro, was distinguished by direct connections with the moderate postwar unions (e.g., *Sodomei* [Japan Federation of Labor Unions] and *Zenrō Kaigi* [Congress of Industrial Unions]); the *Nichiro-kei* lacked such definite ties but had enlisted a higher proportion of intellectuals and was more sympathetic to Marxism.[6] The Marxist-socialist Left-Wing party consisted of the communist-inclined *Koryō-kei* —plus Wada Hirō's faction, unique in its postwar origins and then strongly Marxist oriented—and the large faction led by Suzuki Mosaburo with ties extending to the *Rōnō ha,* which was a central part of the legal left of the prewar proletarian movement.[7] *Sōhyō* (General Council of Trade Unions of Japan), provided strong support for the Left-Wing, so that there was a split in the ranks of organized labor paralleling the party division.[8]

By early 1954, considerable pressure for the unification of the two parties had developed among the Socialists. This grew from a general growth in popular support, growing disunity within the Liberal Party, and the obvious frustrations inherent in continuing as splinter groups. Leadership in the move for merger was taken by the Suzuki and Kawakami *habatsu,* the so-called center factions of the socialist movement. Since a dispute over foreign policy had given rise to the split, adjustment of views in this area was essential for reconciliation. It was achieved through a skillful verbal compromise in the formal merger talks beginning in May 1955. In spite of the intense argument over the platform, compromise over personal differences and party control was an equally important consideration, one which had been basically resolved before the policy debate began.[9] The unified Social Democratic Party which emerged in October 1955 was not a tightly knit group. Structurally it was strikingly similar to the conservatives, a coalition of semi-autonomous *habatsu.* This fragmentation played a significant part in formulation of party policy toward the Soviet Union.

THE PEACE NEGOTIATIONS

Although normalization of ties with the Soviet Union had been advocated by both the Left-Wing and Right-Wing Socialists from the time that Japan gained her independence, it was presented in the form of a slogan, not as a concrete plan for action. The issue was invariably bracketed with the question of Sino-Japanese relations and considered in terms of broad foreign policy objectives: as a move for greater independence from the United States, as a means for easing tensions in East Asia, and as a step essential to paving the way for Japan's neutralization. For the first year after the issue had been opened by Hatoyama, the Socialists continued to treat the question in broad terms, making unequivocally clear only that they favored the restoration of diplomatic ties by some means, as quickly as possible.[10] On the less controversial issues (e.g., detainees, admission to the United Nations), their positions varied only slightly from those of the government, but the Socialists supported the most extreme demands possible concerning the northern territories. They asked for return of them all. However, this claim was linked with the simultaneous restoration of the United States occupied Ryukyu and Ogaswara Islands, as a *quid pro quo* for the concession by the Russians.[11] Such a suggestion, clearly unacceptable to both the Soviet Union and America, nevertheless had nationalist as well as neutralist appeal and was retained as official party policy until just before Shigemitsu's trip to Moscow.

Furthermore, even before the formal talks had opened, the Socialists proposed that a provisional agreement restoring diplomatic relations and repatriating wartime detainees be substituted for a treaty, should an impasse be reached—seemingly anticipating the final form of settlement.[12] But this was merely an ambiguous, appended proviso, underscoring the premium the Socialists placed on achieving an early agreement. As demonstrated by the events in the summer of 1956, it was not a carefully considered recommendation enjoying the unified support of the party.

Despite the differences of detail, the Socialists' Soviet policy was virtually identical in principle with Hatoyama's,[13] and they refrained from strong attacks on the government's stand until after the conservative merger. During the general election in February 1955, the Socialists were robbed of what they had hoped to use as a major campaign slogan because of the initiative taken by the Prime Minister on this issue. Instead, they were only able to question the "sincerity" of Hatoyama and his ability to effectuate rapprochement in the face of opposition within his own party.[14] Although criticizing the tactics of Hatoyama, the Socialists, unlike the Liberals, gave general support to the first London talks as a positive step toward normalization.

After the Socialist merger, the broad goals of party policy toward Russia remained unchanged, but their tactics shifted, particularly as the issue became an important factor in domestic politics. First, their part of the policy dialogue became much more specific in content, with point-by-point discussions of a possible agreement and attacks on specific moves undertaken by the government.[15] Opportunities for criticism of this sort became plentiful as the rift between the Prime Minister's position and the official policy of the newly merged conservative party, and the attendant confusion, grew. The Socialists sought to demonstrate that the conservative insistence that all outstanding problems be settled before restoration of diplomatic ties in effect obviated the possibility of any positive action. Yoshida's continued intransigence, Shigemitsu's categorical rejection of a provisional agreement, and the collapse of the second London talks in March lent support to their charges. Although the Socialists generally approved Kōno's fishery pact, they also published a detailed appraisal of the agreement indicating the areas in which the rights of Japanese fishermen were not sufficiently guaranteed against future encroachment by the Russians.[16] From late 1955 until the dispatch of Shigemitsu's mission, the Socialists served as constructive critics of Japan's foreign policy, acting as pragmatic nationalists and displaying little evidence of ideological rigidity. One reason that they assumed this posture, which they were unwilling or perhaps unable to take during the Security Treaty debates in 1960, lay in their fundamental agreement with the policy goals of the conservative mainstream faction. Yet, there was another factor behind this behavior, in addition to substantive policy consensus.

With the unification of the Left-Wing and Right-Wing parties, the Socialists seemed poised to challenge the conservatives for control of the government. Their combined share of the popular vote had risen from twenty-one to over twenty-nine percent in the general elections held since independence, and as a unified, single party, the prospects for still more rapid rise seemed bright. In 1956, the results of the House of Councillors and local elections as well as the opinion polls seemed to bear out these hopes.[17] As important as this tangible evidence of strength was the optimistic atmosphere in which the party operated. It clearly seemed to possess an upward momentum while the Liberal-Democrats were stagnating in an internecine factional struggle. Under these conditions, the Socialists naturally sought to capitalize on conservative intraparty strife for their own political advantage. Such efforts inevitably became involved with the question of Soviet relations, which had become the focal point of Liberal-Democratic *habatsu* rivalries.

Consequently, the pragmatic tactics of the Socialists concerning Soviet policy were at least in part aimed toward stoking the fires of the policy controversy within the conservative party. To this end, they addressed criticism to the modus operandi of the Liberal-Democrats, not just their substantive policies. For example, the abrupt change in government policy in August 1955 (even before the conservative merger), resulting from a compromise with the Liberals, was immediately criticized on the grounds that conservative disunity and factional wrangling prevented effective or responsible action.[18] Subsequently, all evidence of intraparty differences were publicized and efforts were made to provoke dramatic incidents illustrating this condition.[19] Again, the Socialists joined with Yoshida's "go slow" faction in criticizing Kōno's "irresponsible" methods in negotiating the fishery pact.[20] These tactics required considerable discretion since they created a dilemma for the Socialists which was not easily resolved. On the one hand, they genuinely favored an early settlement with Russia and supported all measures to promote it, on the other, they were attempting to use the conflict within the conservatives over this issue—conflict which would end or diminish with a settlement—to strengthen their own position. To pursue both of these aims simultaneously required a highly flexible policy, one which successfully anticipated the direction in which both the Soviet negotiations and conservative party politics were moving.

In an unusual display of bipartisanship, the Socialists gave full support to the Shigemitsu mission to Moscow just prior to its departure in late July.[21] In view of the party's sharp gains in the upper house election earlier in the month, strong public enthusiasm for the trip, and the likelihood that some sort of acceptable agreement would emerge, the move seemed politically advisable. However, public and direct participation in the efforts to settle Soviet relations demanded equally open and full participation in the turbulent political controversy over this issue which followed the unexpected failure of the Shigemitsu mission in mid-August.

Collapse of the Moscow negotiations over Soviet intransigence on the territorial question left the Socialists with still another dilemma—this time concerning the substance of policy. Official party policy had consistently laid claim to all the lost northern territories. It had also advocated early restoration of diplomatic ties. How could Japanese *national* territorial rights be pursued against the unyielding posture of a supposedly friendly socialist country? In contest here were the effect of ideology (Marxist) and the impact of nationalist loyalties on a specific party policy. Confronted with this choice the party divided, and the broad divisions corresponded roughly to the factional lines. The non-Marxist right, led by Nishio Suehiro, Matsuoka Komakichi, and Nishimura Eiichi, echoed the "official" government policy—that the minimum conditions for a settlement of any kind was the return of the Southern Kurile Islands.[22] On the far left of the party, the strongly Marxist *Koryō-kei* favored abandoning the Socialists' earlier territorial position and acceding completely to the Soviet terms for establishing relations.[23] In the moderate Marxist center factions, reactions varied, but few were willing to sacrifice national interest and honor to the Russians, particularly since this would involve repudiation of past party policy. Suzuki Mosaburo, Socialist Party Chairman, expressed the typical attitude. He condemned the Soviets' stand as "unfitting of a socialist nation," but emphasized that diplomatic ties should still be restored soon, by means of a provisional agreement postponing solution of the territorial question.[24] Others in his faction (e.g., Akamatsu Imasu and Okada Soji) together with Kawakami Jotarō, head of the *Nichiro-kei,* shared this position.[25] Thus there seems to have been some correlation between the intensity of Marxist ideological commitment and the policy position of individual Socialists, but other considerations were also involved. Personal and territorial factors (e.g., the strongly nationalist stand by representatives from Hokkaido) contributed to divisions within the party, some of which cut across factional lines.[26] Consequently, at the time the Socialists had to take a public position, they were as divided internally as the conservatives.

With this background, Socialist behavior in the turbulent weeks following Shigemitsu's recall take on fuller meaning. During this period a series of statements were issued elaborating the official position. All except the final one gave only qualified endorsement to a provisional agreement (as the best way to achieve early restoration of relations under the existing circumstances) and a forthright stand on the territorial question was scrupulously avoided.[27] Because of their ambiguity, these statements provided few guidelines for immediate action, and were widely criticized in the press as "irresponsible" acts of political opposition.[28] Yet there were several factors which virtually barred a more positive stand.

The most important of these was, of course, the situation within the party. Concerning the territorial issue, the Socialists were a house badly divided and official party policy could not have embodied a clear, strong position and maintained party unity. Secondly, the hard line taken by the Soviets seems to have thrown the party off stride to the extent that they were hesitant to declare boldly for specific conditions for normalization until Moscow's minimum conditions were clearer. Finally, the comprehensive style of the discussion, the question was juxtaposing Soviet relations with Japan's international position, while seemingly obfuscating the specific policy recommendations, merely reflected the ideological flavor of all Socialist policy stands.

It would be incorrect, however, to explain the nature of Socialist actions in purely determinist terms. Calculation was involved, for from the Socialists' viewpoint the potential benefits of an ambiguous policy posture were considerable. The collapse of Shigemitsu's talks aggravated the already rapidly deteriorating political position of the Liberal-Democrats. Bitter intraparty strife, sagging popular support, and sharp criticism from business groups seemed to herald the fall of the government and augur success for the Socialists. An effort was made to further enhance the party's position by anticipating the nature of the final settlement in order to claim some credit for solving the most critical political problem of the day. Thus the spate of policy statements represented attempts to steal the thunder of the conservatives, and this, too, accounted for the rather indefinite form of the proposals.[29] The last of these statements, which gave specific support to a provisional agreement, was drafted in an all-night emergency session of the party Central Executive Committee on September 5, so that it could be rushed into print before the government took a similar stand.[30] It appeared first, but with no discernible effect on either the party's fortunes or the nation's policy. By this time, an Adenauer-type agreement was the only path of action open to the government for an early settlement, and in the swirl of political events at the time, the Socialists' move did not take on much significance.

It is somewhat ironic that the ideologically doctrinaire Socialist party sought to participate in policy formation in such a highly opportunistic fashion, rather than mobilizing mass support around a clearly articulated policy. Even after the party had agreed to support a provisional agreement as the most suitable policy, they turned down a bid by Hatoyama for bipartisan unity, proposing instead a special session of the Diet ostensibly to unite public opinion, but in fact to put the raging internal battle of the Liberal-Democrats onto a public stage.[31] Only on the eve of Hatoyama's departure, after he had forced his policies through the cabinet, did Chairman Suzuki agree to support his mission.[32] Thus, Socialist maneuvers during the crucial weeks of the Soviet-Japanese negotiations embodied a response to the domestic challenge, not to the diplomatic one.

SOME CONCLUSIONS

Three aspects of the Socialists' role in the Soviet negotiations have particular significance. First, the strong ideological orientation of the party provided the theoretical framework in which policies were discussed, and it was responsible for the internal party divisions which shaped the Socialist actions. However, because there was basic agreement on government and Socialist policy aims, this framework did not become a straitjacket, narrowly restricting the tactics of the party. Second, by turning to expediential tactics, the Socialists vitiated any positive influence they might have exerted on the formation of Soviet policy. Through the Shigemitsu mission, the Socialists acted as constructive policy critics and ultimately gave full support to what seemed to be the government's final effort for an agreement in the Moscow talks. However, following the collapse of these negotiations, while still in a unique position to aid Hatoyama to achieve the favored early settlement, the Socialists used the question of Soviet policy to harass the Liberal-Democrats and to strengthen their own political position. Since political power seemed to be within reach of the Socialists during this period, the implications of such behavior for "responsible" opposition are noteworthy. As the Socialists seemed to be approaching power they exhibited in extreme form the purely opportunistic behavior normally associated with the conservatives. Thirdly, by their actions the Socialists served only to reinforce that aspect of the conservative decision-making pattern which viewed Soviet policy in terms of domestic politics rather than the international situation.

The Socialists left the Liberal-Democrats' control of policy largely unaffected. If not the opposition, who then was able to touch in some way the conservatives' decision-making? Let us turn to those groups with whom the conservatives have their strongest and most intimate connections—the business interests.

VII

Business Interest Groups

The negotiation of the peace agreement exposed with unusual clarity the capabilities and limitations of the Japanese business community, the most powerful single force behind the Liberal-Democratic Party, in influencing foreign-policy In addition to personal, individual contacts with party leaders (which cannot be meaningfully appraised), two types of business groups were active, each using distinctly different techniques to pursue distinctly differing goals. Together, the four major employers' associations served as the national spokesmen for the largest, most respectable corporations, and concerned themselves with Soviet policy from the broad viewpoint of Japan's national interest. As previously indicated,* they initially acted as an opinion group, concentrating on mobilizing public support behind a "rational" policy. However, as the issue became further embroiled in domestic politics in August 1956, their concern broadened to stabilizing the general political situation as well, and they moved to influence the government from their position as the largest interest group supporting the conservative party. In contrast to the employers' associations, the fishery industry acted as a special, not a national, interest group, being concerned with promoting and protecting their fishing activities in the northern seas. Having dissimilar goals, and with obvious variations in their structures and the channels of influence available, the two groups adopted radically different tactics for influencing policy-making. These two dimensions of the activities of the business interests in the formulation of Japanese policy require separate consideration.

* See Chapter V on business opinion and interest groups

EMPLOYERS' ASSOCIATIONS

BACKGROUND

The development of powerful national business organizations is a postwar phenomenon in Japan. Just as the new constitution and purge directive had reshaped the conservative political world, so the Occupation's *zaibatsu*-busting, the rise of the labor movement, and the demands of total reconstruction altered the structure of Japan's economy and the nature of organized business groups. In the prewar era, a few huge *zaibatsu* combines dominated the nation's economy and provided a centralized base on which close business ties with the political parties were built.[1] There was little need for business federations to coordinate in a formal manner for effective political action. Connections with the parties and the government were more intimate—that is, business influence and funds passed through personal channels, involving a minimum of public pressure.[2] Nonetheless, three formal groups existed: the *Nihon Keizai Renmei* (Japan Economic League) organized for harmonizing political tactics on specific issues; the *Zenkoku Sangyō Dantai Renmei Kyogikai* (National Industrial Communication Association), which dealt with the growing labor movement in the thirties; and the *Nihon Shōkō Kaigijo* (Japanese Chamber of Commerce and Industry) which parallels the purposes and activities of similar organizations in Western nations.[3] Although these groups laid the foundation for their postwar counterparts, they were weak and ephemeral compared to the organizations which developed later.

Three new conditions lay behind the emergence of the stronger postwar business federations. First, the ravages of war and the breaking up of old monopolies led to a far more decentralized and heterogeneous economy in the rapid recovery that followed. If business wished to present its position to the government through a unified voice, there was a need for an explicit effort to bring order to this dispersal. Second, the greatly strengthened role of the parties in policy-making required that more pressure be placed directly on them, making particularly useful organizations to coordinate and publicize the business position on specific issues. Finally, the enormous growth of the labor movement demanded a strong, independent organization to deal with the new and multiplying problems of this area.[4]

A brief sketch of the exact origins and the composition of the four employers' associations is a necessary preface to a specific appraisal of their political role. Keidanren,[5] a national federation of the leading enterprises and industrial and commercial associations, is the most powerful of these organizations. It was formed in August 1946 from remnants of the three prewar groups, and its members include leading officers of the most responsible men from the largest corporations. (Membership is on a company not an individual basis.) It embodies the attitudes of the most conservative, established business interests. Normally, Keidanren's political activities are limited to matters of economic policy, broadening to encompass other issues only in crises which threaten the stability of the government.[6] The second of the national employers' associations, Nikkeiren, was established under the sponsorship of Keidanren in April 1948. Since its inception, it has been almost exclusively concerned with the problems of labor-management relations (*e.g.*, to counter the annual labor "wage offensives"), and follows the lead of its parent organization on other issues.[7] Still another national group with a prewar antecedent sprang full grown from Keidanren in 1952, the Japanese Chamber of Commerce (Nissho). Nissho serves as the spokesman for the small and medium sized enterprises from which its membership is predominantly drawn.[8] During its early years, Fujiyama Aiichirō dominated the organization and shaped what political actions were undertaken. Keizai Dōyūkai stands somewhat apart from others. It is distinct in the absence of prewar ties, in a membership of individuals (not companies), and in its origin in an open rebellion against the remnants of the prewar business establishment for "their inept attempt to preserve the old-type capitalism despite their lip service to formal democracy." [9] Although Keizai Dōyūkai has lost much of its reformist temper, it remains more progressive and aggressive than either Keidanren or Nissho, largely because it is led by younger men, who have matured in the postwar period and are much more flexible in responding to the rapidly changing society. Despite diversity on specific issues, these business organizations tend to approach politics with the same attitudes and seek to harmonize their actions on major questions. In this sense they constitute the voice of business in Japan.

What are the specific bonds linking the business world with the conservative party? First, and most important, is the massive financial backing, amounting to some seventy-five percent of party funds.[10] Until the merger in 1955, all donations passed directly from businesses and businessmen to an individual politician or his *habatsu*—a pattern in part due to the variety of interests within the business community. One important result was the reinforcement of the factions' independence within the party, while another was the obstruction of unified business political pressure. As illustrated in subsequent discussion of the fishing industry, this pattern also enhanced the power of special interests to shape party policy. Following the establishment of the Liberal-Democratic Party, political leaders, together with Keidanren and Keizai Dōyūkai, set up the *Keizai Saiken Kondankai* (Economic Reconstruction Council) to centralize control of party finances with the aim of reducing factionalism and the potential for corruption scandals.[11] This arrangement, lasting until 1961, was to prove only partially successful and certainly in the period under consideration here, the basic nature of business-conservative financial ties remained unaltered. Thus, although the conservatives were vitally dependent on the business world for money, the diffuse nature of such connections inhibited the easy translation of this dependence into policy influence.

Another link between the businessmen and the conservatives (and the upper echelon bureaucracy) lies in their similar attitudes toward economic and political principles. Both favor modified capitalism and a "democracy," controlled by the conservatives, which strives to maintain traditional values in the context of a modern setting.[12] In part this is based upon a common professional and educational background. It has been shown that in the postwar years consistently more than half of the conservative representatives have had some association with business.[13] The overwhelming majority attend the same select set of universities, acquiring attitudes and personal ties that are amazingly durable in the elite society centered in Tokyo. Business and conservative leaders (again together with the top bureaucrats) are members of the Japanese establishment. Their commitment to preserving the status quo is reinforced in Japan by a tightly woven web of personal relations which bind together and set apart this strata of society. Although it is questionable whether these men constitute a functional "power elite" comparable to that which Mills ascribed to the United States,[14] the Japanese situation may be aptly compared with the tightly knit British establishment in the modern era. This community of sympathies has paved the way for powerful informal channels of communication linking the business and political worlds. The strongest political actions by businessmen which call into full play these special ties have occurred when the imminent fall of a conservative government seemed to present the possibility of the left-wing's rise to power. Then they have moved forcefully "to stabilize the political situation." [15] Shared values and the supporting patterns of interaction give the business community enormous potential influence on politics and buttress the hold of the conservative elite on Japan's postwar order, but it cannot assure business control over each policy decision taken by the government.

Most actions on particular issues essentially political in nature are not taken through the associations but occur on a private basis and involve personal ties with individual politicians.[16] Both the variety of opinions among businessmen and the explicitly non-political posture the national organizations consistently seek to assume [17] contribute to this pattern of participation. The resulting disparate and uncoordinated maneuvers leave no clear impression of the business position. These individual actions, however, are highly important in terms of the factional strategies within the party and in this way indirectly contribute to policy formulation.

In one area, domestic economic policy, business influence is formidable if not decisive, through a close working relationship with the bureaucracy. This intimate cooperation is not a recent phenomenon, for the Japanese government has played a positive, integral role in the industrialization of the country since the Meiji Restoration. Reciprocally, Japanese capitalism has grown up hand in hand with the government and lacks a strong *laissez faire* tradition.[18] Japan's statist, paternalist history has been reinforced by the requirements of fashioning a modern welfare state in the postwar era. In Japan, in much the same way as in Western European democracies, technical and administrative requirements have given the various ministries, not the parties in the legislature, the crucial role in formulating such policies.[19] Consequently, in the one area in which Japanese business has acquired effective access to policy-making, it is the bureaucracy, not the conservative party, that rules.

Indisputably, these multiple channels of contact have given the businessmen the most powerful single outside voice in Japanese politics. It does not necessarily follow, however, that they can and do dominate or even substantially influence every specific policy. The extent of the influence depends on the nature of the issue. Business success is likely to be greatest when a concrete domestic economic interest is in question and the bureaucracy integrally involved. However, when a policy matter is international, not domestic, essentially political rather than economic, and the party not the bureaucracy is the dominant force, the established channels of business contacts are comparatively limited in value. The nature and extent of such limits are suggested by the role of Japanese business in the Soviet negotiations.

Soviet Negotiations

The business associations were reluctantly drawn deeply into the controversy over Soviet policy in August and September 1956, partly as a result of their earlier endorsement of the Shigemitsu mission and a provisional settlement formula.* At the time, the statement seemed merely an assertion of the inevitable; but failure of the mission constituted a partial repudiation of their position, leaving an obligation to reopen their pub-

* See Chapter V on business opinion and interest groups.

lic discussion of the issue. More important, however, was the mounting chaos within the Liberal-Democratic Party and the party's dwindling popular support, both related to the handling of the Russian negotiations. Unless checked, the loss of support forebode a quick rise to power for the Socialists, a portent which moved the business associations to direct political intervention in a way which called into question their basic relation to the conservative party.

Business leaders were left surprised and bewildered by the rapid collapse of the Moscow talks. They remained unalterably opposed to any further territorial concessions, but were somewhat baffled at the total impasse. The reaction to Hatoyama's proposed trip was mixed, reflecting this uncertainty; but in the succeeding days, business opinion hardened against further negotiations in the near future, as the factional wrangling in the party raged out of control.[20]

Discontent with the Hatoyama government grew among the businessmen after the setback in the House of Councillors election in July. Their disillusionment steadily gained momentum in the following weeks as the party absorbed itself in *habatsu* maneuvering in anticipation of Hatoyama's early retirement. With the recall of Shigemitsu, the criticism which had been expressed mainly at private, informal meetings [21] was voiced more openly; the government's Soviet policy and the stability of the general political situation were considered conjunctively.[22] Indeed, it was asserted that conservative disunity as much as the Soviet attitude was a major impediment to normalization of relations.[23]

When Shigemitsu's return to Tokyo failed to settle in any way the factional strife, the business associations openly intervened. On September 3, Fujiyama Aiichirō, the president of Nissho and heretofore the leader of businessmen favoring early restoration of Soviet relations, announced that negotiations should remain suspended until the internal party struggle was resolved. Specifically condemning Hatoyama's proposed visit, he further demanded the immediate resignation of the Prime Minister so that stronger hands could take the reins of government.[24] The next day Ishizaka Taizo, president of Keidanren, joined with

Fujiyama in denouncing the Liberal-Democrats for using a policy issue "like a plaything" and again called on Hatoyama ("sick in body and limited in mental abilities") to step down as party president.[25]

Then, on September 6, seventy representatives from the four employers' associations held a special meeting to adopt a formal business position. The meeting unanimously passed a carefully worded resolution asking that order be re-established within the conservative party. Clothed in more discrete language, the strong criticisms and demands concerning Hatoyama and Soviet policy expressed earlier by Ishizaka and Fujiyama were also reiterated.[26] This in effect constituted a blatant attempt by a single interest group to overthrow the cabinet and force a change in a major foreign policy issue simply by means of a public proclamation. In an effort to legitimatize this action, the businessmen purported to speak not for themselves alone (although the situation was "intolerable to the men who control the greater part of the nation's economy"), but for a "united public opinion." Moreover, they pointedly denied any intention of participating in politics, but merely sought "to save the political situation." [27] On the next day, Fujiyama and Ishizaka met with three Liberal-Democratic Party leaders, Kishi, Ishii Mitsujirō, and Mizuta Mikio, to convey officially the opinions of the business association embodied in their resolution.[28] Here they rested their case.

Party reaction was immediate and strong. Despite business protests to the contrary, their actions were interpreted as direct interference with intraparty politics. An emergency meeting of the mainstream faction leaders passed a counter-resolution condemning business' "unwarranted intervention" which tended "to corrupt the democratic political order." [29] Even more significant than this stinging rebuke was the total ineffectiveness of the action on policy or on the *habatsu* struggle. Hatoyama successfully continued his plans for a trip to Moscow, scarcely breaking stride to notice the extreme opposition of the conservatives' closest supporters, although Kōno and Kishi did attempt to make peace with the business leaders. The associations pledged continued cooperation with the party, but refused to support Hatoyama's Soviet policy—even on the eve of his departure for Moscow.[30]

It is hardly surprising that a frontal assault by the business associations to force a change in Japan's Soviet policy proved a humiliating failure. Success required full capitulation by the government, in the face of a public plea based on little more than a vague desire to "stabilize" the political situation. In its timing as well as its substance, this approach demonstrated a basic miscalculation or misunderstanding of the dynamics of conservative politics. By late August and early September, the process of decision-making within the party, had gained a momentum of its own, which clearly set it free from the kind of pressure the business leaders sought to apply. Intense personal and factional considerations were preeminent, precluding the effectiveness of a nebulous appeal for reform. Furthermore, even if the businessmen had successfully forced the Prime Minister's resignation, it is highly unlikely that this would have brought fulfillment of their broader aims. Hatoyama's retirement at that time could only have exacerbated the factional strife still more and might well have fully discredited the conservatives in the eyes of the public. Their tactical naiveté corroborates the apolitical attitudes which the businessmen displayed earlier in campaigning to mold opinion on Soviet relations.

That public pronouncements rather than private talks were brought to bear on a matter so serious as seemingly to jeopardize the conservative majority indicated the business associations' lack of established channels to policy-making with the Liberal-Democratic Party. Neither the fragmented financial ties, the diffuse personal contacts, the sharing of common political ideals (which underlay the business intervention and remained basically unaffected), nor close bureaucratic connections proved effective on this issue which was truly political in nature. On the question of Soviet relations, the Liberal-Democrats' decision-making process functioned quite free from any substantial influence of the party's major supporting interest group.

FISHING INDUSTRY

One economic issue, Japan's fishing rights in the northern seas, did figure significantly in Soviet relations. Accordingly, the Japanese fishing industry actively participated in the negotiations, seeking access to the policy process primarily as an interest group working for its own benefit. Partly because of the way the Soviets used this issue for political purposes and partly because of special ties with the Liberal-Democratic Party, this group did play an effective role in the formulation of Japanese policy.

Before World War II, a substantial proportion of Japan's world-leading catch came from the northern seas, but it was drastically reduced in the postwar period, creating an economic problem of considerable magnitude. Loss of the Kuriles and southern Sakhalin, together with strict Russian enforcement of their right to exclusive control of twelve miles of coastal waters, made the richest fishing grounds inaccessible to the Japanese. Moreover, the Russians' effort to develop their own fishing industry led first to competition and ultimately to restrictions of Japan's catch on the high seas as well.[31] Under these circumstances, with Japanese vessels constantly harassed and often seized by the Soviets and the expansion of their operations dependent on the good will of Moscow, the fishing industry was among the first promoters of the normalization of relations.

With the broader question of diplomatic relations under active consideration, the industry worked toward promoting an early settlement, while at the same time holding open the possibility of a separate fishing agreement. As previously noted, to this end several prominent leaders such as Hiratsuka Tsunejiro and Ōnishi Rensaka, directors of the *Dai Nippon Suisankai* (Japanese Fishery Association), had joined with leading leftists as charter members of the National Council for the Restoration of Diplomatic Relations with China and the Soviet Union.*

* See Chapter IV on policy groups.
The Japanese Fishery Association is a nationwide federation of fishing companies In this chapter, the term "fishery interests" refers loosely to the companies and individuals of the fishing industry—not just to this association or coordinated activities of the industry.

These men served an important liaison function between the unofficial Soviet mission in Tokyo and the mainstream of the conservative party, with whom they had particularly close connections. It was through Hiratsuka that the Domnitsky note reached Hatoyama, and Ōnishi was instrumental in informing the government in January 1956 that an Adenauer-type agreement was acceptable to the Soviets—before this had been made clear in the London talks,[32] However, once the Russians moved to impose specific restrictions on fishing in the north seas, the industry stepped up its activities.

Ostensibly, quotas on the catch were imposed by the Soviets for the purpose of conservation, but both the timing of the move (the day following suspension of the London talks) and the substance of the agreement ultimately signed in May indicate that the paramount aim was political. Thus the fishery industry in seeking to further its own interests by urging an immediate fishing agreement was abetting the cause of the Soviet Union. In this way, the actions of a domestic pressure group became directly involved in foreign policy formulation, the specific nature of its role being determined by its ties with the conservative party.

Personal and financial connections linked fishery circles and the Hatoyama-Kōno mainstream faction. At the vortex was Kōno, whose contacts extended to the days when he was a young reporter covering agricultural and fishery affairs for the *Asahi Shimbun*. At that time he became intimate with Hiratsuka and subsequently served as a director in the latter's firm, the Nichiro Gyogyo Kaisha (Japan-Russian Fishing Company). In this capacity, Kōno established friendships throughout the industry, contacts which were strengthened during his term as Agricultural and Forestry Minister in the Hatoyama Government [33] Extensive financial bonds reinforced these personal ties. Lacking strong support among the "orthodox" leaders of the Japanese business world, Kōno, who bore the main responsibility for fund raising for the faction, relied heavily on his former business associates for contributions.[34] In short, Kōno's position as a *jitsuryokusha* was heavily dependent on his close relations with the fishing industry and this in turn gave the industry special access to policy-making. Indeed, even on an issue as important as Soviet relations, Kōno's intense interest and active participation was in large part based on his concern for the fisheries question.[35]

It was through these established channels with a *habatsu ryoshū,* not through a dramatic public plea, that the main effort to shape the government's policy was exerted, but one other factor also was of importance. The fishing industry had an electoral value that could be accurately gauged by the conservatives. The response to government policy of the fishing population would be clearly more intense than that of the general public, as their way of life was directly involved.[36] There was evidence that feeling on the subject within fishing circles was deep, if not desperate; their first spontaneous reaction to the Soviet restrictions had called for a private agreement directly with Moscow.[37] Consequently, in the eyes of the government the threat of electoral reprisal was real and measurable, providing further incentive for an early settlement.

In response to these pressures, an emergency fishing conference was convened in Moscow at the end of April, on the insistence of the Japanese government. Selection of Kōno to head the delegation met with broad approval, but he was nominated by the Prime Minister with the hope of broadening the talks to diplomatic matters, not out of consideration for the fishing industry.[38] The agreement signed on May 14 did open the northern seas to Japanese vessels for that year, but by making future access dependent on the restoration of diplomatic ties, the Soviets, with the acquiescence if not support of Kōno and Hatoyama, had forced open the door for new normalization talks. Perpetuation of the fishing issue was to lead the Japanese government again to the "water" of the negotiating table. Whether it would drink was to depend on other factors. The turbulent events of August and September saw the fisheries question obscured by the *habatsu* machinations which had come to dominate the direction of party policy.

Nevertheless, the fishery interests, by virtue of their close ties with a particular faction, had gained access to the foreign policy formulation process at a crucial time, and their actions significantly altered the direction of government policy. In fact, a dimension can be said to have been added to this process in that the Soviet Union in effect used a domestic pressure group to achieve a diplomatic aim which had been denied in formal governmental negotiations. The peculiarly loose nature of party policy-making and Kōno's unique role as *jitsuryokusha* of the cabinet facilitated the effectiveness of the Soviet actions. It is indeed ironic, but indicative of the diffuse nature of post-independence Japanese politics, that one special interest group was able to affect foreign policy with a success denied to all other political groups outside the conservative party.

VIII

The Formal Institutions

The formal governmental institutions directly concerned with international affairs form the final major component of the foreign policy formulation process. Their roles in the Soviet negotiations further illustrate the fluidity which characterized Japanese politics during this period. The wide gap between the effective processes of decision-making, elaborated in the preceding chapters, and the formal structures and procedures set up for this purpose fully demonstrated the absence of established channels for communication and policy control. Indeed, rather than facilitating policy leadership, the Foreign Office (Gaimushō), and to a much lesser extent the Diet, inhibited the operations of the government. In the formulation of policy toward Russia, the Foreign Office actually came to be a rival to the government, often differing with and occasionally openly challenging the "official" policy. Underlying the competition were a variety of factors: personal political rivalries, concrete policy disagreements, and the strong dislike of prewar diplomats in the Gaimushō of both Prime Minister Hatoyama's pragmatic negotiating tactics and his constitutionally sanctioned attempts to take policy leadership into his own hands. Instead of serving as a stabilizing force, the Gaimushō further compounded the complexities of formulating Soviet policy.

In contrast, the plenary Diet sessions and committee meetings dealing with Soviet policy played relatively modest parts in the negotiations. They provided additional stages for debate over the issue, but did not go much beyond that role and its limited influence. Decision-making was thus extended to include the legislature only in a formal sense and at the periphery of the effective process through which Soviet policy was formulated.

THE FOREIGN OFFICE

To understand the unusual role of the Foreign Office in the Soviet negotiations it is first necessary to appreciate the circumstances under which it operated in the first years following independence. During this period the ministry was deeply absorbed in the process of rebuilding after the disaster of the war and the hiatus of the Occupation. The resulting introversive focus and debilitated condition inhibited major participation in policymaking. Furthermore, this was a period of quiescence for Japan in international affairs and no serious effort was made to alter the close, quasi-dependent relationship with the United States. Having neither the impetus nor the opportunity for a Gaimushō renaissance, the ministry occupied a subordinate position with little autonomous influence.

At the same time, Prime Minister Yoshida took firm and full control over all aspects of Japan's foreign affairs. In reconstructing the Foreign Office, the veteran diplomat built up a staff which was personally loyal and shared his policy sympathies. All international problems of any consequence were resolved by the prime minister himself; and his only foreign minister, Okazaki Katsuo, was a close friend and confidant. Consequently, the Gaimushō worked smoothly with the government as a clearing-house for Yoshida's policies.[1] However, the closeness of this association, its basis in personal ties with the prime minister, and its connection with an undeviatingly pro-American policy orientation sowed the seeds for the discord which followed Yoshida's downfall.

With the advent of the Hatoyama cabinet, harmony between the government and the Foreign Office quickly deteriorated. The two actions which precipitated this collapse—the change in policy toward the Soviet Union and the assertion of party leadership over foreign affairs—struck at the foundations of the special relationship that Yoshida had nurtured. Immediately after the Democrats took office, a broad shift in Japan's foreign policy was announced, and within two weeks Hatoyama was publicly pressing for early normalization of Soviet relations.

This constituted a repudiation of a position to which not only Yoshida but leading Gaimushō officials had been openly committed. For the latter, the new policy posture was a source of embarrassment and strained relations with the government. Nevertheless, had the only conflict been over the substance of policy, the breach might well have proved reparable. It was soon supplemented by another controversy, however, which made the split between the Hatoyama and Foreign Office leaders deeper and lasting.

Hatoyama early made clear his intentions to secure the reins of policy leadership in the hands of the prime minister, inevitably, at the expense of certain functions and prerogatives previously held by the Foreign Office. Most conspicuously, leading conservative politicians rather than Gaimushō diplomats were placed in charge of major international negotiations. In May 1955, Takasaki Tatsunosuke, head of the Economic Planning Agency and a close friend of Hatoyama, negotiated the Philippine reparations agreement. Matsumoto Shunichi, the plenipotentiary in London, had had a distinguished career in the Gaimushō, but resigned to become a Hatoyama Democrat in the Diet and a close diplomatic advisor of the prime minister. Both of these appointments were opposed by the Foreign Ministry on the grounds that this "politicized" functions rightfully belonging to it.[2] When Foreign Minister Shigemitsu was dispatched to Washington for a general review of Japanese-American relations, party leaders Kishi and Kōno were also sent to insure that he satisfactorily presented the government's opinion.[3] Another aggravating innovation was the requirement that all ambassadors and ministers be passed upon by the Democratic Party leaders.[4]

Foreign Office officials were further provoked by Hatoyama's expediential tactics in dealing with the Soviets. Almost immediately the issue was noisily incorporated into the Democrat's campaign for mass support in preparation for the general election imminent in February 1955. It remained a matter of open partisan controversy for the next two years, and the resulting broader, more public policy-making process further curtailed the role of the Gaimushō. Still another source of irritation were the informal contacts maintained by Kōno and Hatoyama with the unofficial Soviet mission in Tokyo. This arrangement not only provided a continuous liaison, but permitted initiation of the formal talks as a direct result of the Domnitsky note, and through this connection the government also learned of the Russian's desire for an Adenauer-type agreement well before the ministry was even aware of its existence.[5] To the self-conscious and protocol-bound prewar Gaimushō elite, such challenges to accepted diplomatic procedures and to the role of the ministry in policy-formulation were at least as aggravating as their substantive differences with the government regarding the Soviet Union.

As Foreign Minister, Shigemitsu provided the catalyst through which these sources of disaffection were transformed into a concrete challenge to the government. His appointment, ironically dictated by party considerations, placed the nation's most prestigious diplomat at the head of the Foreign Office. Shigemitsu himself had a strong faction of supporters within the Foreign Office which was distinct from the Yoshida group, and this was reflected in the reshuffling of positions that occurred shortly after he took office.[6] Nevertheless, as the dispute over Soviet policy intensified, Shigemitsu's close personal and professional ties with virtually all of the upper echelon Gaimushō officials took on greater importance. The Gaimushō was divided regarding Soviet policy, but opposition to the Prime Minister's position was strongest among the leading ministry officials, those most sensitive to the party challenge to the bureaucracy, often having strong American sympathies. Despite the fact that the ministry was not of a single mind on this issue, it came into sharp conflict with the government over policy toward the Soviet Union with Shigemitsu as its standard bearer.[7]

Overt manifestation of this conflict first came into the open in January 1955 over the Domnitsky note, which the Russians had initially sought to transmit through the Foreign Office. Shigemitsu, strongly supported by other members of the ministry, refused to receive it because it did not come from an official diplomatic source.[8] In view of the friendly overtures from Mos-

cow in December and Tokyo's positive response, it is dubious
that this formal reason was the basic consideration for rejecting
the key to a major opening in foreign affairs. Whatever the real
explanation, suspicion was cast on the motives of the Foreign
Office because of this rebuff to the Soviet emissary. Domnitsky,
with Sugihara Arita as the main intermediary, delivered the note
directly to the Prime Minister. Hatoyama not only accepted the
message but immediately proclaimed a breakthrough in relations.

This incident undermined the Foreign Office–government
relationship in a threefold manner. Both Shigemitsu and the
Gaimushō came to be identified with the supporters of a "go-
slow" policy toward Russia, casting strong doubts on their capacity to serve as neutral agents of the government. Secondly,
their alienation encouraged the Prime Minister and Kōno to
adopt pragmatic, free-wheeling tactics in their diplomatic
maneuvers. Finally, it ignited the rivalry between the conservative party leaders and the Gaimushō bureaucracy, which flared
up intermittently for the duration of the talks.

From the first contacts with the Soviets until the Kōno fishery
mission in 1956, Gaimushō opposition to the government falls
into two stages. During the first part of the negotiations it centered around the previously discussed public differences between Shigemitsu and Hatoyama. Once Japan shifted to stiffer
territorial demands in August 1955,[9] the Foreign Office
adopted more conservative, defensive tactics. Again with Shigemitsu as the spokesman, strongly supporting the official line
and inveighing against any suggestion for a provisional agreement, the ministry aided in temporarily frustrating the Prime
Minister's efforts to gain an early settlement. At this time, the
role of the Gaimushō was not a crucial influence on the government's policy; the breakdown of the London talks and the com-
promises necessary to support the merger of the Liberal and
Democratic parties were more important. However, the schism
between the Prime Minister and the Ministry steadily widened.

As it became clear that the two leading branches of government responsible for foreign affairs were advocating different
policies toward the same issue, the phrase "dual diplomacy"

was increasingly used to describe the situation. In Japan, this phrase carries a peculiarly invidious connotation, for it is commonly applied to the period in the 1930's when the military and the Gaimushō vied for control of foreign policy—with the victory of the former leading directly to World War II. For this reason the conflict during the Soviet negotiations, although only crudely analogous to the earlier situation, drew added and derogatory attention. The full extent of the discord and its meaning for policy-formulation was dramatically clarified in the controversy surrounding Kōno's fishery mission and the succeeding debate over "amateur diplomacy."

The circumstances surrounding the fishery trip to Moscow have a bizarre cast, especially in the open jousting between the Foreign Minister and the government for policy control. Shigemitsu foresaw that Kōno would attempt to use the fishing talks to break the deadlocked diplomatic negotiations. To forestall this, he initiated two counter moves. First, the Gaimushō took the lead in gaining formal and public guarantees that Kōno would negotiate only regarding a temporary fishing pact.[10] There was, however, general doubt concerning the effectiveness of such assurances in view of Kōno's mercurial personality and his strong commitment to an early settlement. Consequently, when Domnitsky was recalled to Russia for the obvious purpose of expanding the talks to diplomatic matters, the Foreign Office made a desperate effort to halt the fishing mission, then en route to Moscow. Shigemitsu wired Kōno in Stockholm requesting him to stay there while Tokyo considered a new policy to meet this unexpected ploy by the Soviets. Perplexed by this turn of events, Kōno requested further clarification through formal channels. However, suspecting Gaimushō duplicity, he also had a reporter surreptitiously telephone Hatoyama's private secretary in Tokyo. Countermanding the orders from the Foreign Office, the Prime Minister urged Kōno to proceed to the Soviet Union immediately and, further, stated that he would assume full responsibility for any settlement that might be reached.[11] Thus, the Gaimushō was circumvented, and Shigemitsu's hopes for preventing the talks were finally dashed.

What transpired in Moscow fulfilled the worst expectations of the Foreign Office, both in terms of the substance of the agreement and the manner in which it was negotiated. The fishery accord did indeed force reopening of diplomatic talks under conditions which made some sort of settlement likely. This was fully in accord with what Hatoyama (and the Soviets) desired and precisely the sort of agreement the Gaimushō had sought to prevent.[12]

Equally distressing to the Foreign Office was the unorthodox nature of the negotiations. Accepted diplomatic techniques and protocol were totally abandoned. Kōno himself describes with swashbuckling bravado and in considerable detail the informal tactics by which he "triumphed" over the Soviets as had no other Western diplomat. In Kōno's own portrayal of the Moscow talks, the tactics guiding the meetings strikingly resembled those operative in Japanese conservative *habatsu* decision-making. To him the negotiations were essentially individual confrontations in which the major considerations were the personal relations of the participants, not the issues.[13] In such a system, indispensable for any agreement is the establishment of *shinjitsu* (sincerity or mutual trust) between the parties. Apparently it was in part through a desire to demonstrate his sincerity that Kōno attended a crucial conference with Bulganin without an interpreter from Japan. This procedural *gaffe* had serious repercussions, for it was at this meeting that the Soviets first attached to the fishery agreement the proviso for new diplomatic normalization talks.[14] It gave the Gaimushō officials an opening to criticize Kōno's "amateur diplomacy." Indeed, in Tokyo this charge became the focus of a campaign to discredit the agreement and to bolster the position of the Foreign Office.

The sharp public controversy concerning "amateur diplomacy" touched off by the Moscow talks was a final act of resistance before Gaimushō leaders acknowledged the passing of foreign policy control to the party politicians. In a basic sense, the dispute reflected a generational problem; the bitterest criticism came from *Taishō* diplomats, men nurtured in the "tailcoat, top hat, and white gloves" era in Japanese diplomacy.[15] Kōno's actions culminated the pragmatic diplomacy of the Hatoyama government, a style unseemly in the eyes of these men. To them, "amateur diplomacy" was not only ill-mannered, it almost inevitably led to poor representation of Japan's position.[16] What is noteworthy is not that such procedural objections were made, for they were to be expected in view of the radically altered roles of the Foreign Office and the parties under the new constitution, but that they were of so little effect. In part, their ineffectualness was due to the aggressive efforts and skill of Hatoyama and Kōno, but it was also shaped by the clumsy Gaimushō efforts to promote a hard policy toward the Soviet Union.

We have already seen that Foreign Office opposition to the fishery pact was not only on procedural grounds. This was clear from previous efforts to obstruct an early settlement and was now made explicit through statements by Shigemitsu and the "senior diplomats." The Gaimushō sought to press its case through the only avenues open, public appeal and alliance with the anti-mainstream party faction. Both tactics held out little hope for success and required actions far beyond the domain of diplomacy, thereby compromising the professional prestige they ostensibly sought to protect. Consequently, the conclusion of the Soviet peace agreement was doubly disastrous. It constituted a defeat for the Gaimushō not only in the sense that a disapproved policy was enacted, but that the Foreign Office could not control foreign policy-making.

The Gaimushō's role in the final stages of the Soviet talks was increasingly obstructionist. Shigemitsu's selection to head the Moscow delegation, although a product of party compromise, temporarily seemed partial vindication for the minority. With the failure of this mission, however, the Foreign Office again moved into a position at odds with the government. Hatoyama's visit to Moscow was opposed from the first, and the private talks between Kōno and Soviet fishery representative Sergei Tichvinsky in September 1956 (paving the way for the final peace agreement) again fanned into flames the smoldering issue of "amateur diplomacy." [17]

In a sense, the peace agreement of 1956 marked the passing of an era Unlike the prewar period, the Japanese Foreign Office proved incapable of directly competing with the ruling party in the making of policy. As intended in the 1947 constitution the prime minister and his party were in control—the old gave way to the new, the politician replaced the bureaucrat.

THE DIET

An appraisal of the Diet's role in the Soviet negotiations completes the picture of the foreign policy-making process. Although the ruling party ultimately controlled the formal decisions of the Diet, the plenary sessions and especially the committee meetings of the House of Representatives and the House of Councillors added a significant dimension to this process. Not only did the Diet debates clarify the issues, but the rift among the conservatives took on concrete meaning in terms of party discipline when the vote for ratification of the peace agreement took place.[18]

To view the role of the Diet in proper perspective, it is first necessary to understand the place that the Foreign Affairs committees of both houses hold in the government. Each of these committees is a standing committee, with membership allocated in strict proportion to party strength and training and experience (not seniority in the Diet) the formal criteria of selection. In practice, however, committee membership is determined by the leaders of the parties and similarly, the chairmen are chosen by the prime minister and his closest advisers—thus personal and factional considerations enter the picture. The crucial decisions on all major issues of foreign affairs are made in the party caucuses, depriving the committees of any real autonomy in policy-formulation and making interpellation during hearings their main line of access to policy influence.

A comparison of the Japanese foreign affairs committees with their counterparts in the House and Senate in the United States is instructive. Both of the American committees are prestigious groups and assignment to them is sought after by congressmen. Both take positions that, on the one hand, reflect the bipartisan tone of United States policy and, on the other, demonstrate the independence from party discipline of individual committee members. The more important and powerful Senate committee has carved out a unique niche for itself in the governmental structure. Composed of unusually distinguished personalities, normally enjoying informal ties and special privileges with the executive, and commanding enormous respect from both the public and Congress, the ability of the Senate Foreign Relations Committee to shape American policy greatly transcends the formal power it commands. In contrast, the relatively new Japanese foreign affairs committees were in 1955 and 1956 lacking in any comparable power base beyond the authority formally granted to them. They did not have established ties with the Foreign Office, were under tight party control, and necessarily lacked an established tradition of competence in the general area of foreign policy. The Japanese committees were passive actors in a policy-formulation process dominated by conservative *habatsu* rivalries and involving the sharp partisan split between the Socialists and the Liberal-Democrats.

Hearings on Soviet policy were conducted by both Foreign Affairs Committees during the Diet sessions of 1955 and 1956. Unlike the practice in the United States, where significant foreign policy debate often occurs in plenary sessions,[19] the important Diet discussion was focused in the committee meetings. Several aspects of this debate have been selected for further elaboration: the issues which received greatest attention, the role of partisanship, the relation to and impact of these discussions on the overall policy dialogue.

The style of the hearings was fundamentally shaped by the persons who were called upon to testify. There was an occasional staff member from the Foreign Office, but the four men who directly took part in the negotiations,* Prime Minister Hatoyama, Foreign Minister Shigemitsu, Plenipotentiary Matsumoto, and Agricultural Minister Kōno virtually monopolized

---

* The question of Soviet policy played a relatively minor part in the 21st Diet session (December 1954 to January 1955) and 22nd session (March to July 1955) compared with the prominent place this issue claimed in the 23rd session (November to December 1955), 24th (December 1955 to June 1956) and 25th (November to December 1956) There was debate on Soviet policy in the Budget as well as the Foreign Affairs Committees, but it was rather limited and did not differ significantly from that in the latter groups.

the witness stand. One result was that in testimony before these committees, the most complete public report of current developments in the negotiations was provided by the men directly engaged in the talks. Furthermore, the overwhelming proportion of the testimony came from the Prime Minister and the Foreign Minister, and they were called upon in direct and pointed terms to defend the various changes in government policy, the differences between themselves on this issue and the related tangled conservative factional battle. In sum, the committee hearings provided the occasion both for significant additional explanation of the issues involved in the Soviet talks and a sharper focus on the internal political considerations that continuously enveloped the policy-making process.

The most interesting and significant debate took place during the short 23rd Special Session and the 24th Ordinary Session of the Diet, which together met from December 1955 through June of 1956. The opening and early collapse of the second London talks, the Soviet ban on Japanese fishing, and Kōno's fishery pact all took place in this period. A more overt manifestation of the policy split between Hatoyama and Shigemitsu, an intensification of the conservative factional battle, and the first meetings of the Diet since the party mergers were the major domestic political developments. All of these matters were reflected in the interpellations in the Diet.

An issue about which Socialist and conservative questions consistently focused and which caused considerable embarrassment to the government was the delicate matter of policy differences between the Prime Minister and Foreign Minister. To the attentive observer these differences had long been obvious, but the committee hearings made abundantly clear in specific terms the extent of the split. Partly because both men were available for personal challenge, this was the subject most frequently raised in the interpellations. Even in the face of a web of contradictory statements (e.g., Hatoyama's desire for early normalization by provisional agreement if necessary and Shigemitsu's categorical insistence on a treaty [20]) the existence of differences was repeatedly denied. Typical of the oblique responses accompanying these denials is the Foreign Minister's reply to a persistent Socialist questioner in the House Foreign Affairs Committee.

> I have said again and again that my views and those of the Prime Minister do not differ. The Prime Minister is the head of the cabinet and as a cabinet member I would not have different views from the Premier's. There may be different feelings (about the Japanese-Soviet talks), but we try to reach the same conclusions.[21]

The effect of these exchanges was to muddy still more an already murky policy dialogue and to re-emphasize the image of a government deeply divided.

Except for some questions dealing with the status of the northern territories, the committee debates centered on issues in a way that fanned the political fires within the conservative party. This is well illustrated by the interpellations concerning Kōno's mission to Moscow. First, Shigemitsu was forced into an ambiguous and ineffectual explanation of the limited scope of Kōno's powers and then into a half-hearted defense of the agreement Kōno had signed, an agreement at odds with Shigemitsu's earlier remarks, both in substance and in the procedure by which it was negotiated.[22] Similarly, Kōno was prodded into an area of controversy in a committee hearing on his return from the Soviet Union. At a time when the rift between the Foreign Office and the government was at its broadest, he aggravated the situation by strongly defending his concept of "amateur diplomacy." [23] Such exchanges in the Diet exacerbated divisions within the Liberal-Democratic Party and contributed to the fractious pattern of decision-making previously described.

Regarding the territorial claims, the Diet hearings did take the lead in clarifying the legal issues at stake and the relation of this question to a general diplomatic settlement. Since this was the basic question on which the talks with the Soviets had stalled, it became the departure point for general criticism by Socialist committee members of the "intent" of the government regarding a settlement and, as previously noted, an easy entrée to exploiting the policy divisions within the conservatives. Additionally, both Socialist and conservative members of the House Foreign Affairs Committee tried to obtain a fuller and clearer explanation of Japanese claims to the Southern Kuriles. Despite the importance of this matter, the government position in early 1956 was still unclear; as one Liberal-Democratic member of the committee stated, "not many people inside or outside the Diet know on what basis Japan claims the South Kurile Islands." [24] The government's response, largely delivered by the Foreign Minister, was vague and ambiguous, and the Socialist members of the committee persisted in their questioning with very telling effect.[25] Committee hearings in this case fulfilled their intellectual-political function of clarifying the policy dialogue, but the result was to bare weaknesses in Japan's legal case for the Southern Kuriles. In statements in 1951 before the House of Representatives and a special committee on the San Francisco Peace Treaty, Prime Minister Yoshida and a spokesman for the Gaimushō had stated unequivocally that Japan's renunciation of the Kurile Islands (Article II, Section 3) included the Southern Kuriles.[26] It is rather ironic that the behavior of the Diet most in keeping with the deliberative role implied in the constitution, and envisioned by many,[27] should have the effect of undercutting official policy.

Partisan differences were clearly manifest in the debates. Despite the Socialists' basic agreement with the Prime Minister's policy of early normalization and several public statements purporting bipartisan collaboration, the committee hearings were primarily used by the opposition party to criticize the conservatives. With minor exceptions this criticism was restrained, but in both the Lower and the Upper House Foreign Affairs Committee hearings, over eighty percent of the questions came from the Socialists. The main aim was to turn faltering government policy and conservative intraparty division into domestic political advantage. Rather surprisingly the factional rivalries that loomed so large in conservative decision-making were barely evident in the Diet hearings. Only when the 25th Diet was convened in November 1956 to ratify the agreement did these intraparty differences become significant.

The procedure by which both Houses of the Diet ratified the Soviet-Japanese Joint Peace Agreement took on a comic opera air. However, it also gave insight into the meaning of party discipline, the style of Japanese decision-making, and the important place of formal governmental institutions in Japanese politics.

The Peace Agreement was introduced into the Diet in the form of four resolutions on the main points at issue, and these were assigned to the consideration of a Special Committee of the Lower House. Representation on this committee included several members of the Yoshida faction of the Liberal-Democratic Party, who after a week of deliberation were still opposed to the resolutions. Although they could have been reported out of the committee with Socialist support, the conservatives wanted a unanimous vote. In consequence, the party leadership simply replaced those members of the committee who opposed the resolutions with men who favored them—and the committee gave its unanimous approval on November 27.[28]

Meanwhile the problem of party loyalty for the plenary session on ratification was dealt with. In a secret party caucus the still sizable Yoshida bloc in the party had voted against the proposed agreement, which prompted a behind-the-scenes move to prevent overt opposition. Since the Yoshida group adamantly refused to vote for the resolutions, the goal was achieved by convincing them not to attend the Diet session. The vote was 365-0, but not before a speech "offensive to the Socialists" had been struck from the record and Socialist Katsumata Inoue had said (outside of the Diet) that "such intraparty opposition should not exist in a parliamentary democracy." [29]

In the House of Councillors the script was modified only slightly. The resolutions were submitted directly to the plenary session. Lack of full party control, notably over a group of independent Diet members called the Green Breeze Society, led to the casting of three opposition votes. However, the Socialists at one point threatened not to vote at all because one member of the Green Breeze Society voted against the resolutions after another had *spoken* in their favor.[30] Even unanimity in opposition was demanded! To the end the Socialists took every occasion to harass the government through the institutions of the Diet, but with a peculiarly Japanese style.

Although the Diet debates and hearings did add substantially to the public debate over Soviet policy, these actions, like those of the Gaimushō, did not basically alter the pattern of policy-making. The institutions formally responsible for foreign affairs played clearly subordinate roles in the process by which policy toward the Soviet Union was formulated.

IX

Conclusions

THE PARTY

The most striking feature of the Soviet negotiations is the extent to which control of policy was concentrated within the Liberal-Democratic Party. Other components of Japanese politics were able to affect the formulation of policy only insofar as they were able to reach conservative decision-making. Through close connections with a powerful party leader, the fishery interests were able to exercise peripheral influence on the intraparty decision-making process, but the employers' associations, lacking such a channel, were shut off. At the same time, the other half of the party system, the Socialists, avoided positive participation in policy-making at the crucial moment, concentrating instead on exploiting the conservatives' confusion for their own political advantage. Furthermore, as neither a clear public sentiment nor a broadly based articulate opinion emerged, public opinion did not leave the mark that might have been expected. Also, the formal governmental institutions dealing with international affairs found themselves unable to exercise their defined roles in the process. Foreign policy formulation not only centered in the intraparty decision-making process of the conservatives, but this process functioned virtually free from the influence of all other major elements in Japanese politics.

This closed aspect of the policy-making process rested upon a wide variety of forces peculiar to the postwar Japanese political scene, the most important of which being the structure and modus operandi of the conservative party. However, it must first be noted that underlying the party's central role in the talks was the formal structure of the government. Decision-making in prewar Japan also had an elitist cast, but it was the Occupation-sponsored constitutional reforms which led to a new elite of leaders drawn from the ruling party in the Diet. Within the Liberal-Democratic Party itself, two structural aspects were particularly influential in encouraging a closed decision-making process—the lack of a mass base and the factional divisions among the party Diet members. The conservatives were essentially a parliamentary party, and therefore free from the checks that a broad organizational base might impose on the representatives' behavior. Furthermore, the personality-centered *habatsu* of the Liberal-Democratic Diet members were not vertically linked with basic political or economic cleavages in the society —as are the factions within the Congress Party of India and those characterizing the Third and Fourth Republics in France. Control of almost two-thirds of the Diet seats removed the immediate threat of electoral defeat, and thus another potentially mitigating influence on intraparty decision-making. Left virtually free from "outside" checks on their behavior, the *habatsu* became fully engaged in an absorbing competition for power and position. Clearly, the self-contained manner in which conservative politicians formulated policy toward Russia was directly related to the nature of the Liberal-Democratic Party in 1955 and 1956.

There was no meaningful foreign policy debate involving the government, the Diet, and the public. It is difficult to affix specifically the responsibility for this omission. No serious effort was undertaken by the government to explain the official policy to the legislature and to the public, which stands in marked contrast to the elaborate efforts of American administrations to clarify their positions on major foreign policy questions. Hatoyama did not categorically object to open discussion nor was the issue systematically kept from public debate; but political (i.e., party) considerations had priority, and the momentum of the decision-making process gave emphasis to them. Although the issue was "used" by the Democrats to gain public support in the general election in early 1955, eighteen months later in the House of Councillors' election, conservative candidates were barred from discussing the subject because of intraparty differences. The Japanese press also did little to promote a constructive policy dialogue; it reported without discrimination the complicated details of the issues and the negotiations and became a sounding board for the tangled factional struggle. It scrupulously avoided a positive role in the policy-formulation process, refusing to lend editorial support to any firm policy position. Whatever the cause, the bewildered unresponsiveness of the public to the issue, as seen in the results of the opinion polls, demonstrates that the foreign policy debate was indeed a discussion among a small elite with a narrow audience.

That the Socialists did not positively participate in foreign policy-making is not surprising. Why they did not, is. It was not because the party was systematically excluded from discussion by the conservatives. Unlike the issues involved in the United States Security Treaty and the restoration of ties with the Republic of Korea, the Socialists in this case were not previously committed to a policy or ideological position that precluded their cooperation with the government. Rather, the Socialists chose to be left out of the foreign policy-making process in order to use the issue to strengthen their place on the Japanese political scene. Ideological rigidity, which is often used as an explanation for their tactical weakness and permanent minority position, was only indirectly influential on party behavior during the negotiations. Such inflexibility did underlie factional cleavages within the party and made agreement on a single policy difficult. However, the degree to which the Socialist posture was pragmatically determined is striking; the party directly sought its own benefit, not the fulfillment of lofty principles.

Most difficult to reconcile with the standard interpretations of postwar Japanese politics is the failure of the major business organizations to influence party decision-making to any great extent. It is also one of the most conclusive findings, because of the public nature of the business pressure and the equally open and dramatic rebuffs. In part, business impotence may be attributable to the unusual absence of close ties between the prime minister and the dominant elements of the Japanese business world; but it also seems to have been rooted in the basic nature of the connections between the conservative party and their main supporting interest group. The highly fragmented financial ties, the lack of continuing and clear procedures for consultation regarding major non-economic policy questions, the vague opinions voiced by the businessmen regarding this essentially political foreign policy issue, and, above all, the self-contained nature of party policy-making exaggerated by the intensity of the factional struggle, aborted the considerable efforts undertaken by the businessmen to influence Soviet policy. Unless the form of ties with the Liberal-Democratic Party is substantially altered, business influence on major Japanese foreign policy decisions seems likely to continue to be limited despite its commanding position on domestic economic issues and essential financial backing given to the conservatives.

Are serious problems for the Japanese political system posed if this closed aspect of the policy-making process is perpetuated? The wide gap between the elitist practice and the democratic ideals embodied in the constitution and now integral to the political socialization process could be a highly destabilizing influence. Unless modification occurs through broadening the channels of communication and access, each major foreign policy decision will become a potential crisis in which not only policy but the viability of the system itself is called into question. Although experience in Western democracies also suggests that effective widespread political participation in foreign policy formulation is a difficult if not impossible goal, it is doubtful that an open society with democratic ideals can for long sustain a decision-making process which functions autonomously from all other articulate and organized elements of its political system. Tensions generated from this situation could lead to a violent challenge to the foundations of the system. The 1960 Security Treaty incident, when the gap between government policy and the position of both articulate opinion and the opposition party exceeded tolerable bounds, provides a good example. Although the Soviet negotiations constitutes a special case, displaying to an extreme degree the potential autonomy of conservative decision-making, nevertheless, the underlying structural and attitudinal forces operative in 1955 and 1956 have seen little change in the last decade. The problem which dramatically emerged in the Hatoyama era is still pertinent to foreign policy-making.

Despite the danger to the political system inherent in a decision-making process largely restricted to a party elite, this may well be the characteristic pattern for Japan. A party-centered pattern similar to that seen in the Soviet negotiations characterized the decision to normalize relations with South Korea and has dominated the continuing moves regarding ties with Communist China. The mass involvement in the 1960 Security Treaty incident represents, in one sense, a deviation from this pattern; but effective policy control remained in the hands of the Prime Minister, and it is doubtful that such widespread violent actions could recur in future Japanese foreign policy decisions without producing basic changes in the political order. Short of such revolutionary upheaval, in Japan, as in the open societies of the West, the style of foreign policy making is best understood by concentrating on the apex of the political order and on the political culture of the elite, not on the more visible mass base.

EFFICACY OF THE SYSTEM

To evaluate the efficiency of the Japanese political institutions and processes in the peace negotiations, the most useful criteria are those of policy leadership and control. In this regard the crucial question is to what extent the Hatoyama government's accommodation of domestic attitudes and pressures weakened Japan's position in bargaining with Moscow? Although Japan was internationally in a weak position vis-à-vis the Soviet Union, this was a period of thaw in the Cold War, leaving some latitude for diplomatic maneuver. To understand the almost wholly passive and reactive role of Japan in the negotiations, it is necessary to ascertain whether the limits imposed on policy leadership by the domestic political process left open even the possibility of another kind of agreement.

With the locus of power in Japan so centered in the ruling Liberal-Democrats, the foreign policy formulation process was virtually identical with party decision-making. The task of balancing the semi-autonomous factions within the party in order to maintain conservative unity continuously served as a check on strong policy leadership by Hatoyama. As the question of Soviet policy became a focal point for factional contention, the issue became deeply involved in the struggle for party control. Government policy eventually was determined as much by *habatsu* maneuvers as by international considerations. Indeed the timing and the content of the changes in the Japanese position came about almost totally independent of the bargaining at the negotiating table—almost, it would seem, independent of the substantive issues involved. This focus on intraparty problems induced a kind of international myopia and, at the same time, produced *immobilisme* in decision-making. Hatoyama eventually succeeded in forcing a decision, but only at the cost of his political life and after the issues in the party power struggle had been concomitantly resolved. Under these circumstances, Japan could not but play a passive role, for the prime minister was effectively denied the opportunity for maneuver toward any form of agreement other than that desired by the Soviets. International constraints left Japan in a weak negotiating position, but passivity was assured by the nature of her foreign policy formulation process.

Several of the factors underlying this policy *immobilisme* were unique to the Soviet negotiations. First, the peace talks occurred during a period of extreme fluidity, at a time when the new political institutions were undergoing their first major test after the Occupation. In established constitutional states having relatively permanent institutions, the duties of officials in policy formulation are carefully defined, placing inexorable restraints on their actions. No such limitations were operative during the Soviet negotiations. Conservative leaders consistently circumvented the Foreign Office and the formal diplomatic channels; the official party institutions and policies were ignored or bypassed; even leaders in the fishing industry dealt directly with the Soviet representatives. Institutional procedures were largely circumvented, and foreign policy-making came to depend on the actions of, and rivalries between, politically powerful individuals and groups. The resulting unregulated pattern of decision-making is characteristic of a system in which the roles of the political participants are not clearly established, of a transitional society in which there is a sizeable gap between the constitutional and actual patterns of politics. Japanese politics continues to undergo change, but the structure and processes of the political system have become more settled with the passage of time. Barring a major political or economic upheaval, a recurrence of the turbulence of 1955 and 1956 seems quite remote.

Secondly, the prewar party leaders and bureaucrats who dominated conservative politics at that time have since passed from the political scene. To most of these individuals (e.g., Hatoyama, Shigemitsu, and Yoshida) the old ways were most natural, and functioning in the new political milieu was a profoundly difficult and unsettling experience. Inevitably, their confusion aggravated the confusion of the entire political process and, as previously suggested, at least partially explains the inordinate concern for power and position displayed by conservative party leaders. Future foreign policy decisions will rest in the hands of men more adapted to and skilled in politics of the post-independence period.

Because normalization of Soviet relations did not basically challenge the alliance with the West, Japan was left relatively free from international pressures and internal political forces were undoubtedly allowed exceptional latitude for policy influence. Even if the Japanese had explicitly intended to use a Soviet settlement as the basis for a more independent foreign policy, in the context of the mid-fifties such a move could have been only symbolic. With the development of a polycentric international order and Japan's sharply rising importance in Asia and the world, a major foreign policy decision in Tokyo would not necessarily involve greater and more varied outside influences. This may not diminish the effect of domestic politics on foreign policy, but it means that an important dimension virtually absent in 1955 and 1956 will also have to be taken into account.

In these ways, the Soviet peace negotiations are a special

case; in other ways, they are not. That the issue became the shuttlecock of conservative politics is only partially attributable to the special circumstances of the immediate post-independence period. The conditions within the political world in general and the conservatives in particular were unsettled, but this is properly viewed as an extreme not a unique situation. The inextricable commingling of domestic politics with foreign policy formulation is simply the result of the form in which the postwar Japanese political system has developed. The absence of established institutions for resolving conflict in an ordered fashion, the nature of the *habatsu* struggle and the peculiar relationship between the government and opposition, the parties and the interest groups, the public and the government, all had the combined effect of drawing this issue into the center of domestic politics. Moreover, these have become permanent features of the Japanese political landscape (albeit in slightly altered or attenuated forms) and integral to all major foreign policy decisions.

It is important to emphasize that this pattern of decision-making did not emerge *de novo* in the post-independence political world, but, owing to the persistence of traditional Japanese attitudes and behavior, had direct links with the past. A reciprocal relationship existed between these vestiges of tradition and the "modern" political institutions (e g., the party, the Diet) in which they operated, producing distinct hybrid political practices. Because these new patterns of behavior were the product of the political and organizational forces of the national government and the central party organs, they are correctly viewed as parts of the political sub-culture of the upper echelon of Japanese politics. Particularly significant examples of modernized-traditional political phenomena were the *habatsu* and the concept of consensual authority. The former underlay the fragmented structure of the Liberal-Democratic Party, while the latter exacerbated the problem of policy leadership in the conservative coalition by demanding the participation of all the leading political actors and at least their tacit acquiescence on major decisions. There are surprising parallels between the procedural values and practices of the conservatives and the general pattern of decision-making in the immediate prewar period as described by F. C. Jones:

> Policy was formulated by discussion and compromise between various groups in the ruling caste. It was a system which militated against swift decisions and clear cut policies as well as against sudden changes of front.[1]

In the Soviet negotiations, the party *ha* replaced the then ruling oligarchy of the military, the Court officials, the Gaimushō, and the party leaders; but the process of policy formulation was strikingly analogous in form as well as result.

This diffuse style of Japanese decision-making which proscribes strong policy leadership, may well become an obstacle to any future efforts to play a more positive part in world politics. Policies involving greater independence from the United States, whether neutralist or as an armed intermediate power in East Asia, will require a kind of effective direction which a conservative government or a conservative-dominated coalition will find extreme difficulty in providing. Unless the pattern of policy formulation and leadership displayed in the Soviet negotiations is radically reversed, Japan seems destined to remain a passive actor on the international stage, reacting to, not leading events despite increasing potential for autonomous action.

To what extent was the Japanese decision-making process displayed in the Soviet negotiations consistent with the aim of the Occupation to create a democratic political order? In certain ways the system was clearly deficient. There was no broad participation by the public or organized groups since effective channels of communication with the government were never opened. Neither did the Diet serve as a forum for careful and reflective policy deliberation. Yet certain fundamental aspects of this political system were undeniably democratic. The essential elements of an open society were maintained, including the popular elections, free speech, and free assembly guaranteed by the constitution. Japan must be classified as a species of the genus democracy. Indeed, the inevitable complexities we have herein examined illustrate de Tocqueville's dictum on democracy:

> In the conduct of foreign relations, . . . democratic governments appear to be decidedly inferior to governments carried on upon different principles.

Particularly, it seems, the species found in the Soviet-Japanese peace negotiations.

Appendix
Notes
Bibliography

Appendix

JOINT DECLARATION BY THE UNION OF SOVIET SOCIALIST REPUBLICS AND JAPAN. SIGNED AT MOSCOW, ON 19 OCTOBER 1956

From 13 to 19 October 1956 negotiations were held at Moscow between the Delegations of the Union of Soviet Socialist Republics and Japan.

The following representatives of the Union of Soviet Socialist Republics took part in the negotiations:

N. A. Bulganin, Chairman of the Council of Ministers of the USSR,

N. S. Khrushchev, Member of the Presidium of the Supreme Soviet of the USSR,

A. I. Mikoyan, First Vice-Chairman of the Council of Ministers of the USSR,

A. A. Gromyko, First Deputy Minister of Foreign Ministers of the USSR, and

N. T. Fedorenko, Deputy Minister of Foreign Affairs of the USSR.

The following representatives of Japan took part in the negotiations:

Prime Minister, Ichiro Hatoyama,

Ichiro Kono, Minister of Agriculture and Forestry, and

Shunichi Matsumoto, Member of the House of Representatives.

In the course of the negotiations, which were held in an atmosphere of mutual understanding and co-operation, a full and frank exchange of views took place. The Union of Soviet Socialist Republics and Japan were fully agreed that the restoration of diplomatic relations between them would contribute to the development of mutual understanding and co-operation between the two States in the interests of peace and security in the Far East.

As a result of these negotiations between the Delegations of the Union of Soviet Socialist Republics and Japan, agreement was reached on the following:

1. The state of war between the Union of Soviet Socialist Republics and Japan shall cease on the date on which this Declaration enters into force and peace, friendship and good-neighbourly relations between them shall be restored.

2. Diplomatic and consular relations shall be restored between the Union of Soviet Socialist Republics and Japan. For this purpose, it is intended that the two States shall proceed forthwith to exchange diplomatic representatives with the rank of Ambassador and that the question of the establishment of consulates in the territories of the USSR and Japan respectively shall be settled through the diplomatic channels.

3. The Union of Soviet Socialist Republics and Japan affirm that in their relations with each other they will be guided by the principles of the United Nations Charter, in particular the following principles set forth in Article 2 of the said Charter:

(a) To settle their international disputes by peaceful means in such a manner that international peace and security, and justice, are not endangered;

(b) To refrain in their international relations from the threat or use of force against the territorial integrity or political independence of any State, or in any other manner inconsistent with the Purposes of the United Nations.

The USSR and Japan affirm that, in accordance with Article 51 of the United Nations Charter, each of the two States has the inherent right of individual or collective self-defence.

The USSR and Japan reciprocally undertake not to intervene directly or indirectly with each other's domestic affairs for any economic, political, or ideological reasons.

4. The Union of Soviet Socialist Republics will support Japan's application for membership in the United Nations.

5. On the entry into force of this Joint Declaration, all Japanese citizens convicted in the Union of Soviet Socialist Republics shall be released and repatriated to Japan.

With regard to those Japanese whose fate is unknown, the USSR, at the request of Japan, will continue its efforts to discover what has happened to them.

6. The Union of Soviet Socialist Republics renounces all reparations claims against Japan.

The USSR and Japan agree to renounce all claims by either State, its institutions or citizens, against the other State, its institutions or citizens, which have arisen as a result of the war since 9 August 1945.

7. The Union of Soviet Socialist Republics and Japan agree that they will enter into negotiations as soon as may be possible for the conclusion of treaties or agreements with a view to putting their trade, navigation and other commercial relations on a firm and friendly basis.

8. The Convention on deep-sea fishing in the north-western sector of the Pacific Ocean between the Union of Soviet Socialist Republics and Japan and the Agreement between the Union of Soviet Socialist Republics and Japan on co-operation in the rescue of persons in distress at sea, both signed at Moscow on 14 May 1956, shall come into effect simultaneously with this Joint Declaration.

Having regard to the interest of both the USSR and Japan in the conservation and rational use of the natural fishery resources and other biological resources of the sea, the USSR and Japan shall, in a spirit of co-operation, take measures to conserve and develop fishery resources, and to regulate and restrict deep-sea fishing.

9. The Union of Soviet Socialist Republics and Japan agree to continue after the restoration of normal diplomatic relations between the Union of Soviet Socialist Republics and Japan, negotiations for the conclusion of a Peace Treaty.

In this connexion, the Union of Soviet Socialist Republics, desiring to meet the wishes of Japan and taking into consideration the interests of the Japanese State, agrees to transfer to Japan the Habomai Islands and the island of Shikotan, the actual

transfer of these islands to Japan to take place after the conclusion of a Peace Treaty between the Union of Soviet Socialist
Republics and Japan.

10. This Joint Declaration is subject to ratification. It shall
enter into force on the date of the exchange of instruments of
ratification. The exchange of the instruments of ratification shall
take place at Tokyo as soon as may be possible.

IN WITNESS WHEREOF the undersigned plenipotentiaries have
signed the Joint Declaration.

DONE in two copies, each in the Russian and Japanese lan-
guages, both texts being equally authentic.

Moscow, 19 October 1956.

<table>
<tr><td>By authorization
of the Presidium of the Supreme
Soviet of the Union of Soviet
Socialist Republics:</td><td>By authorization
of the Government
of Japan:</td></tr>
<tr><td>N. BULGANIN
D. SHEPILOV</td><td>I. HATOYAMA
I. KONO
S. MATSUMOTO</td></tr>
</table>

United Nations Treaty Series, Vol 263 (1957), pp 112–117.

Notes

Complete bibliographical information for the sources cited in these notes is given in the Bibliography, pages 183 to 194 For the reader's convenience, each source item has been keyed to the Bibliography by a bracketed number, thus, [136] refers to the Bibliography entry numbered [136].

CHAPTER I

1. A number of widely-differing approaches have been used to study foreign policy-making Among the most significant works are· Bernard C. Cohen, *The Political Process and Foreign Policy. The Making of the Japanese Peace Settlement* [136]; Karl W. Deutsch and Lewis J. Edinger, *Germany Rejoins the Powers* [144]; Gabriel Almond, *The American People and Foreign Policy* [129], Richard C. Snyder, H. W. Bruck, and Burton Sapin, *Foreign Policy Decision-Making* [166]; James N. Rosenau, *Public Opinion and Foreign Policy* [163]; and Frederick S. Dunn, *Peace-Making and the Settlement with Japan* [146].

2. In keeping with Herbert McCloskey's apt caveat concerning the insurmountable difficulties of measuring effective influence "scientifically," in terms of a comprehensive model (e g , that proposed by Snyder, et al.), the present approach is explicitly interpretative and is built around a simplified picture of Japanese decision-making. (Herbert McCloskey, "Concerning Strategies for a Science of International Politics," in Snyder, *et al.*, *Foreign Policy Decision-Making* [166], pp. 201–202.)

3. See especially Cohen, *The Political Process* [136].

4. Walter Lippmann, *Essays in the Public Philosophy* [156], pp. 23–24.

5. See, for example, George F. Kennan, *Realities of American Foreign Policy* [153], *passim*, and Hans J. Morgenthau, *Politics Among Nations* [160], pp 146–147.

6. Morgenthau, *ibid.*

7. Lippmann, *Essays* [156], p 28.

8. This point is elaborated in Kenneth N. Waltz, *Foreign Policy and Democratic Politics* [169], pp. 267–269.

9. See, for example, *ibid.*, pp. 254–257 and Chapter 10, and Cohen, *The Political Process* [136], pp. 29–30, 62–63.

10. For an elaboration of this distinction see Cohen, *The Political Process* [136], p. 29, Chapter 3 through 6, and 10.

11. Sir Ivone Kirkpatrick, *The Inner Circle* [155], p. 199.

12. Hazel G. Erskine, "The Polls: The Informed Public" [184], *Public Opinion Quarterly*, 26, 4 (Winter 1962), 675.

13. A. I. P. O. poll published in March 1955, cited in *ibid.*

14. The pyramidal conception of public opinion is treated in Almond, *The American People* [129], Chapter 4 through 6, and especially pp. 138–139. Also see Cohen, *The Political Process* [136], Chapter 3, and Rosenau, *Public Opinion* [163], pp 33 ff.

15. Rosenau, *Public Opinion* [163], pp. 19–26.

16. See, for example, Douglas H. Mendel, *The Japanese People and Foreign Policy· A Study of Public Opinion in Post-Treaty Japan* [159]. This book provides a useful description of Japanese public opinion, but fails to give the description meaning by demonstrating how opinion is integrated into the policy-making process.

17. V. O. Key, Jr., *The Responsible Electorate* [154], pp. 50–51, 74–76, 130–135, and Waltz, *Foreign Policy* [169], pp. 274–297

18. See Robert A. Scalapino and Junnosuke Masumi, *Parties and Politics in Contemporary Japan* [165], Chapter V, for an excellent general discussion of this incident; and see George W. Packard, III, *Protest in Tokyo: The Security Treaty Crisis of 1960* [161], *passim.*

19. Scalapino and Masumi, *Parties and Politics* [165].

20. For elaboration see Cohen, *The Political Process* [136], pp. 62–63, and Almond, *The American People* [129], pp. 136–143.

21. See, for example, Samuel H. Beer, "The Representation of Interests in British Government: Historical Background" [177], *American Political Science Review*, LV (September 1957), 628–645

22. See Packard, *Protest in Tokyo* [161], pp. 262 ff.

23. Bernard C. Cohen, *The Press and Foreign Policy* [137], pp. 3–16.

24. Edward P. Whittemore, *The Press in Japan Today . . . A Case Study* [170], pp. 1–2, and Ardath W. Burks, *The Government of Japan* [135], pp. 61–65.

25. For elaboration on the role of elites in foreign policy-making see Deutsch and Edinger, *Germany Rejoins the Powers* [144], pp. 3–8, and Elie Able, *The Missile Crisis* [128], especially pp. 95–130, for an example of how the United States government brought both domestic and foreign public opinion into a major foreign policy decision.

26. Regarding Prime Minister Yoshida and the United States Peace Treaty, see Kōsaka Masataka, "Saishō Yoshida Shigeru ron" [43], *Chūō kōron*, 79, 2 (February 1964), 80–85 and 105; regarding Kishi and the 1960 Security Treaty see, Packard, *Protest in Tokyo* [161], Chapter VII; and regarding Hatoyama and the Soviet Peace Agreement see my discussion in Chapter IV of conservative party attitudes.

27. See Robert A. Scalapino, "The Foreign Policy of Modern Japan" [201], in Roy C. Macridis (ed.) *Foreign Policy in World Politics*, pp. 237–241, and Yale C. Maxon, *Control of Japanese Foreign Policy: A Study of Civil-Military Rivalry, 1930–1945* [158], especially Chapter IV.

28. See, for example, Ezra F. Vogel, "Migration to the City" [207], in R. P. Dore (ed.), *Aspects of Social Change in Modern Japan*, pp. 108–109.

29. A concise discussion of the political meaning of Japanese social values and institutions is found in Nobutaka Ike, *Japanese Politics. An Introductory Survey* [151], pp. 10–36. "Japan" [209] by Robert E Ward, in Lucian Pye and Sidney Verba (eds.), *Political Culture and Political Development*, pp. 71–73, Scalapino and Masumi, *Parties and Politics* [165], pp. 18–19 (See also Ruth Benedict, *The Chrysanthemum and the Sword* [133], especially Chapters 6 and 7.)

30. For elaboration on this point see Oka Yoshitake, "Seitō to seitō seiji" [64], in Oka Yoshitake (ed.), *Gendai Nihon no seiji katei*, pp 93–98. Although some factions do become identified with a single policy issue (e.g., the commitment of the current Matsumura Kenzo faction to closer ties with Communist China), most typically "policy factions" concerned with foreign affairs draw their members from a number of the personality-centered *habatsu*, leaving the latter substantially intact. (See, for example, Murakami Kaoru, "Jimintō kakuha no bōei kankaku" [53], *Jiyū*, 8, 7, (July 1966), 105–113.

31. Watanabe Tsuneo, *Habatsu* [20], pp. 46–48, and George O. Totten and Tamio Kawakami, "The Functions of Factionalism in Japanese Politics" [206], *Pacific Affairs*, XXXVIII, 2 (Summer 1965), 111–112.

32. Frank C. Langdon, "Organized Interests in Japan and Their Influence on Political Parties" [189], *Pacific Affairs*, XXXIV (Fall 1961), 272–274.

33. See Hans H. Baerwald, "Factional Politics in Japan" [174], *Current History*, April 1964, pp. 225–226.

34. Scalapino and Masumi, *Parties and Politics* [165], pp. 85–86.

35. On this point see Michael Leiserson, "Factions and Coalitions in One Party Japan: An Explanation Based on the Theory of Games" [190], (paper delivered at the annual meeting of the American Political Science Association, September 5–9, 1967). This paper provides a superb discussion on the role of factions in selecting party leaders.

36. See, for example, discussion of the maneuvers which occurred in Kōno Ichirō's faction in the year following his death. *Mainichi shimbun*, June 29, 1966.

37. Maurice Duverger, *Political Parties· Their Organization and Activity in the Modern State* [147], pp. 63–64.

38. See especially, R P. Dore, *Land Reform in Japan* [145], pp. 343–349, and Scalapino and Masumi, *Parties and Politics* [165], p 6.

39. For a similar interpretation, see Takeshi Ishida, "Interest Groups in Japan" [186], pp. 34, 72

40. Kawamura Kinji (ed), *Gaimushō* [5], pp. 29–49, provides a good summary of the Gaimushō's activities during the first ten postwar years. See also Katsuo Okasaki, "Japan's Foreign Relations" [197], *Annals of the American Academy of Political and Social Science*, No. 308 (November 1956), 156–159.

41 Hosoya Chihiro, "Taishō gaikō ni okeru seitō to itan—Katō Takaaki to Gotō Shimpei" [36], *Nihon oyobi nihonjin*, 1430 (1966), 18–25; Uchiyama Masakuma, "Senzen no gaimu daijin—Shidehara Kijūro to Matsuoka Yōsuke" [75], *Nihon oyobi Nihonjin*, 1430 (1966), pp. 26–37.

42. Imai Shinnichi, "Shidehara gaikō ni okeru seisaku kettei" [37], *Nihon seijigaku nenpō, 1959,* entitled *Taigai seisaku no kettei katei,* pp. 93–94.

43. See Chapter VIII below and Ohtari Keisuke, "Hanayaka na bōrei: gaikokan" [63], *Bungei shunjū,* July 1956, pp. 122–127.

44. Packard, *Protest in Tokyo* [161], pp. 233–242.

CHAPTER II

1. Roger Swearingen, "A Decade of Soviet Policy in Asia, 1945–56" [204], *Current History,* 32 (February 1957), 91–92.

2. The text of this agreement appears in the *New York Times,* February 15, 1950.

3. *Conference for the Conclusion and Signature of the Treaty of Peace with Japan: Record of Proceedings* [213], published by the U.S. Department of State, pp. 119–122.

4. *New York Times,* January 26, 1955; *Press Releases* (*December 1954–December 1955*) [211], from the Japanese Ministry of Foreign Affairs, p. 5.

5. James W. Morley, *Soviet and Communist Chinese Policies Toward Japan, 1950–1957* [192], pp. 8–9.

6. These conditions were publicly renounced by Foreign Minister Molotov on December 16, 1954, *Pravda,* December 17, 1954, translated in *The Current Digest of the Soviet Press* [217], VI: 50, 19, and in *Ni-So kokkō chōsei mondai kiso shiryōshū* [88], published by the National Diet Library Legislative Research Bureau, pp. 231–232.

7. *Pravda,* September 13, 1954, in *The Current Digest of the Soviet Press* [217], VI: 34, 16.

8. New China News Agency, Peking, October 12, 1954 in *Survey of the China Mainland Press* [212], published by the American Consulate General in Hong Kong, No 906 (October 12, 1954), 3–4.

9 *Pravda,* December 17, 1954, in *The Current Digest of the Soviet Press* [217], VI: 50, 19, and *Ni-So kokkō chōsei mondai* [88], pp. 231–232.

10. *Press Releases* [212], p. 65.

11. For example, in a poll by the Yoron Kagaku Kyōkai (Public Opinion Institute) in September 1954, 56 4% of the sample positively stated that Yoshida should retire. Allan B. Cole and Nakanishi Naomichi (eds.), *Japanese Opinion Polls with Socio-Political Significance* [139], p. 188.

12. *Yomiuri shimbun,* December 10, 1954; *Asahi shimbun,* December 13, 1954.

The intention to seek quick restoration of diplomatic relations with Communist China was abandoned in January 1955. In a Diet speech, Foreign Minister Shigemitsu indicated that contact with Peking would be limited to economic and cultural interchange (*Asahi shimbun,* January 22, 1955).

13. Matsumoto Shigeharu, *et al., Kindai Nihon no gaikō* [10], pp. 144–146.

14. On normalization see *Mainichi shimbun*, December 19, 1954 and on the latter point see *Asahi shimbun*, January 24, 1955.

15. *Asahi shimbun*, January 23 and 24, 1955.

16. For a summary of the Soviet actions during this period, see *The Current Digest of the Soviet Press* [216], VII; 14, 30, and *Ni-So kokkō chōsei mondai* [88], pp. 234–241.

17. *Mainichi shimbun*, June 18, 1955.

18. In Article 2 (para. c) of the treaty, Japan specifically renounced all rights to the Kurile Islands and the southern part of Sakhalin. *Conference for . . . Treaty of Peace with Japan* [212], U.S. Department of State, p. 314.

19. Interview with Matsumoto Shunichi, January 20, 1963 [122].

20. *The Northern Islands* [210], published by the Japanese Ministry of Foreign Affairs.

21. *Asahi shimbun*, August 20, 1955.

22. *Ibid.*, November 13, 1955.

23. *Tokyo shimbun*, December 13, 1955.

24. *New York Times*, January 29, 1956.

25. *Asahi shimbun*, March 21, 1956.

26. *Ibid.*, March 22, 1956.

27. *Tokyo shimbun*, May 16, 1956.

28. *Yomiuri shimbun*, May 25, 1956.

29. See, for example, Hatoyama's statement at a press conference on June 6 (*Asahi shimbun*, June 7, 1956).

30. *Ibid.*, July 17, 1956.

31. *Ibid.*, August 2, 1956.

32. *Mainichi shimbun*, August 12, 1956.

33. *Asahi shimbun*, August 14, 1956.

34. *Ibid.*, August 20, 1956.

35. *Mainichi shimbun*, August 23, 1956.

36. An *Asahi* poll of August 27–28 showed 41% of the public favored a cabinet change, a figure equaled only in the last days of the Ashida Hitoshi cabinet in 1945 and the period immediately prior to the collapse of Yoshida in 1954 (*Asahi shimbun*, September 7, 1956). The attitude of the businessmen will be dealt with in Chapter VII.

37. *New York Times*, August 30, 1956.

38. *Asahi shimbun*, September 7, 1956, *Japan Times*, September 9, 1956; *Mainichi shimbun*, September 23, 1956.

39. *Tokyo shimbun*, October 7, 1956.

40. *Ibid.*, October 20, 1956. An interesting, although biased, description of the talks is Kōno Ichirō, *Ima dakara hanasō* [9], Chapter 7.

41. See Appendix I for a translation of the Joint Declaration.

42. *Ibid.*

CHAPTER III

1. For elaboration see Kenneth E. Colton, "Pre-War Political Influences in Post-War Conservative Parties" [182], *American Political Science Review*, XLII (October 1948), 940–957.

2. See Hans H. Baerwald, *The Purge of Japanese Leaders Under the Occupation* [131], pp. 21–24.

3. Naka Masao, *Kaisō no sengo seiji* [14], pp. 74–76.
4. Yoshida Shigeru, *The Yoshida Memoirs* [172], pp. 72–75.
5. Watanabe Tsuneo, *Tōshu to seitō* [21], pp. 83–87.
6. The conservatives opposed to the Liberals went by a variety of party names As mentioned above, the first such group was known as the Progressive Party. In 1947, it became the Democratic Party (*Minshutō*); in 1950, the name was changed to the People's Democratic Party (*Kokumin Minshutō*); finally in February 1952, it was designated the Reform Party (*Kaishintō*). Each change was accompanied by minor shifts in membership or leadership, but the basic personnel and nature of the organization remained fairly constant. In addition to this major group, a variety of splinter groups sporadically appeared.

For a chronology of this complicated series of events, see Watanabe Tsuneo, *Habatsu* [20], pp. 220–221.
7. For elaboration of Hatoyama's maneuvers in this period, see Tatamiya Eitaro, *Hatoyama būmu no budai ura* [17], pp. 25–110, and "Hatoyama to Ogata" [34], *Sande mainichi*, December 12, 1954.
8. Detailed discussion of these developments are found in Tatamiya, *Hatoyama* [17], pp. 155–184; "Uwasa no otoko Hatoyama Ichirō" [78], *Shūkan yomiuri*, August 1, 1954, pp. 4–16, "Seikai 'shintaifū no me' Kishi Nobusuke" [70], *Shūkan yomiuri*, October 3, 1954, pp. 4–12.
9. Tatamiya, *Hatoyama* [17], pp 113–154.
10. Watanabe Tsuneo, *Daijin* [19], pp. 254–255.
11. "Yodantobi seijika, Shigemitsu Mamaro" [80], *Shūkan asahi*, June 8, 1952, p. 3.
12. For Shigemitsu's career and his record as a party politician see *ibid.*, pp. 2–6; *Mainichi shimbun*, June 6, 1953; Asahi shimbun seijibu, *Nihon no kyūjūkunin* [1], pp. 136–138.
13. For a discussion of the negotiations between the Hatoyama Liberals and the Kaishintō just prior to the founding of the Democratic Party, see Tatamiya, *Hatoyama* [17], pp. 184–201. It is clear that the resulting agreement involved cabinet posts for Kaishintō faction leaders, Watanabe, *Daijin* [19], pp. 254–255.

The simplified account of the turmoil among the conservatives during 1954, given here, does not deal with the many and complicated behind-the-scenes moves taken to solve the recurrent crises. In particular, efforts were made to promote rapprochement between Yoshida and Hatoyama, and Yoshida and Shigemitsu—maneuvers demonstrating the comprehensive web of close personal ties pervading the entire conservative camp beneath the factional cleavages. A detailed account is found in Kokuritsu kokkai toshokan shimbun kirinuki shiryōshitsu, *Hoshu gōdō shichigatsu kara jūichigatsu made 1954* [110]. Hereafter this collection will be cited as Kirinuki.
14. In his memoirs, Hatoyama stated that he "hoped" to make Shigemitsu the next prime minister because of the latter's concessions in the talks leading to the formation of the Democratic Party. Hatoyama Ichirō, *Hatoyama Ichirō kaikoroku* [2], pp. 139–140.
15. Watanabe, *Daijin* [19], pp. 254–257.

16. *Yomiuri shimbun*, December 10, 1954; *Asahi shimbun*, December 13, 1954.

17. See especially, *Asahi shimbun*, December 19, 1954, January 4 and 23, 1955, and February 5, 1955.

18. *Ibid.*, March 5, 1955.

19. *Ibid.*, May 26, 1955.

20. For the roles of Miki and Ōhno in the conservative merger, see Mikikai, *Miki Bukichi* [11], pp. 426–449; Mitarai Tatsuo, *Miki Bukichi den* [12], pp. 437–441; Ōhno Bamboku, *Ōhno Bamboku kaisōroku* [15], pp. 170–174.

For a good, brief summary of the factors behind the merger, see R. P. Dore, "Left and Right in Japan" [183], *International Affairs*, XXXIII (January 1956), 13–16.

21. "Atama no nai hoshu shintō" [29], *Ekonomisuto*, November 19, 1955, p. 8.

22. For the text of the statement on the party's organization, see Kokuritsu kokkai toshokan rippō-chōsashitsu, *Shuyōkokka no seitō koyaku* [89], pp. 4–14.

23. Watanabe, *Daijin* [19], pp. 259–261.

24. Robert A. Scalapino, *Democracy and the Party Movement in Prewar Japan* [164], pp. 117–119, 132–134.

25. Undoubtedly the most famous manifestations of this pattern of behavior were the *Genrō* and their successors, the *Jūshin*, informal groups of elder statesmen who exercised de facto control over many aspects of Japanese government througout most of the modern era.

26. Watanabe, *Habatsu* [20], pp. 132–135, provides an excellent, brief discussion of this subject. On conservative *ha* in general and the role of the *jitsuryokusha* in particular, I am heavily indebted to the stimulating analysis given by Professor Masumi Junnosuke in numerous personal conversations.

27. Watanabe, *Daijin* [19], pp. 259–260; Watanabe, *Habatsu* [20], pp. 197–199.

Miki, interestingly, supported early restoration of relations with the Soviet Union despite his opposition to the mainstream faction, *Asahi shimbun*, May 16, 1956. For elaboration of Miki's opposition to the merger see Dore, "Left and Right in Japan" [183], pp. 14–15.

28. Information concerning the size and maneuvers of factions inevitably involves conjecture. However, by sifting through the most authoritative of the many sources, a fairly satisfactory picture of the party's structure can be reconstructed—certainly one of sufficient accuracy for the present analysis. In addition to the previously cited books by Watanabe, the following articles proved particularly useful: Kanazaki Kō, "Kane no mado kara seikai mireba" [39], *Shin seikai*, March 1956, pp. 38–43; Arimura Uhei, "Jiyūminshutō no uchimaku" [26], *Chūō kōron*, June 1956, pp. 151–161; "Gaikō wa gaikōkan ni" [32], *Shūkan shinchō*, August 6, 1956, pp. 26–31; Karashima Kochizō, "Habatsu no dorashō seikai" [40], *Bungei shunjū*, November 1956, pp. 71–83.

29. *Asahi shimbun*, April 7, 1956.

30. Hatoyama explicitly indicated that Kōno should deal with all basic problems outstanding between the two countries. Kōno Ichirō, *Ima dakara hanasō* [9], p. 9.

31. See, for example, two public statements by Hatoyama in *Asahi shimbun*, January 29, 1956, and June 7, 1956.

32. "Nı-So gyogyō kōshō tokushū" [56], *Sande mainichi*, May 27, 1956, pp. 14–18, *Sankei jıji*, May 26, 1956; *Nıppon Tımes*, May 13, 1956.

33. See *Asahi shımbun*, June 8, 9, and 14, 1956.

34. See Mıkıkai, *Mıki Bukichı* [11], pp. 450–482, for an outline of Mıki's role in the merged conservatıve party. See also Uehara Hisazō, "Nerawareta Jimintō sōsai no isu" [76], *Jimbutsu ōrai*, September 1956, pp. 7–9.

35. *Asahi nenkan, 1957* [106], pp. 274–275.

36. For discussıon of the controversy over the make-up of the Moscow delegatıon, see *Asahı shımbun*, July 10–15, 1956.

37. *Yomırıu shimbun*, December 10, 1954.

38. For a clear statement of Yoshıda's polıcy toward the Soviet Union, see Jiyutō, *Futatsu no sekai to Nıhon gaıkō no arıkata* [82], pp. 41–43.

39. Interview with Wakamiya Kotarō, private secretary to Hatoyama, April 9, 1962.

40. See Chapter II, especıally note 14.

41. *Asahi shimbun*, January 31, 1955.

42. *Yomıuri shimbun*, May 23 and 25, 1955, and *Asahı shimbun*, May 26, 1955.

43. The ınformation on which this paragraph is based was obtained in an ınterview with Matsumoto Shunichi, January 20, 1963.

44. Under the provısions of the San Francisco Peace Treaty, Japan renounced sovereignty over these territorıes, and theır status was to be determined by an ınternatıonal conference ınvolving all the allıed nations. See Chapter II, note 17 and reference cited therewıth.

45. Interview with Matsumoto Shunıchi, January 20, 1963.

46. Intervıew wıth Matsumoto Shunichi, July 21, 1962.

47. See the discussıon by Vernon A. Aspaturian, "Soviet Foreign Policy" [173], in Roy C. Macridis (ed.), *Foreıgn Polıcy ın World Polıtıcs*, pp. 150–156.

48. See Kōno, *Ima dakara hanasō* [9], pp. 16–17; Arimura Uhei, "Jiyūmınshutō no uchımaku" [26], *Chūō kōron*, June 1956, p. 159, and the elaboration of this subject in Chapter VII.

49. See *Asahi shımbun*, April 13, 14, and 17, 1956.

50. Interview wıth Matsumoto Shunıchi, January 20, 1963. Kōno, ın particular, was eager to take a strong stand and proposed a cabinet reshuffle to control intraparty opposıtion. See also *Asahı shımbun*, June 6, 1956.

51. See, for example, Shūgiin, *Gaimu iinkai giroku* [96], No. 3, 22nd Diet, 6–7, *Maınichi shimbun*, December 19, 1954 and *Asahı shımbun*, June 7 and 8, 1956.

52. Interview with Matsumoto Shunichi, January 20, 1963; *Asahı shimbun*, June 16, 1955; and Nırazawa Yoshio, "Gaımushō no tenraku" [54], *Chūō kōron*, July 1956, p. 62.

53. This is evident both in Shigemitsu's actions and statements during the negotiations and was clear even before Soviet relations became a central issue. See *Mainichi shimbun,* December 19, 1954.

54. This appraisal, implicit in numerous magazine and newspaper reports, was corroborated in an interview with Nakasone Yasuhiro, a prominent Liberal-Democratic Party leader, July 30, 1962.

55. For elaboration, see *Japan Times,* August 12, 1956, and Kōno, *Ima dakara hanasō* [9], pp. 55–56.

56. *Ibid.,* August 29, 1956, and *Asahi shimbun,* September 2, 1956.

57. See, for example, *Asahi shimbun,* August 27 and 31, 1956, and *Yomiuri shimbun,* August 31, 1956.

58 *Asahi shimbun,* August 21, 1956; *Mainichi shimbun,* August 23, 1956

59. Watanabe, *Daijin* [19], p. 260; *Japan Times,* September 28 and October 4–6, 1956; *Asahi shimbun,* October 8, 1956.

60. *Asahi shimbun,* August 21, 27, and September 9, 1956; *Japan Times,* September 14, 1956.

61 *Asahi shimbun,* August 29, 31, and September 2, 3, 1956.

62. *Ibid.,* September 9, 13, 23, 1956.

63. "Ni-So kōshō—Nichi-Nichi kōshō taishō nisshi" [57], *Chūō kōron,* October 1956, pp 70–74.

64 *Asahi shimbun,* September 14 and 15, 1956.

65. See Watanabe, *Habatsu* [20], pp. 195–199, and *Asahi shimbun,* October 4, 1955, and January 30, 1956.

66 See, for example, *Asahi shimbun,* May 11, 25, and September 5, 1956, and *Nihon keizai shimbun,* May 24, 1956

67 *Asahi shimbun,* April 14 and 17, 1956.

68. *Ibid.,* September 5, 12, and October 2, 3, 1956, *Japan Times,* September 12, 13, and October 3, 1956.

69. "Ni-So kōshō—Nichi-Nichi kōshō [57], pp 70–74.

70. *Asahi shimbun,* October 2–4, 1956; *Japan Times,* October 2, 4–6, 1956.

71. Robert E. Ward, "Political Modernization and Political Culture in Japan" [208], *World Politics,* XV (July 1963), 573–574.

72 Gabriel A. Almond and James S. Coleman, *The Politics of the Developing Areas* [130], pp 19–23.

73. Robert E. Ward, "Japan The Continuity of Modernization" [209], in Lucian W. Pye and Sidney Verba (eds.), *Political Culture and Political Development,* p. 72.

74. For Hatoyama's own concept of political responsibility, see Shūgiin, *Gaimu iinkai giroku* [96], No. 24, 24th Diet, 2.

75. For this point and a general summary of decision-making, see Fred M. Kerlinger, "Decision-Making in Japan" [188], *Social Forces,* XXX (October 1951), 36–41.

CHAPTER IV

1. This period of Russo-Japanese history is summarized in Chitoshi Yanaga, *Japan Since Perry* [171], especially pp. 250–258, 275–289; and David J. Dallin, *The Rise of Russia in Asia* [143], pp. 36–41, 70–123.

2. Yanaga, *Japan Since Perry* [171], pp. 457–462.
3. David J. Dallin, *Soviet Russia in the Far East* [142], pp. 22–44.
4. *Ibid.*, pp. 160–166, 174–189.
5. Jiji News Agency Survey, May 1–4, 1949, cited in Allan B. Cole and Nakanishi Naomichi (ed.), *Japanese Opinion Polls with Socio-Political Significance* [139], p. 648.
6. *Asahi shimbun*, June 24, 1953.
7. *Ibid.;* and Cole and Nakanishi, *Japanese Opinion Polls* [139], p. 694.
8. *Asahi shimbun*, June 24, 1953.
9. For surveys concerning the question of rearmament, see *Asahi shimbun*, February 9, 1953, and *Mainichi shimbun*, April 6, 1953. Polls indicating over 50% favorable to ties with Communist China appear in *Asahi shimbun*, May 17, 1952 and June 24, 1953.
10. A survey in *Mainichi shimbun*, October 24, 1955, dealt separately with the general problem of normalizing relations, and 51 percent of the sample favored a quick solution, while only 8 percent thought it undesirable to reach any settlement.
11. *Mainichi shimbun*, October 24, 1955; *Yomiuri shimbun*, December 1, 1955.
12. This whole problem, especially the interconnections between the fishery interests and Kōno, is explored in detail in Chapter VII.
13. *Asahi shimbun*, December 5, 1955
14. *Yomiuri shimbun*, December 1, 1955.
15. *Ibid.*, April 20, 1956.
16. For a sharply contrary opinion see Douglas H. Mendel, *The Japanese People and Foreign Policy* [159], p. 202.
17. Council on Foreign Relations, *The American Public's View of U.S. Policy Toward China: A Report Prepared for the Council on Foreign Relations by the Survey Research Center, University of Michigan* [141], Table 1, p. 5 and Table 6, p. 11.
18. *Ibid* , Table 23, p. 42.
19. *The Japan Times Weekly*, July 22, 1967.
20. Kenneth N. Waltz, *Foreign Policy and Democratic Politics* [169], pp. 267–269.
21. *Asahi shimbun*, September 2, 1956.
22. *Ibid.*, June 9, 1956.
23. *Ibid.*, June 14, 1956.
24. Survey of August 27–28, *Asahi shimbun*, September 7, 1956. The results seemed to have portentous implications, on two earlier occasions in postwar Japan, polls showed more than 40 percent of the cabinet (the Ashida Hitoshi cabinet in July 1948 and the Yoshida cabinet in May 1954), and they signaled the imminent collapse of the government.
25. Survey of August 27–28, *Asahi shimbun*, September 2, 1956.

CHAPTER V

1. Bernard C. Cohen, *The Political Process and Foreign Policy* [136], p. 29.

2. This question will be considered at length in Chapter VIII. It is given good, brief treatment in Nirazawa Yoshio, "Gaimushō no tenraku" [54], *Chūō kōron*, July 1956, pp. 58–63, and Ohtari Keisuke, "Hanayaka na bōrei. gaikōkan" [63], *Bungei-shunjū*, July 1956, pp. 122–127.

3. *Asahi shimbun*, May 25, 1956.

4. *Ibid.*, July 3, 1956.

5. *Ibid.,* October 1, 1956.

6. *Sankei jiji*, May 26, 1956; *Asahi shimbun*, July 22, 1956.

7. *Asahi shimbun*, May 16, 1956.

8. For the speeches given by Ashida and Nomura at a mass rally in August 1956, see Preparatory Committee for a People's League on the Territorial Problem, *Ryōdo mondai kokumin taikai kiroku* [86], pp. 89–99 and 39–48 respectively. For another statement by Nomura, see *Asahi shimbun*, October 24, 1956. See also Ashida Hitoshi, "Ni-So kōshō ni tsuite shinchōron no tachiba kara" [28], *Sekai*, November 1956, pp 65–70.

9. For elaboration of this point see Kawamura Kinji (ed.), *Gaimushō* [5], pp. 45–47.

10. *Nihon keizai shimbun*, May 29, 1956.

11. See, for example, David B Truman, *The Governmental Process* [168], Chapter 2.

12. A breakdown of the persons affiliated with each group is given in Kikuchi Hidehiro, "Ni-So fukkō· zaikai ten'yawan'ya" [42], *Jimbutsu ōrai*, August 1956, pp. 30–32.

13. For Ishizaka's statement see the *Asahi shimbun*, July 25, 1956. The general position of this group is well summarized in the *Asahi shimbun*, July 16, 1956.

14. Fujiyama, who pushed for an early settlement, was closely connected with Kishi Nobusuke, then Secretary General of the Liberal-Democrats and sympathetic to Hatoyama's policy. This, in part, explains the policy leadership Fujiyama sought to assume in the business world. See *Mainichi shimbun*, May 28, 1956.

15. For a good summary of this group's position, see the *Yomiuri shimbun*, June 5, 1956.

16. *Yomiuri shimbun*, June 5, 1956.

17. *Mainichi shimbun*, June 26, 1956. Two days later, Kōno spoke in Osaka to a meeting of the *Kansai Keidanren*, a separate, influential organization of the leading figures from the second most important business center in Japan (*Yomiuri shimbun*, June 28, 1956).

18. *Mainichi shimbun*, July 3, 1956.

19. *Asahi shimbun*, July 4, 1956.

20. *Ibid.*

21. *Ibid.*, July 7, 1956.

22. *Ibid.*, July 24, 1956.

23. *Nihon keizai shimbun*, May 29, 1956.

24. See, for example, *Sankei jiji*, June 27, 1956.

25. Japan-Soviet Society, *Ni-So kyōkai no oitachi to gonen no ayumi* [85], p. 1.

After the restoration of diplomatic ties, this association continued to operate, pursuing the same general goals in similar ways. Since June 1957, it has been known as the *Nı-So Kyōkaı* (Japan-Soviet Society).

26. Takahura, "Nı-So shınzen kyōkai no naimaku" [74], *Zenbō*, August 15, 1956, pp. 29–32.

27. *Ibid.*, p. 29.

28. See, for example, *ibıd.*, p. 34, and *Akahata shımbun*, November 29, 1955.

29. Majima Ken, "Nı-So kokkō wa saikai sarete yuku" [45], *Chūō kōron*, March 1955, pp 224–227.

30. For discussion of Kuhara's role see "Mamiama nı chokketsu suru mınkan gaıkō no hıtobıto" [46], *Keızaı ōıaı*, April 1956, p 52, and *Japan Tımes*, October 2, 1956.

31. "Mamiama ni chokketsu suru" [46], pp. 51–52.

32. These ıncluded the *Daı Nıhon Suısan Kaı* (Japan Fishery Association), *Sōhyō* (General Council of Trade Unıons), and *Kokusaı Bōeki Sokushın Kai* (International Trade Promotion Socıety), *ibıd*, p. 52.

33. "Mamiama no shujınkō Domunıtsuki to yūnō na hosakantachı" [47], *Keizai ōrai*, April 1956, pp. 43–44

34. "An-yaku no chūshın jımbutsu, Majıma Ken to Baba Yusuke" [24], *Keizai ōrai*, Aprıl 1956, pp 57–61.

35. *Asahi shimbun*, January 31, 1955.

36. After Kōno's mission had departed, the Soviets attempted to re-call Domnitsky to Moscow to participate in the talks. However, Shige-mitsu violently protested, denıed him an exit visa, and tried to recall Kōno from Stockholm. *Nıhon keızaı shımbun*, Aprıl 24, 1956

Also see "Minkan gaikō no suishin botai taru, suısan gyōkai to Ōnishı Rensaku" [51], *Keızaı ōraı*, Aprıl 1956, pp 53–57

37. Interview with Matsumoto Shunichi, January 20, 1963

38 Elıe Abel, *The Missıle Crısıs* [128], pp. 155–158

39. In Kuwahara Terumichı, "Hoppō ryōdo no henkan yōkyū undō" [44], *Kokusaıhō Gaıkō Zasshı*, LX (March 1962), 429–474, the move-ment is chronicled in detaıl and the followıng dıscussıon is largely based on the facts cited ın this article.

40. *Ibıd.*, pp. 435–436.

41. *Ibıd.*, p. 443.

42. See *ibid.*, pp. 446–458, and the *Asahi shımbun*, June 22, 1955.

43. Kuwahara, "Hoppō ryōdo no henkan" [44], p. 459.

44. See Preparatory Committee [86], *passım, Asahi shımbun*, August 17, 1956; and *Tokyo shımbun*, August 17, 1956

45. See *Asahı shımbun*, March 30 and 31, 1956, and James W. Mor-ley, "Japan's Image of the Soviet Union, 1952–61" [191], *Pacific Affairs*, XXXV (Spring 1962), 54.

46. See *Sankeı jıjı shimbun*, March 26, 1956; *Tokyo shımbun*, April 10, 1956; and *Maınıchı shimbun*, April 10, 1956.

47. The role of the press in the United States is well treated in Bernard C. Cohen, *The Press and Foreign Policy* [137], and in James N. Rosenau, *Public Opınıon and Foreign Polıcy* [163], especially pp. 77–83.

48. For a stimulating dıscussıon of the press as an advocate of policy ın the United States, see Cohen, *The Press and Foreign Policy* [137], pp. 36–39.

49. For elaboration, see "Japanese Press Today," *Japan Times,* November 1, 1958, and "Japanese Newspapers and Magazines," *Japan Report,* VI (January 15, 1960), 4–8.

50. See Hessel Tiltman, " 'Fourth Estate' in Japan," *Asahi Evening News,* October 4, 1958; Ardath W Burks, *The Government of Japan* [135], pp. 63–64; and Edward P. Whittemore, *The Press in Japan Today . . . A Case Study* [170], pp. 11–12

51 The contrary view is supported in Whittemore, [170]

52 For elaboration of the relation between press coverage and mass opinion, see Cohen, *The Political Process and Foreign Policy,* [136], pp. 110, 120–121.

53. "Gaikō to shimbun" [31], *Sekai,* October 1956, pp. 225–226.

54. See for example, Chiba Yujirō, "Shimbun to aikokushin no mondai" [30], *Bungei shunjū,* November 1956, pp. 56–63, "Ni-So kōshō to shimbun" [59], *Shin seikai,* October 1956, pp. 106–109, Kido Mataichi, "Ni-So kōshō to shimbun" [41], *Sekai,* November 1956, pp. 71–76, and "Shimbun no arikata wo ureu" [71], *Kokoro,* November 1956, pp. 23–42

55 For an excellent discussion of this subject, see Cohen, *The Press and Foreign Policy* [137], pp. 3–16

CHAPTER VI

1. See Yamada Kōki, *Nihon Shakaitō* [22], pp 45–68, for a good summary of the Socialist movement in the immediate postwar years. This book provides a description of the postwar history of the Socialists, particularly in terms of the factional structure of the party Another useful general discussion of this period is Yamazaki Hiroshi, *Nihon Shakaitō jūnen shi* [23]. In English, see Evelyn S. Colbert, *The Left Wing in Japanese Politics* [138], pp. 75–94, and Allan B. Cole, George O. Totten, and Cecil H. Uehara, *Socialist Parties in Postwar Japan* [140].

2. An excellent account of the relations between labor and the Socialists in the postwar period is Robert A. Scalapino, "Japan," in Walter Galenson, (ed.), *Labor and Economic Development* [199], pp. 116–132 and 136–142.

3 Robert A. Scalapino and Junnosuke Masumi, *Parties and Politics in Contemporary Japan* [165], pp. 76–77, 96–97.

4. The Socialist conceptions of neutralism are summarized in J A. A. Stockwin, " 'Positive Neutrality'—The Foreign Policy of the Japanese Socialist Party" [203], *Asian Survey,* II (November 1962), 33–38.

5. Scalapino and Masumi, *Parties and Politics* [165], pp 69–72, 97–98.

6. Yamada, *Nihon Shakaitō,* [22], pp. 86–87.

7. *Ibid ,* pp. 87–88. For an excellent discussion in English of the prewar Socialist movement, see George O. Totten, III, *The Social Democratic Movement in Prewar Japan* [167]

8 *Ibid.* A similar split in the labor movement recurred in 1958 when the Nishio faction broke away to form the *Minshu Shakaitō* (Democratic-Socialist Party).

9 Interview with Fujimaki Shimpei, Deputy Director, Secretariat of

178 Notes to Pages 114–118

the Policy Research Board, Japan Socialist Party, January 12, 1962. For an excellent, brief summary of the relations between the two wings of the divided Socialists from 1951 to 1955, see Oka Yoshitake, "Seitō to seitō seiji" [64], in *Gendai Nihon no seiji katei*, pp. 98–100.

10 The broad development of Socialist policy toward the Soviet Union was traced primarily in the *Jōhō tsūshin* (News Bulletin), an official publication of the Right-Wing Socialists, which became the *Shakai tsūshin* (Socialist Bulletin), the official organ of the unified party. See especially *Jōhō tsūshin* editions of January 25, March 25, August 25, 1955, and *Shakai tsūshin*, October 15, 1955.

11. *Jōhō tsūshin*, January 25, 1955, pp. 1–4. There were virtually no basic differences between the Left and Right wings.

12. *Ibid.*, p. 2.

13. Sone Eki and Sata Tadataka, "Shigemitsu gaikō wo hihan suru" [72], *Chūō kōron*, February 1956, p. 130.

14. *Jōhō tsūshin*, January 25, 1955, p 1, and *Nippon Times*, February 6, 1955.

15. See, for example, *Shakai sūshin*, February 25, 1956, pp 1–4, April 17, 1956, pp. 1–4, July 1, 1956, pp. 4–6, *Nihon shakai shimbun* (Japan Socialist Newspaper), June 4, 1956; *Asahi shimbun*, December 14, 1955.

16. *Shakai tsūshin*, July 1, 1956, p. 6

17. See *Asahi nenkan, 1957* [106], pp. 273–279, and *Japan Times*, August 29, 1956.

18. *Jōhō tsūshin*, August 25, 1955, p 1.

19. See, for example, *Asahi shimbun*, December 14, 1955, on the Diet interpellation of Foreign Minister Shigemitsu, which forced him to emotionally condemn any type of provisional agreement with Russia; also *Nihon shakai shimbun*, May 21, 28, and June 4, 1956.

20. *Shakai tsūshin*, July 1, 1956, pp 4–5, and *Nihon shakai shimbun*, June 4, 1956.

21. *Mainichi shimbun*, July 21, 1956, *Asahi shimbun*, July 25, 1956

22 "Ni-So kōshō ni tai suru shakaitō no taido wo bunseki suru" [58], *Minshu shakaishugi*, October 10, 1956, p. 20; *Yomiuri shimbun*, August 26, 1956.

23. *Tokyo shimbun*, August 30, 1956 In particular, Tanaka Toshio and Hozumi Shichirō openly expressed this opinion.

Among the Left-Wing Socialists there had always been a considerable number who were willing to play down, if not ignore, the problems of the territorial issue in order to establish ties with the Soviet Union Indeed, some compromise was necessary on this point at the time of the merger. Interview with Yamaguchi Fusao, International Affairs Bureau, Socialist Party of Japan, January 30, 1962.

24. *Yomiuri shimbun*, August 17, 1956.

25. "Ni-So kōshō tai suru shakaitō" [58], pp. 19–20; *Yomiuri shimbun*, August 17, 1956.

26. Interview with Fujimaki Shimpei, January 12, 1963.

27. See *Asahi shimbun*, August 14, 30, 26, 30, and September 6 and 15, 1956.

28. See, for example, August 30, 1956, editions of *Mainichi shimbun*,

Tokyo shimbun, and *Nihon keizai shimbun.* "Ni-So kōshō tai suru
shakaitō" [58], pp. 16–17. Ōuchi Hyōe, "Zenmen kōwaron no tachiba
kara" [66], *Sekai,* November 10, 1956, pp. 10–16.
   29. Interview with Yamaguchi Fusao, January 30, 1962.
   30. *Ibid.,* and *Shakai tsūshin,* September 13, 1956, pp. 1–4. The latter
contains a summary of the party's past policies as well as a comprehensive statement of its current position.
   31. *Asahi shimbun* and *Japan Times,* September 23, 1956.
   32. *Asahi shimbun,* October 4 and 5, 1956, and *Nihon shakai shimbun,* October 8, 1956.

CHAPTER VII

   1. For a good summary of prewar business-party relations see Robert
A. Scalapino, *Democracy and the Party Movement in Prewar Japan*
[164], Chapter VII, especially pp. 289–293. See also Keizai dantai
rengōkai, *Keindanren no jūnen* [6], pp. 10–20.
   2. Takeshi Ishida, "Interest Groups in Japan" [186], p. 35.
   3. Noguchi Yūjirō, "Yottsu no keieisha dantai" [61], *Chūō kōron,*
October 1956, p. 159.
   4. *Ibid.,* p. 158; Sakamoto Fujiyoshi, "Nihon keieisha no seikaku"
[68], *Chūō kōron,* October 1960, pp. 142–156.
   5. For the full Japanese title and the English translation of this and
the other employers' associations, see Chapter II, note 10 and the section on "The Businessmen."
   6. Keizai dantai rengokai, *Keidanren no jūnen* [6], pp. 1–10, 31–58.
   7. In effect the establishment of Nikkeiren was merely the reactiva-
tion on a grander scale of the parallel prewar organization, *Zensanren.*
Noguchi, "Yottsu no keieisha dantai" [61], p. 161.
   8. *Ibid.,* p. 161.
   9. *Ibid,* p 160; Keizai dōyūkai, *Keizai dōyūkai junenshi* [7], *passim*
Keizai Dōyūkai paralleled the organization and activities of the
American Committee for Economic Development. In 1963 formal ties
were established and it became the Japanese Committee for Economic
Development (*Keizai Kondankai*).
   10. James R. Soukup, "Japan" [202], *Journal of Politics,* XXV (November 1963), 748–749.
   11. Frank C. Langdon, "Organized Interests in Japan and their Influence on Political Parties" [189], *Pacific Affairs,* XXXIV (Fall 1961),
271–278.
   12. A summary of these principles is found in Shintō soshiki iinkai
(New Party Formation Committee), *Shintō shimei, seikaku, seikō*
(New Party Nominations, Policy, and Program), (Tokyo: August 1955)
cited in R. P. Dore, "Left and Right in Japan" [183], *International Affairs,*
XXXIII (January 1956), 18–19.
   13. Robert A Scalapino and Junnosuke Masumi, *Parties and Politics
in Contemporary Japan* [165], Appendix: Chart 8.
   14. For a contrary view, see Hayashi Shōzō, "Nihon no pawā eriito"
[35], *Chūō kōron,* January 1960, pp. 146–157.
   15. In addition to their actions connected with Soviet policy, the

businessmen also directly and effectively intervened in 1954 when the Yoshida Cabinet lost popular support and was threatened by the intra-party revolt led by Hatoyama (see "Hatoyama naikaku to zaikai" [33], *Ekonomisuto*, December 19, 1954). A similar, but less significant move to "stabilize" politics was made in 1960 over the crisis caused by the Security Treaty riots.

16. This paragraph is in large part based on an interview with Ono Tatsuo, Deputy Chief of the International Affairs Division, Federation of Economic Organizations, December 7, 1962.

17. See, for example, the statement of Wada Kōsuke, a director of Keidanren, on the need for caution in political activities, in *Keidanren geppō* [109], September 1956, p. 21.

18 See Scalapino, *Democracy and the Party Movement* [164], pp. 270–273 and 292.

19. For a summary of the broad development of Japanese pressure groups in general and the business groups in particular, see Ishida Takeshi, "Atsuryoku dantai hassei no rekishiteki jōken to sono toku-shitsu" [38], in *1960 Nihon seijigaku nenpō* entitled *Nihon no atsuryoku dantai*, pp. 30–44.

20. *Nihon keizai*, August 11, 20, and 31, 1956; *Sankei jiji*, August 16, 1956; *Asahi shimbun*, September 7, 1956.

21. *Nihon keizai*, August 31, 1956; *Japan Times*, August 30, 1956.

22. Suzuki Ken, "Hatoyama shushō yo sumiyaka ni intai seyo" [73], *Daiyamondo*, August 21, 1956, pp 18–21.

23. *Nihon keizai*, August 20 and 31, 1956.

24. *Mainichi shimbun* and *Japan Times*, September 4, 1956

25. *Asahi shimbun*, September 5, 1956.

26. *Ibid.*, September 7, 1956. For an interesting summary of the events leading to this meeting, see "Zaikai 'bakudan sengen' no heikei" [81], *Seiji keizai*, October 1956, pp. 13–15.

27. *Asahi shimbun*, September 7, 1956. To emphasize that they had entered politics solely to protect the "public interest," not their own, the businessmen recommended that Hatoyama's successor be chosen in an unprecedented open, democratic party election.
See also, *Keidanren geppō* [109], October 1956, p. 10

28 *Asahi shimbun*, September 7, 1956.

29. *Ibid.*, September 8, 1956

30 *Japan Times*, September 20 and October 4, 1956.

31. For a summary of the postwar history, see George Ginsburgs and Scott Shrewsbury, "The Postwar Soviet-Japanese Fisheries Dispute" [185], *Orbis*, VII (Fall 1963), 596–604. See also "Ōzume no Ni-So kōshō to hokuyō gyogyō" [67], *Ekonomisuto*, February 18, 1956, pp. 42–45.

32. *Asahi shimbun*, January 29, 1955; *Nippon Times*, March 1, 1956; "Ōzume no Ni-So kōshō" [67], p. 42.

33. This history of Kōno's relations with the fishery industry is out-lined in Kōno Ichirō, *Ima dakara hanasō* [9], pp. 6–8.

34. See Arimura Uhei, "Jiyūminshutō no uchimaku" [26], *Chūō kōron*, June 1956, pp. 153–154, 158–159, Yamada Gorō, "Seizaikai wo masabu chikarosen" [79], *Shin seikai*, March 1956, pp. 21–22; "Nihon

no shio" [55], *Sekai*, March 1956, pp 168–169; Nukita Tsuneki, "Hatoyama wo meguru yōun" [62], *Shinron*, December 1955, p. 113.
35. Interview with Wakamiya Kotarō, private secretary to Hatoyama, April 9, 1962.
36. The government and particularly Kōno, the responsible minister, were extremely vulnerable on this issue since they had ordered an increase in the operation of fishing boats for the coming season. *Sankei jiji*, March 26, 1956.
37. See *Mainichi shimbun*, March 22, 1956, *Yomiuri shimbun*, March 23, 1956; *Sankei jiji*, March 26 and 30, 1956; and *Nihon keizai*, March 25 and 27, 1956, for the initial strong reaction by the fishing industry
38. Kōno, *Ima dakara hanasō* [9], p. 9.

CHAPTER VIII

1. For a summary of relations between Yoshida and the Foreign Ministry, see Kawamura Kinji (ed.), *Gaimushō* [5], pp. 31–34.
2. Nirazawa Yoshio, "Gaimushō no tenraku" [54], *Chūō kōron*, July 1956, pp. 60–61.
3. Hatoyama Ichirō, *Hatoyama Ichirō kaikoroku* [2], pp 162–164; Kawamura, *Gaimushō* [5], p. 31
4. Kawamura, *Gaimushō* [5], p. 17.
5. *Nihon keizai*, January 28, 1956 and *Nippon Times*, January 29, 1956.
6. Matsumoto Seichō, "Gaimu kanryō ron" [48], *Bungei shunjū*, 43, 10 (October 1965), 152.
7. Ohtari Keisuke, "Hanayakana no bōrei· gaikōkan" [63], *Bungei shunjū*, July 1956, pp. 122–124, and Kawamura, *Gaimushō* [5], pp. 37–38.
8. For elaboration see, Kōno Ichirō, *Ima dakara hanasō* [9], pp. 17–18; Matsumoto Shunichi and Fujiyama Aiichirō, "Nihon no gaikō wa kore de yoi ka?" [50], *Bungei shunjū*, July 1956, pp. 64–65; Hatoyama Ichirō, *Hatoyama Ichirō kaikoroku* [2], p. 162; *Nippon Times*, October 21, 1955 and Nirazawa, "Gaimushō no tenraku" [54], pp. 59–60.
9. *Asahi shimbun*, January 30, 1955; Nirazawa, "Gaimushō no tenraku" [54], p. 59.
10. Although the basic cause for this shift lay in party compromise, it was abetted by conservative Yoshida supporters within the Foreign Ministry. Matsumoto and Fujiyama, "Nihon no gaikō" [50], p. 65.
11. *Mainichi shimbun*, April 21, 1956.
12. Kōno, *Ima dakara hanasō* [9], pp. 15–18
13. Mugino Ippei, "Gaimu kanryō ron" [52], *Chūō kōron*, 71, 8, p. 85.
14. Kōno, *Ima dakara hanasō* [9], pp. 34–39, 46–48, and 75–80.
15. *Ibid.*, p. 39; *Asahi shimbun* and *Nihon keizai*, May 14, 1956.
16. Sangiin, *Sangiin honkai giroku* [90], No. 56, 24th Diet, 811–814 and Ohtari, *Hanayaka na bōrei* [63], pp. 122–126.
17. "Gaikō wa gaikokan ni" [32], *Shūkan shinchō*, August 6, 1956, pp. 26–31.
18. Kōno, *Ima dakara hanasō* [9], pp. 58–64.

19. For a comprehensive summary of the Diet actions see "Ni-So kōshō wo meguru kokkai gijiroku" [60], *Chūō kōron,* October 1956, pp. 75–87.

20. See, for example, Shūgiin, *Gaimu iinkai giroku,* 24th Diet [98], No. 12, 2–7; No. 17, 2–3 and Sangiin, *Gaimu iinkai giroku* [94], No. 5, 24th Diet, 2–3.

21. Shugiin, *ibid.,* No. 44, 24th Diet, 13.

22. See *ibid.,* No. 31, 24th Diet, 2–3; No. 34, p. 6; and No. 42, 5–7.

23. Shūgiin, *Yosan unkai giroku* [102], No. 15, 24th Diet, 3–5.

24. Shugiin, *Gaimu iinkai giroku* [98], No. 9, 24th Diet, 10.

25. See, for example, *ibid.,* No. 18, 9–10; No. 22, 3–4.

26. Shūgiin, *Heiwa jōyaku oyobi Nichi-Bei anzen hōsho jōyaku tokubetsu iinkai giroku* [100], No. 4, 12th Diet, 18–19, and *Shugiin giroku* [101], 11th Diet, p. 3.

27. For an interesting critical review of the Diet's overall role in the negotiations from this perspective see Matsumoto Shunichi, "Gaikō to kokkai" [49], *Chūō kōron,* July 1956, pp. 52–57.

28. *Asahi shimbun,* November 27, 1956.

29. *Ibid.*

30. *Ibid.,* December 6, 1956.

CHAPTER IX

1. F. C Jones, *Japan's New Order in East Asia, Its Rise and Fall, 1937–1945,* [152], p. 110.

Bibliography

I. JAPANESE SOURCES

A. Books

[1] Asahi shimbun seijıbu (Political Section, Asahi Newspaper). *Nihon no kyūjūkunin* (Ninety-nine Men of Japan). Tokyo Sōjusha, 1954. 290 pp.

[2] Hatoyama Ichirō. *Hatoyama Ichirō kaıkoroku* (The Memoırs of Hatoyama Ichirō). Tokyo Bungei shunju shinsha, 1957. 224 pp

[3] Inoki Masamichı (ed). *Nıhon no nıdaıseıtō* (The Two Parties of Japan). Tokyo Shımbunka sensho, 1956. 317 pp.

[4] Ishida Takeshı. *Sengo Nıhon no seiji taiseı* (The Postwar Japanese Political System). Tokyo. Miraisha, 1961. 253 pp.

[5] Kawamura Kinjı (ed.). *Gaimushō* (The Foreign Ministry). Tokyo. Hobunsha, 1956. 231 pp.

[6] Keizai dantai rengōkai (Federation of Economic Organizations). *Keidanren no jūnen* (Ten Years of the Federation of Economıc Organizations). Tokyo· 1956. 264 pp.

[7] Keızaı dōyūkai (Economic Friends Association). *Keızaı dōyūkai gonen shi* (A Fıve-Year History of the Economic Friends' Association). Tokyo: 1951. 398 pp

[8] ———. *Keızaı dōyūkai jūnen shi* (A Ten-Year History of the Economic Friends' Associatıon). Tokyo: 1956. 599 pp.

[9] Kōno Ichirō. *Ima dakara hanasō* (Now I Can Speak). Tokyo: Shunyōdō shoten, 1958 220 pp.

[10] Matsumoto Shigeharu, *et al. Kindai Nihon no gaıkō* (The Diplomacy of Modern Japan). Tokyo. Asahi shimbunsha, 1962. 271 pp.

[11] Mıkikai (Mıkı Society). *Mıki Bukıchi*. Tokyo: 1958 570 pp.

[12] Mıtarai Tatsuo. *Miki Bukıchı den* (The Biography of Miki Bukichi). Tokyo: Shikisha, 1958. 526 pp.

[13] Miyamoto Yoshio. *Shın hoshutō shi* (History of the New Conservative Party). Tokyo: Jıjı tsushinsha, 1962 640 pp.

[14] Naka Masao. *Kaisō no sengo seıjı* (Reflections on Postwar Polıtics). Tokyo· Jitsugyō no sekaisha, 1957. 322 pp.

[15] Ōhno Bamboku. *Ōhno Bamboku kaisōroku* (The Memoirs of Ōhno Bamboku). Tokyo: Kōbundō, 1962. 264 pp.

[16] Royama Masamichi. *Kokusaı seıjı to Nihon gaıkō* (International Politics and Japan's Diplomacy). Tokyo: Chūō kōronsha, 1959. 306 pp.

[17] Tatamiya Eitarō *Hatoyama būmu no budai ura* (Behind the Scenes of the Hatoyama Boom). Tokyo· Jitsugyō no sekaisha, 1955. 222 pp.

[18] Togawa Isamu. *Seiji shikin* (Political Funds). Tokyo: Rokakuhō, 1961. 237 pp.
[19] Watanabe Tsuneo. *Daijin* (Cabinet Ministers). Tokyo: Kōbundō, 1959. 284 pp.
[20] ———. *Habatsu* (Factions). Tokyo· Kōbundō, 1958. 235 pp.
[21] ———. *Tōshu to seitō* (Party Leaders and Political Parties) Tokyo. Kōbundō, 1961. 233 pp.
[22] Yamada Kōki. *Nihon Shakaitō* (The Japanese Socialist Party). Tokyo· Hōbunsha, 1956 297 pp.
[23] Yamazaki Hiroshi *Nihon Shakaitō jūnen shi* (A Ten-Year History of the Japanese Socialist Party). Tokyo. Taibunkan, 1956. 262 pp.

B ARTICLES

[24] "An-yaku no chūshin jimbutsu, Majima Ken to Baba Yusuke" (Majima Ken and Baba Yusuke, the Central Figures Behind the Scenes), *Keizai ōrai*, April 1956, pp. 57–63.
[25] Arimura Uhei. "Hatoyama gaikō no jittai" (The Realities of Hatoyama's Diplomacy), *Chūō kōron*, August 1956, pp 38–49.
[26] ———. "Jiyūminshutō no uchimaku" (Inside the Liberal-Democratic Party), *Chūō kōron*, June 1956, pp. 151–161.
[27] ——— "Kore ga hatashite gaikō ka?" (Is This Really Diplomacy?), *Chūō kōron*, October 1956, pp. 62–68
[28] Ashida Hitoshi. "Ni-So kōshō ni tsuite shinchōron no tachiba kara" (Soviet-Japanese Negotiations from the "Prudent" Viewpoint), *Sekai*, November 1956, pp. 65–70.
[29] "Atama no nai hoshu shintō" (The Leaderless New Conservative Party), *Ekonomisuto*, November 19, 1955, p. 8
[30] Chiba Yujirō "Shimbun to aikokushin no mondai" (The Press and the Question of Patriotism), *Bungei shunjū*, November 1956, pp. 56–63.
[31] "Gaikō to shimbun" (Diplomacy and the Press) (editorial), *Sekai*, October 1956, pp 224–226.
[32] "Gaikō wa gaikōkan ni" (Diplomacy Should be Entrusted to Career Diplomats) (editorial), *Shūkan shinchō*, April 6, 1956, pp. 26–31.
[33] "Hatoyama naikaku to zaikai" (The Hatoyama Cabinet and Financial Circles) (editorial), *Ekonomisuto*, December 18, 1954, pp. 11–15.
[34] "Hatoyama to Ogata" (Hatoyama and Ogata), *Sande mainichi*, December 12, 1954.
[35] Hayashi Shōzō. "Nihon no pawā eriito" (Japan's Power Elite), *Chūō kōron*, January 1960, pp. 146–157.
[36] Hosoya, Chihiro. "Taishō gaikō ni okeru seitō to itan-Katō Takaaki to Gotō Shimpei" (Orthodoxy and Heresy in Taishō Diplomacy-Katō Takaaki and Gotō Shimpei), *Nihon Oyobi Nihonjin*, No. 1430 (1966), pp. 18–25.
[37] Imai Shinichi. "Shidehara gaikō ni okeru seisaku kettei" (Decision-Making in the "Shidehara Diplomacy"), in *Nihon seijigaku nenpō, 1959* (Japanese Political Science Annual, 1959), entitled *Taigai seisaku no kettei katei* (Aspects of Foreign Policy-Making).

[38] Ishida Takeshi. "Atsuryoku dantai hassei no rekishiteki jōken to sono tokushitsu" (Historical Factors and Special Conditions in the Development of Pressure Groups), in *1960 Nihon seijigaku nenpō* (1960 Japan Political Science Association Annual) entitled *Nihon no atsuryoku dantai* (Japanese Pressure Groups).

[39] Kanazaki Kō. "Kane no mado kara seikai mireba" (The Political World Viewed from the Window of Money), *Shin seikai*, March 1956, pp. 38–43.

[40] Karashima Kochizō. "Habatsu no doroshō seikai" (The Political World, a Quagmire of Factions), *Bungei shunju*, November 1956, pp. 76–83.

[41] Kido Mataichi "Ni-So kōshō to shimbun" (The Soviet-Japanese Negotiations and the Press), *Sekai*, November 1956, pp. 71–76.

[42] Kikuchi Hidehiro. "Ni-So fukkō: zaikai ten'yawan'ya" (Confusion within the Financial World Concerning the Restoration of Soviet-Japanese Diplomatic Relations), *Jimbutsu ōrai*, August 1956, pp. 30–32.

[43] Kōsaka Masataka. "Saishō Yoshida Shigeru ron" (Premier Yoshida Shigeru), *Chūō kōron*, February 1964, pp. 76–111.

[44] Kuwahara Terumichi. "Hoppō ryōdo no hendan yōkyū undō" (The Movement Demanding Return of the Northern Territories), in *Kokusaihō Gaikō Zasshi* (Journal of International Law and Diplomacy), LX (March 1962), entitled *Hoppō ryōdo no chii* (Status of the Northern Islands), 429–474.

[45] Majima Ken. "Ni-So kokkō wa saikai sarete yuku" (Reopening of Soviet-Japanese Diplomatic Relations), *Chūō kōron*, March 1955, pp. 224–227.

[46] "Mamiama ni chokketsu suru minkan gaikō no hitobito" (The People of Private Diplomacy Having Direct Connections with Mamiama), *Keizai ōrai*, April 1956, pp 50–53.

[47] "Mamiama no shujinkō Domunitsuki to yūnō na hosakantachi" (The Master of Mamiama, Domnitsky, and His Capable Assistants), *Keizai ōrai*, April 1956, pp. 43–45.

[48] Matsumoto Seichō, "Gaimu kanryō ron" (Foreign Ministry Bureaucrats), *Bungei shunjū*, 43, 10, (October 1965), pp. 142–154.

[49] Matsumoto Shunichi "Gaikō to kokkai" (Diplomacy and the Diet), *Chūō kōron*, July 1956, pp. 52–57.

[50] ——— and Fujiyama Aiichirō. "Nihon no gaikō wa kore de yoi no ka?" (Japan's Diplomacy Criticized), *Bungei shunjū*, July 1956, pp. 60–72.

[51] "Minkan gaikō no suishin botai taru, suisan gyokai to Ōnishi Rensaku" (Basic Promoters of Private Diplomacy, Fishery Circles and Ōnishi Rensaku), *Keizai ōrai*, April 1956, pp 53–57.

[52] Mugino Ippei. "Gaimu kanryō ron" (Foreign Ministry Bureaucrats), *Chūō kōron*, 71, 8 (August 1956), pp. 78–88

[53] Murakami Kaoru. "Jimintō kakuha no boei konkaku" (Liberal-Democratic Party's sense of Defense), *Jiyū*, 8, 7 (July 1966), pp. 105–113.

[54] Nirazawa Yoshio. "Gaimushō no tenraku" (Fall of the Foreign Office), *Chūō kōron*, July 1956, pp. 58–63.

[55] "Nihon no shio" (Current of Japan), *Sekai*, March 1956, pp. 164–170.

[56] "Ni-So gyogyō kōshō tokushō" (A Special Collection on the Soviet-Japanese Fishery Negotiations), *Sande mainichi*, May 27, 1956, pp. 14–18.

[57] "Ni-So kōshō—Nichi-Nichi kōshō taishō nisshi" (A Chronicle Comparing the Soviet-Japanese Negotiations and the Japanese-Japanese Negotiations), *Chūō kōron*, October 1956, pp. 70–74.

[58] "Ni-So kōshō ni tai suru shakaitō no taido wo bunseki suru" (An Analysis of the Attitude of the Socialist Party Toward the Soviet-Japanese Negotiations) (editorial), *Minshu shakaishugi*, October 10, 1956, pp. 14–20.

[59] "Ni-So kōshō to shimbun" (The Soviet-Japanese Negotiations and the Press) (editorial), *Shin seikai*, October 1956, pp 106–109.

[60] "Ni-So kōshō wo meguru kokkai gijiroku" (The Diet Record Concerning the Soviet-Japanese Negotiations), *Chūō kōron*, October 1956, pp. 75–87.

[61] Noguchi Yūjirō. "Yotsu no keieisha dantai" (The Four Employers' Associations) *Chōū kōron*, October 1956, pp. 155–165.

[62] Nukita Tsuneki. "Hatoyama wo meguru yōun" (An Ominous Cloud Threatening Hatoyama), *Shinron*, December 1955, pp. 110–115.

[63] Ohtari Keisuke. "Hanayaka na bōrei: gaikōkan" (Diplomats: Grand Figures from a Bygone Era), *Bungei shunjū*, July 1956, pp. 122–127.

[64] Oka Yoshitake. "Seitō to seitō seiji" (Political Parties and the Politics of Political Parties), in Oka Yoshitake (ed.), *Gendai Nihon no seiji katei* (The Political Process in Modern Japan). Tokyo: Iwanami, 1961.

[65] One Masao. "Ni-So fukkō no genzai to shōrai" (The Restoration of Japanese-Soviet Diplomatic Relations: Present and Future), *Kokusai seiji*, Summer 1957, pp. 21–34.

[66] Ōuchi Hyōe. "Zenmen kōwaron no tachiba kara" (From Standpoint of an Over-all Peace Treaty), *Sekai*, November 1956, pp. 10-16.

[67] "Ōzume no Ni-So kōshō to hokuyō gyogyō" (Final Stage of the Soviet-Japanese Negotiations and the Northern Seas Fisheries), *Ekonomisuto*, February 18, 1956, pp 42–45.

[68] Sakamoto Fujiyoshi. "Nihon keieisha no seikaku" (The Nature of Japanese Employers), *Chūō kōron*, October 1960, pp. 142–156.

[69] "Seikai no tōbaku sannin otoko" (Three Behind-the-Scenes Political Party Men), *Jimbutsu ōrai*, August 1954, pp 44–52.

[70] "Seikai 'shintaifū no me' Kishi Nobusuke" (The Focal Point of the New Movement in the Political World, Kishi Nobusuke), *Shūkan yomiuri*, October 3, 1954, pp. 4–17.

[71] "Shimbun no arikata wo ureu" (Anxiety over the Ways of the Press), *Kokoro*, November 1956, pp 23–42.

[72] Sone Eki and Sata Tadataka. "Shigemitsu gaikō wo hihan suru" (Criticism of Shigemitsu's Foreign Policy), *Chūō kōron*, February 1956, pp. 128–135.

[73] Suzuki Ken "Hatoyama shushō yo sumiyaka ni intai seyo" (Prime Minister Hatoyama, Retire Quickly!), *Daiyamondo*, August 21, 1956, pp. 16–21.

[74] Takahura. "Ni-So shinzen kyōkai no naimaku" (Inside the Japan-Soviet Friendship Association), *Zenbō*, August 15, 1956, pp 28–34.

[75] Uchiyama Masakuma. "Senzen no gaimu daijin—Shidehara Kijūro, to Matsuoka Yōsuke" (Foreign Ministers of the Prewar Era—Shidehara Kijūro and Matsuoka Yōsuke, *Nihon oyobi Nihonjin*, 1430 (1966), pp 26–37.

[76] Uehara Hisazō. "Nerawareta Jimintō sōsai no isu" (Those Who Seek the Presidency of the Liberal-Democratic Party), *Jimbutsu ōrai*, September 1956, pp. 6–11.

[77] Uramatsu Samitarō. "Shimbun ni miru Ni-So kōshō" (Press Reports on the Soviet-Japanese Negotiations), *Bungei shunjū*, October 1956, pp. 78–83.

[78] "Uwasa no otoko Hatoyama Ichirō" (Man of the Moment, Hatoyama Ichirō), *Shūkan yomiuri*, August 1, 1954, pp. 4–16.

[79] Yamada Gorō. "Seizaikai wo masabu chikarosen" (Beneath the Surface Connections between the Political and Financial Worlds), *Shin seikai*, March 1956, pp. 18–22.

[80] "Yodantobi seijika, Shigemitsu Mamaro" (Shigemitsu Mamaro, Fast-Rising Politician), *Shūkan asahi*, June 8, 1952, pp. 2–6.

[81] "Zaikai 'bakudan sengen' no heikei" (The Background of the 'Explosive Statement' of the Business World), *Seiji keizai*, October 1956, pp. 13–15, (signed S. S. K.).

C. PAMPHLETS

[82] Jiyutō (Liberal Party). *Futatsu no sekai to Nihon gaikō no arikata* (The Direction of Japanese Diplomacy with the Two Political Worlds). Jiyutō seichō shirizu (Liberal Party Political Trend Series), No. 24. Tokyo: December 1954. 75 pp

[83] Nihon kyōsantō (Japanese Communist Party). *Ni-So kōshō no keika to sono mondaiten* (The Progress of the Russo-Japanese Negotiations and the Points of Issue). Tokyo. 1956. 92 pp.

[84] Ni-So kyōkai (Japan-Soviet Society). *Ni-So heiwa jōyaku shokushin no tame ni* (A Japanese-Soviet Peace Treaty is Urged) Tokyo· 1959. 6 pp.

[85] ———. *Ni-So kyōkai no oitachi to gonen no ayumi* (The Japan-Soviet Society's Early Days and the Progress of Five Years). Tokyo· 1962. 2 pp.

[86] Ryōdo mondai kokumin remmei jimbikai (Preparatory Committee for a People's League on the Territorial Problem). *Ryōdo mondai kokumin taikai kiroku* (The Proceedings of the National Convention on the Territorial Problem). Tokyo· 1956. 107 pp.

[87] Takahasi Akira and Yufu Sachiko. *Sengo no Nihon ni okeru yōron chōsa no tebiki* (Index to Public Opinion Polls in Postwar Japan, 1945–1956). Tokyo: Tokyo daigaku shimbun kenkyūjo. 1957. 21 pp.

D. GOVERNMENT DOCUMENTS

[88] Kokuritsu kokkai toshokan rippō chōsashitsu (National Diet Library Legislative Research Bureau). *Nı-So kokkō chōseı mondaı kiso shiryōshū* (A Collection of Basic Materıals Concerning the Regulation of Soviet-Japanese Diplomatic Relatıons). Tokyo. 1955. 242 pp.

[89] ———. *Shuyōkokka no seitō koyaku* (The Rules and Regulations of the Political Parties in the Prıncipal Countries). Tokyo: 1961. 174 pp.

[90] Sangıin (House of Councillors). *Sangıin honkai giroku* (Proceedings of the Plenary Session of the House of Councillors), No. 56. 24th Diet. Tokyo: 1956.

[91] Sangiin gaimu ıinkai chōsashitsu (House of Councillors Foreign Affairs Committee Research Bureau). *Nı-So kōshō kankeı shıryō. saıkin no shimbun kıjı* (Materials Concernıng the Soviet-Japanese Negotiations: Recent Newspaper Artıcles). Tokyo: 1956. 161 pp.

[92] Sangıin. (House of Councıllors). *Sangiin gaimu ıinkai kaıgiroku* (Proceedings of the House of Councillors Foreign Affairs Committee). No. 1–20. 22nd Diet. Tokyo. 1955.

[93] ———. ———. No. 1–5. 23rd Dıet. Tokyo. 1955.

[94] ———. ———. No. 1–20 24th Dıet. Tokyo: 1956.

[95] ———. ———. No. 1–10. 25th Dıet. Tokyo: 1957.

[96] Shūgiin (House of Representatives). *Gaimu ıinkai gıroku* (Foreign Affairs Commıttee Proceedings), No. 1–20, 22nd Diet, House of Representatives Committee Proceedıngs. Tokyo 1955.

[97] ———. ———, No. 1–5, 23rd Diet, House of Representatives Committee Proceedings. Tokyo: 1955.

[98] ———. ———, No. 1–51, 24th Dıet, House of Representatives Commıttee Proceedıngs. Tokyo: 1956

[99] ———. ———, No 1–5, 25th Diet, House of Representatıves Committee Proceedings. Tokyo· 1956.

[100] ———. *Heiwa jōyaku oyobi Nichi-Bei anzen hōsho jōyaku tokubetsu ıinkai giroku* (Proceedings of the Specıal Commıttee on the Peace Treaty and the Japan-United States Securıty Treaty), No. 4, 12th Diet, House of Representatives Committee Proceedings, V. Tokyo. 1951.

[101] ———. *11 kokkaı shūgıin giroku* (11th Diet, House of Representatives Proceedings), I. Tokyo· 1951.

[102] ———. *Yosan iinkai giroku* (Budget Commıttee Proceedıngs), No. 26, 22nd Dıet, House of Representatıves Committee Proceedings, VIII. Tokyo. 1955.

[103] Sōrifu (Prime Minister's Office). *Gaimushō* (The Foreign Mınıstry). Tokyo· *Ōkurashō*, 1958. 196 pp.

[104] ———. *Zenkoku yoron chōsa kıkan no genkyō shigatsu 1955-sangatsu 1956* (The Current Findings of the Natıonal Publıc Opınıon Research Agencies, April 1955–March 1956). Tokyo· 1956 73 pp

[105] ——— *Zenkoku yoron chōsa kıkan no genkyō shıgatsu 1956-sangatsu 1957* (The Current Fındings of the National Public Opınıon Research Agencies, April 1956–March 1957). Tokyo. 1957. 84 pp.

E. NEWSPAPERS AND PERIODICALS

[106] *Asahi nenkan, 1957* (Asahi Yearbook, 1957). Tokyo: Asahi shimbunsha, 1958. 642 pp.
[107] *Asahi shimbun*, December 1954–November 1956.
[108] *Jimintō no seisaku geppō* (Monthly Policy Report of the Liberal-Democratic Party), No. 1–10 (February–November 1956).
[109] *Keidanren geppō* (Federation of Economic Organizations' Monthly Report), No. 1–12, IV (1956).

Kokuritsu kokkai toshokan shimbun kirinuki shiryōshitsu (National Diet Library Newspaper Clipping Section). This collection consists of Japanese newspaper clippings bound according to subject. Clippings from the following newspapers are cited in this work
    Akahata   *Tokyo shimbun*
    Mainichi shimbun   *Tokyo taimusu*
    Nihon keizai shimbun   *Yomiuri shimbun*
    Sankei jiji
These articles were found in collections titled as follows
[110] *Hoshu gōdō shichigatsu kara jūichigatsu made 1954* (The Union of the Conservatives, July–November 1954.)
[111] *Nihon gaikō seisaku* (Japanese Foreign Policy), 1954, 1955, 1956.
[112] *21 rinji kokkai* (The 21st Extraordinary Session of the Diet), December 10, 1954–January 24, 1955.
[113] *22 tokubetsu kokkai* (The 22nd Special Session of the Diet), I–III (March 18–July 30, 1955.
[114] *23 rinji kokkai* (The 23rd Extraordinary Session of the Diet), November 22–December 16, 1955.
[115] *24 tsūjō kokkai* (The 24th Ordinary Session of the Diet), I–V (December 20, 1955–June 15, 1956).
[116] *Ni-So gyogyō kōshō* (The Soviet-Japanese Fishery Negotiations), I–IV (February–May 1956).
[117] *Ni-So kōshō* (The Soviet-Japanese Negotiations), I–XXV (December 1954–November 1956).
[118] *Nihon shakai shimbun* (Japan Socialist Newspaper), May 1–October 30, 1956.
[119] *Shakai tsūshin* (Socialist News), January 1955–October 1956.
      This periodical was published at the *Jōhō tsūshin* (News Bulletin) by the Right-Wing Socialist Party until October 15, 1955. Subsequent to the Socialists' merger it became an official party organ, *Shakai tsūshin*.

F. INTERVIEWS

[120] Fujimaki Shimpei. Deputy Director, Secretariat of the Policy Research Board, Japan Socialist Party. Interview: January 12, 1962
[121] Ishii Mitsujirō. Liberal-Democratic Party faction leader. Interview. May 29, 1962.
[122] Matsumoto Shunichi. Japanese plenipotentiary in the Soviet-Japanese negotiations, Interview: July 21, 1962

[123] ———. Interview January 20, 1963.
[124] Nakasone Yasuhiro. Liberal-Democratic Party member. Interview· July 30, 1962.
[125] Ono Tatsuo. Deputy Chief, International Affairs Division, Federation of Economic Organizations. Interview: December 7, 1962.
[126] Wakamiya Kotarō. Private secretary to Hatoyama Ichirō. Interview April 9, 1962.
[127] Yamaguchi Fusao. International Affairs Bureau, Socialist Party of Japan. Interview: January 30, 1962.

II. ENGLISH SOURCES

A. BOOKS

[128] Abel, Elie. *The Missile Crisis.* New York: Bantam Books, 1966. 197 pp.
[129] Almond, Gabriel A. *The American People and Foreign Policy.* New York: Harcourt, Brace, c1950. 269 pp.
[130] ———, and James S Coleman. *The Politics of the Developing Areas.* Princeton. Princeton University Press, 1960. 591 pp.
[131] Baerwald, Hans H. *The Purge of Japanese Leaders Under the Occupation.* University of California Publications in Political Science, VIII. Berkeley University of California Press, 1959 111 pp.
[132] Beloff, Max. *Soviet Policy in the Far East, 1944–1951.* London Oxford University Press, 1953 278 pp.
[133] Benedict, Ruth The *Chrysanthemum and the Sword.* Boston: Houghton Mifflin, 1946. 324 pp
[134] Buck, Philip W, and Martin B. Travis (eds.). *Control of Foreign Relations in Modern Nations.* New York: W. W. Norton, 1957. 865 pp.
[135] Burks, Ardath W *The Government of Japan.* New York· Thomas Y. Crowell, 1961. 269 pp.
[136] Cohen, Bernard C. *The Political Process and Foreign Policy. The Making of the Japanese Peace Settlement.* Princeton: Princeton University Press, 1957. 293 pp.
[137] ———. *The Press and Foreign Policy.* Princeton: Princeton University Press, 1963. 279 pp.
[138] Colbert, Evelyn S. *The Left Wing in Japanese Politics.* New York: Institute of Pacific Relations, 1952. 353 pp.
[139] Cole, Allan B., and Nakanishi Naomichi (eds.). *Japanese Opinion Polls with Socio-Political Significance, 1947–1957.* Ann Arbor University Microfilms, 1960. 3 vols.
[140] Cole, Allan B, George O Totten, and Cecil H. Uehara. *Socialist Parties in Postwar Japan.* New Haven: Yale University Press, 1966. 490 pp.
[141] Council on Foreign Relations. *The American Public's View of U.S. Policy Toward China: a Report Prepared for the Council on Foreign Relations by The Survey Research Center, University of Michigan.* New York: 1964. 61 pp.
[142] Dallin, David J. *Soviet Russia in the Far East.* New Haven: Yale University Press, 1948. 398 pp.

[143] —— *The Rise of Russia in Asia* New Haven: Yale University Press, 1949. 293 pp.
[144] Deutsch, Karl W., and Lewis J. Edinger. *Germany Rejoins the Powers.* Stanford: Stanford University Press, 1959. 320 pp.
[145] Dore, Robert P. *Land Reform in Japan.* London: Oxford University Press, 1959. 510 pp.
[146] Dunn, Frederick S. *Peace-Making and the Settlement with Japan.* Princeton· Princeton University Press, 1963. 210 pp.
[147] Duverger, Maurice. *Political Parties· Their Organization and Activity in the Modern State.* New York: John Wiley, 1961. 439 pp.
[148] Easton, David. *The Political System.* New York: Alfred A. Knopf, 1953. 320 pp.
[149] Ekstein, Harry. *A Theory of Stable Democracy.* Center of International Studies, Woodrow Wilson School of Public and International Affairs, Research Monograph No. 10. Princeton University: 1961. 50 pp. (mimeo.)
[150] Herz, John H. *International Politics in the Atomic Age.* New York. Columbia University Press, 1959. 360 pp.
[151] Ike, Nobutaka. *Japanese Politics, An Introductory Survey.* New York· Alfred A. Knopf, 1957. 300 pp.
[152] Jones, F C *Japan's New Order in East Asia, Its Rise and Fall, 1937–45.* London· Oxford University Press, 498 pp.
[153] Kennan, George F. *Realities of American Foreign Policy.* Princeton· Princeton University Press, 1954. 119 pp.
[154] Key, Vladimir O , Jr. *The Responsible Electorate.* Cambridge: Harvard University Press, 1966. 158 pp.
[155] Kirkpatrick, Ivone. *The Inner Circle.* London: Macmillan and Company, 1959. 275 pp.
[156] Lippmann, Walter. *Essays in the Public Philosophy.* Boston: Little, Brown, 1955. 189 pp
[157] March, James G. and Herbert Simon. *Organizations.* John Wiley and Sons New York, 1958. 262 pp.
[158] Maxon, Yale C. *Control of Japanese Foreign Policy: A Study of Civil-Military Rivalry, 1930–1945.* University of California Publications in Political Science, V. Berkeley. University of California Press, 1957. 286 pp
[159]Mendel, Douglas H. *The Japanese People and Foreign Policy: A Study of Public Opinion in Post-Treaty Japan.* Berkeley. University of California Press, 1961 269 pp.
[160] Morgenthau, Hans J. *Politics Among Nations.* New York· Alfred A. Knopf, 1963 630 pp.
[161] Packard, George W., III. *Protest in Tokyo. The Security Treaty Crisis of 1960.* Princeton Princeton University Press, 1966. 423 pp.
[162] Reischauer, Edwin O. *The United States and Japan.* 3rd ed. Cambridge Harvard University Press, 1965. 396 pp.
[163] Rosenau, James N. *Public Opinion and Foreign Policy.* New York. Random House, 1961. 118 pp.
[164] Scalapino, Robert A. *Democracy and the Party Movement in Prewar Japan.* Berkeley: University of California Press, 1953. 471 pp.
[165] ——, and Junnosuke Masumi. *Parties and Politics in Con-*

temporary Japan. Berkeley· University of California Press, 1962.
190 pp.
[166] Snyder, Richard C., H. W Bruck, and Burton Sapin. *Foreign
Policy Decision-Making.* Glencoe: Free Press, 1962, 274 pp.
[167] Totten, George O., III. *The Social Democratic Movement in
Prewar Japan.* New Haven· Yale University Press, 1966. 455 pp.
[168] Truman, David B. *The Governmental Process Political Interests
and Public Opinion.* New York: Alfred A. Knopf, 1960. 544 pp.
[169] Waltz, Kenneth N. *Foreign Policy and Democratic Politics.*
Boston· Little, Brown, 1967 331 pp.
[170] Whittemore, Edward P. *The Press in Japan Today . . . A Case
Study.* Columbia, S.C.: University of South Carolina Press, 1961.
91 pp.
[171] Yanaga, Chitoshi. *Japan Since Perry.* New York. McGraw-Hill,
1949. 723 pp.
[172] Yoshida, Shigeru. *The Yoshida Memoirs.* London. Heinemann,
1961. 291 pp.

B. ARTICLES

[173] Aspaturian, Vernon A. "Soviet Foreign Policy," in Roy C.
Macridis (ed.), *Foreign Policy in World Politics.* Englewood Cliffs,
N.J : Prentice-Hall, 1958.
[174] Baerwald, Hans H. "Factional Politics in Japan," *Current History,*
XLVI (April 1964), 223–229.
[175] ⸻. "Japanese Politics Since the General Election," *Far
Eastern Survey,* XXV (September 1955), 134–140.
[176] Beer, Samuel H "The Analysis of Political Systems," in Samuel
H. Beer and Adam B. Ulam (eds.), *Patterns of Government.* New
York· Random House, 1962.
[177] ⸻. "The Representation of Interests in British Government:
Historical Background," *American Political Science Review,* LV
(September 1957), 613–650.
[178] Cohen, Bernard C. "Foreign Policy Makers and the Press," in
James N. Rosenau (ed.), *International Politics and Foreign Policy.*
Glencoe: Free Press, 1961.
[179] ⸻. "Foreign Policy-Making: Modern Design," *World Politics,* V (April 1953), 377–391.
[180] ⸻. *The Influence of Non-Governmental Groups on Foreign
Policy Making.* Studies in Citizen Participation in International Relations, II Boston: World Peace Foundation, 1959. 26 pp. (mimeo).
[181] ⸻. *The Press and the Formulation of Foreign Policy.*
Washington: American Political Science Association Meeting, 1962
23 pp. (mimeo).
[182] Colton, Kenneth E. "Pre-war Political Influences in Post-war
Conservative Parties," *American Political Science Review,* XLII (October 1948), 940–957.
[183] Dore, R. P. "Left and Right in Japan," *International Affairs,*
XXXIII (January 1956), 13–16.
[184] Erskine, Hazel G. "The Polls: The Informed Public," *Public
Opinion Quarterly,* 26, 4 (Winter 1962), 669–677.

[185] Ginsburgs, George and Scott Shrewsbury. "The Postwar Soviet-Japanese Fisheries Dispute," *Orbis*, VII (Fall 1963), 596–604.

[186] Ishida, Takeshi. *Interest Groups in Japan*. 80 pp. (mimeo)

[187] Jones, F. C. "Uncertainties in Japan: Parties and Personalities," *The World Today*, X (December 1954), 513–522.

[188] Kerlinger, Fred M. "Decision-Making in Japan," *Social Forces*, XXX (October 1951), 36–41.

[189] Langdon, Frank C. "Organized Interests in Japan and their Influence on Political Parties," *Pacific Affairs*, XXXIV (Fall 1961), 271–278.

[190] Leiserson, Michael. *Factions and Coalitions in One Party Japan: Explanation Based on the Theory of Games*. Paper delivered at the annual meeting of the American Political Science Association. 29 pp. (mimeo).

[191] Morely, James W. "Japan's Image of the Soviet Union, 1952–1961," *Pacific Affairs*, XXXV (Spring 1962), 51–58.

[192] ———. *Soviet and Communist Chinese Policies Toward Japan, 1950–1957*. New York. Institute of Pacific Relations, 1958 46 pp. (mimeo).

[193] ———. "The Soviet-Japanese Peace Declaration," *Political Science Quarterly*, LXXII (September 1957), 370–379.

[194] Morris, I. I. "Japan and the Moscow Negotiations with the Soviet Union," *The World Today*, XII (November 1956), 438–447.

[195] ———. "Politics in Japan," *The World Today*, XIII (March 1957), 127–136.

[196] ———. "Soviet-Japanese Peace Treaty Talks," *The World Today*, XI (August 1955), 357–364.

[197] Okasaki, Katsuo. "Japan's Foreign Relations," *The Annals of the American Academy of Political and Social Science*, No. 308 (November 1956), 156–166.

[198] Robinson, James A. *Some Effects of Information on State Department-Congressional Relations· The Interdependence of Process and Policy*. Evanston. Northwestern University Program in International Relations, 1960. 24 pp.

[199] Scalapino, Robert A. "Japan," in Walter Galenson (ed.), *Labor and Economic Development*. New York. John Wiley, 1959.

[200] ———. "Japanese Socialism in Crisis," *Foreign Affairs*, XXXVIII (January 1960), 313–328.

[201] ———. "The Foreign Policy of Modern Japan," in Roy C. Macridis (ed.), *Foreign Policy in World Politics*. Englewood Cliffs, N.J.: Prentice-Hall, 1962.

[202] Soukup, James R. "Japan," *The Journal of Politics*, XXV (November 1963), 737–756.

[203] Stockwin, J. A. A. " 'Positive Neutrality'—The Foreign Policy of the Japanese Socialist Party," *Asian Survey*, II (November 1962), 33–41.

[204] Swearingen, Roger. "A Decade of Soviet Policy in Asia, 1945–56," *Current History*, XXXII (February 1957), 89–96.

[205] Tiltman, Hessel " 'Fourth Estate' in Japan," *Asahi Evening News*, October 4, 1958

[206] Totten, George O. and Tamio Kawakami. "The Functions of Factionalism in Japanese Politics," *Pacific Affairs*, XXXVIII, 2 (Summer, 1965), 109–122.
[207] Vogel, Ezra F. "Migration to the City" in R. P. Dore (ed.), *Aspects of Social Change in Modern Japan*. Princeton: Princeton University Press, 1967.
[208] Ward, Robert E. "Political Modernization and Political Culture in Japan," *World Politics*, XV (July 1963), 569–596.
[209] ———. "Japan" in Lucian W. Pye and Sidney Verba (eds.), *Political Culture and Political Development* Princeton: Princeton University Press, 1965.

C. GOVERNMENT DOCUMENTS

[210] Japan. Ministry of Foreign Affairs. Public Information Bureau. *The Northern Islands.* Tokyo· Bunshodo, 1955. 28 pp.
[211] ———. ———. ———, Second Section. *Press Releases December 1954–December 1955).* Tokyo. 1956. 141 pp.
[212] U.S. American Consulate General, Hong Kong. *Survey of the China Mainland Press.* No. 906 (October 12, 1954).
[213] ———. Department of State. *Conference for the Conclusion and Signature of the Treaty of Peace with Japan: Record of Proceedings.* Washington: 1951. 468 pp.

D. NEWSPAPERS AND PERIODICALS

[214] *Japan Times* (until July 1, 1956, *Nippon Times*), December 1, 1954–October 31, 1956.
[215] *New York Times,* February 15, 1950 and July 1, 1954–November 30, 1956.
[216] *Nippon Times* (See *Japan Times*).
[217] *The Current Digest of the Soviet Press.* (Joint Committee of Slavic Studies). VI–VII (September 1954–December 1956).

Index

Adenauer-formula settlement, 54, 61, 67, 68, 92, 97, 131, 137; proposed by Soviet Union, 35, Hatoyama-Kōno position, 36-37; and conservatives, 38; public attitudes, 78-79; and Japanese policy-making, 78; and business faction, 96-97; proposed by Socialists, 119

"Amateur diplomacy," 139-141, 145

Articulate opinion, 75; defined, 10-11, 89; opinion groups, 11; individuals, 11; the *demo,* 12; mass media, 12, 105-107; structure in the peace negotiations, 89-90; impact of senior diplomats, 93-94; business groups' influence, 98; issue groups, 101-102, 105; impact on negotiations, 109

Ashida, Hitoshi, 44, 46, 57; chairman of Foreign Policy Research Committee, 67-68; aided senior diplomats, 91-92

Business groups: impact on foreign policy, 22-23, ties with conservatives, 23, 121, 124-126; and Hatoyama's trip, 66; articulate opinion, 94, 96-98; policy factions among, 95-96; access to conservative policy-making, 98; origins and structure of, 122-124; shared attitudes with party leaders, 125; links to the bureaucracy, 125-126; and Soviet negotiations and Hatoyama's retirement, 127-128; role in foreign policy-making, 129, 151-152

Climate of opinion, 74, defined, 8; in the U S., 8-9; impact on policy-making, 9-10; and articulate opinion, 9; and historical image of Russia, 75-76; and Japan-Soviet relations, 76-78; on specific issues in the negotiations, 78-83, effect on territorial policy, 81; instability during the negotiations, 84-86; compared with American opinion, 85; and mass media, 86, influenced by conservative party leaders, 86-89. *See also* Public opinion

Cold War, 111, 153, and Japanese public opinion, 76-77

Communist China, 30, 56, 77, 153; policy toward Japan, 31

Congress of Industrial Unions. See *Zenrō Kaigi*

Consensus: tactics of senior diplomats, 93; reponsibility of press, 107-108; Diet ratification of Peace Agreement, 147-148, style of authority in decision-making, 156-157

Conservatives: post-Occupation history, 29-30, 47n13; pre-Occupation history, 43n6; Liberal-Democratic Party merger and Soviet policy, 35, 59. *See also* Liberal-Democratic Party

Constitution of 1947, 13-14; and Foreign Office, 25-26

Dai Nippon Suisankai. See Japanese Fishery Association

Decision-making· traditional, 71, 156-157; consensual, 70-71, 73;

www.ingramcontent.com/pod-product-compliance
Lightning Source LLC
Chambersburg PA
CBHW031132270326
41929CB00011B/1600